W9-BLS-878

North
of Now

Books by W. D. Wetherell

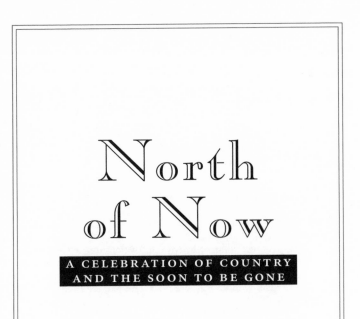

North of Now

A CELEBRATION OF COUNTRY AND THE SOON TO BE GONE

W. D. Wetherell

Illustrated by Matt Brown

The Lyons Press
Guilford, Connecticut
An imprint of The Globe Pequot Press

For Celeste, Erin, and Matthew

Copyright © 1998, 2002 by W. D. Wetherell

ALL RIGHTS RESERVED. No part of this book may be reproduced or transmitted in any form by any means, electronic or mechanical, including photocopying and recording, or by any information storage and retrieval system, except as may be expressly permitted by the 1976 Copyright Act or in writing from the publisher. Requests for permission should be addressed to The Globe Pequot Press, P.O. Box 480, Guilford, Connecticut 06437.

The Lyons Press is an imprint of The Globe Pequot Press.

Printed in the United States of America

10 9 8 7 6 5 4 3 2 1

Library of Congress Cataloging-in-Publication data is available on file.

ISBN 1-58574-647-9

Portions of this book have appeared in *The New York Times, Vermont Life, Dartmouth Alumni Magazine, Green Mountain Review, Yankee, Vermont Woodland Magazine, Sky,* and *Trout.*

"There's something about north," he said, "something that sets it apart from all other directions. A person who is heading north is not making any mistake, in my opinion."

"That's the way I look at it," said Stuart. "I rather expect that from now on I shall be travelling north until the end of my days."

～ E. B. White, *Stuart Little*

Here, nature and life follow a pattern that has so gone out of style it gets rejected in the editorial offices.

～ Anton Chekhov, *Letters*

You and I are the last remembrance of all that immeasureable greatness which has been created in the world in all the thousands of years between them and us, and it is in memory of all those vanished marvels that we live.

～ Boris Pasternak, *Dr. Zhivago*

For us, there is only the trying. The rest is not our business.

～ T. S. Eliot, *Four Quartets*

CONTENTS

The book that follows is an attempt to come to terms with the central dilemma of one person's life: that writing in early middle age, describing as best I can the things, people, and landscapes I love the most and wish most passionately to endure, I am revealing myself to be as extinct as a dinosaur, dead as a dodo, a relic of another era, a footnote to an age that not only rushes ahead in heedless bondage to the new, but tramples in contempt on anyone who stubbornly refuses to keep pace.

I am amazed by this fact, saddened by this fact, victimized by this fact, bemused by this fact, bitter at this fact, and when these responses fail me, at a loss to find any attitude at all. But, borrowing the bitter mode for a single sentence, this is the motive behind much of what follows: to find the right style, the proper expression and posture with which to face extinction.

I lead by what older standards might well be considered an ordinary life, and yet by the movement of our times this life has become extraordinary. A walker in a sedentary age; a lover of quiet in a century that has the volume turned up full blast; a reader in a visual age; a writer in one that is increasingly aliterate. Mastodons, in their last confused moments, must have experienced the same incomprehension—that those very conditions that had enabled them to flourish in life, the ferns and mosses they had eaten with such relish, the high dome of the sunlit sky, had now turned on them to spell their doom.

In trying to record the pleasures of a life that is increasingly made up of the threatened, the soon to be gone, it seems best to celebrate what made these precious in the first place, not to try to convince people to go back to them, restore them to prominence. I write with absolutely no hope of that. Certainly, if I ran the world much would change, but the only thing I have even partial command over are words, and my goal here is to use them to preserve something of the afterglow, the sunset beauty, of what will in a few moments be lost.

There's lots of talk about extinction these days—extinction as a topic will never be extinct—but the candidates I'm writing about are not the usual ones. No condors appear in what follows, no spotted owls, though I wish them both well; nothing so abstract and hypocritical as *competitiveness* or *family values* appears either. Writers have been insisting for such a long time now that the pillars of Western society are shaky that the belief itself has become a pillar of Western society, replacing ones that have otherwise fallen. I can't dismiss these writers as hypocrites; their beliefs and worries I largely share. And yet here in this book it's not the pillars that interest me, but the forgotten spots under the eaves, the shadowy corners, the little decorations and flourishes that go unnoticed by most.

I have parents who are largely responsible for introducing me to much of what I celebrate here; I have children who, coming of age, will know at least some of these pleasures, and will be able, reading this, to learn something more. For all the seriousness with which my generation takes itself, it's clear now that baby boomers are very much a transitional generation between those who, in our grandparents' age, knew the world as it had largely been for centuries and our grandchildren, who will have no inkling of that world save from what portion of the collective memory and wisdom we are able to pass on—our grandparents who were alive in the 1880s; our grandchildren who, fate willing, will see 2080 come in. This is not to dismiss the importance of my generation, but to stress it in a different direction, as keepers of the flame, the vital link between eras.

One of the subjects I won't be pining for is nostalgia. Partly this is a matter of definition—the things I celebrate, while battered, on the ropes, are still very much with us—and partly a matter of taste; there's nothing so sickly sweet, so much a mark of our times, as this longing for the artifacts we were quick enough to trash when we had them in our hands. I will celebrate instead the old-fashioned, the splendidly anachronistic, but not in their usual pejorative senses. In an age that for all its chatter about the new too often remains timid, juvenile, and boring, "old-fashioned" is a term that should be turned on its head, since to my mind it connotes what is ambitious, energetic, mature, and daring, the very qualities that are in such short supply in what passes for contemporary culture.

Many of the pleasures described here are country ones, both by intention and by default. By intention, because I live in rural New England, work hard to make this possible; by default, because so much of the natural world has been driven into exile from what outposts in the city and suburbs it once maintained. Since this is a book largely about country, it seems natural to organize it around the old seasonal pattern that, at least here in these northern hills, still manages to frame and order much of life. And needless to say, in most of our suburban world seasons are threatened too, climate-controlled and stage-managed so they can be ignored entirely. Indeed, seasons have become something to threaten us with, whip us into line. We hear of "nuclear winter," or, with the greenhouse effect, of endless summers of brutal, life-sapping heat. No one ever predicts endless spring, a solid year of autumn. We're promised hell no matter which way we turn, fire or ice, and yet the worst hell is for what most people is already in place: a dead year; a year with no seasonal rhythms at all.

But here I am, flirting with that bitter, ironic mood I'm determined at all costs to avoid. In celebrating the soon to vanish I have found no shortages of subjects, to the point where I've had to leave out many candidates that could otherwise be included. Letters are one of these. Who in these days of E-mail and cellular phones and ready-made cards bothers writing personal letters? Or rather, who under the age of sixty? And yet a few seconds ago, cosmically speaking, the sending and receiving of letters was one of the universal pleasures in life taken for granted both by rich and by poor. Love letters written in anguish and exhilaration, even the corny ones; letters wishing as far as it's possible to wish anything off the page good luck in a new course of life; letters, the words pressed deep, offering consolation for great pain, or at least trying to ... letters that took time to compose, time to mail, time to receive, drawing out the contents over the course of several days and many miles, so they all but echoed.

Where have they gone? In bundles, the lucky ones, tied lovingly with string, stored in attics—to those homes that still have attics. For people who remember them, expose them occasionally to the light, they can bring alive the past in a way no electronic gadget will ever duplicate, since letters are *human* documents, in handwriting that discloses a personality, a mood, on stationery that was carefully chosen, in words that often reveal an entire life.

Only once or twice will I mention another candidate for extinction, one that is harder to give a shorthand label to or place in any category, but the passing of which will perhaps be saddest of all. I refer to the kind of man or woman, never very common, who you could count on meeting with a fair degree of regularity in any town you happened to live in, any place you went to visit. Often this would be a person of some affluence, not in money or property, but in *time,* with a certain broad margin to his or her life that could be embellished and enhanced in all sorts of unexpected ways. Self-educated in the most important parts, they combined both great breadth of view and intensely specific knowledge—of specific places, specific skills, specific wonders. Their manners were apt to be of the old school—manners, that is, that ornamented an already instinctive gentleness and tact. Often, not always, this would be a country man or country woman. Invariably, they were storytellers, good ones, letting the past wrinkle their face up in disgust or widen it in laughter, consumed by the telling, knowing by instinct just where to start their stories, just where to finish—throwbacks to the days Céline recalls "when not being able to sing or tell a story properly was looked upon as stupid, shameful, and sick."

Their race, nationality, looks, political allegiance—all these could be filled in almost any way you wanted to, but the essentials remained. Most of all, these were people who, in a culture all but deliberately designed to crush it, maintained their childish capacity for curiosity and wonder—and wanted to share with you what time had brought their way, whether it was the most reliable spot to find raspberries on a hot August afternoon, the history of the abandoned farm off the rockiest of the town's back roads, what a small patch of Belgian earth had looked like on a cold December day in 1944, the whys and wherefores of boiling sap, or the inner mysteries of an old Ford truck. They had no use for fads or styles or fashions. They were the ones twentieth-century America could not seduce.

I think of them, picture their faces all but glowing in excitement, as if they possessed an extra nerve ending to receive and broadcast *joie de vivre.* I value them too well to think I could ever share their kind of freedom and ease. And yet something of their wonder, their delight in sheer living, is what this book aspires toward and hopes to share.

I write this at the close of a century few will bother lamenting, near the start of a new century that is as frightening and hopeful, to use the simile that lies closest at hand, as a blank sheet of paper. I look forward to the future, wake up to it each morning with the greatest anticipation, and yet. . . . Well, like many others, irrespective of age, I've the sense I will go into the new century with the best part of myself left behind, decapitated by the remorseless trip wire that, like it or not, extends between the numbers 1999 and 2000.

And if someone were to ask me where I'd like to see the old millennium out, the new one in, it would be a difficult choice. At home with my family, going outside at midnight to look at the way our trees split apart the moonlight? On a mountain top, the summit of October, the hill my window faces, the companion to my days? There are people who will do that, climb Katahdin and camp there so as to take advantage of that high easterly facing, be the first Americans the sun will shine on in the new century, brag for decades on that fact.

Or perhaps, to go to the other extreme, see it out in a bar—the kind of small neighborhood bar where the furnishings are threadbare but mellow, the music country but soft, the beer locally brewed and ice cold, the patrons all friends of long standing who share most of your interests, understand a few of your passions, indulge almost all of your quirks. By midnight, with those beers under our belts, all seems even more mellow, to the point where the thought of ever having to leave the scene of such coziness and conviviality is not to be borne. Like in the old days, someone starts a story, someone else joins in, stories of great things, important things, foolish things—the kind of stories where, listening, you don't know whether to laugh or cry, and so end up managing the hardest balancing act of all, doing both at once.

Closing time, for so much now. A moment to midnight—but what a hell of a fine moment we'll make that be.

REMEMBRANCE

The eleventh hour of the eleventh day of the eleventh month is almost always cloudy here, pensively so, with the kind of dark gray stratus that can drive thought inward. Six weeks past the equinox, six weeks to solstice, the feel is very much of intermission, a resting point where autumn, in the course of playing its bittersweet composition, has deliberately left room to draw its breath. A quiet, even clement mood this one. In the pause, no leaves are left to rattle in tree tops, and even if there were the wind seems temporarily to have blown out its lip. The clouds, gray as they are, press the warmth to the earth, creating a ceiling under which all sorts of seasonal postscripts manage to linger on. Bluebirds helping themselves to what berries the earlier migrants missed; monarch butterflies, enough of them that my four-year-old kicks apart the leaves searching for his net, races off in pursuit; asters, purple ones, acting as the meeting point where butterfly and butterfly chaser, after much exuberant swooping, converge.

An intermission, too, in my own daily routine. Usually I take my first break from writing around ten, having put in a good two or three hours before this. But not today. Today I'm taking my break at precisely 10:55, and what's more, taking it outside facing the brown-gray ridges—the khaki-colored ridges—that shape the horizon to our east.

Armistice Day, though I don't suppose there are a dozen people in this village who remember it by this name. *Veterans Day* it's called now, robbed of its specificity and hence much of its meaning, but it's hardly even commemorated as that. Carlton

Tabor, for a few more years anyway, can be counted on to lower the flag outside the smaller of our town's two churches (and remember to haul it up again sometime after Christmas), but other than that, and the inconvenience of not being able to get your mail, the day passes unremarked. There are Veterans Day sales at the malls well south of us, but there are sales all the time now, and even the most ironically eyed commentators don't waste their time trying to understand the connection between young boys dying overseas and discounts on widgets. Then, too, the schools stay open here, and almost no one takes the day off even to go hunting—in this part of rural New England, work is still the religion *franca,* and not many of the other lesser holidays are celebrated either.

But me I'm out here in gum boots, jeans, and a sweater standing at the edge of our field facing east toward our local mountain and through it toward Flanders. A reader, a person born in 1948 who knows something of what happened in the world thirty years earlier and, knowing something, feels something, I stand observing the ritual that once upon a time was all but universal. A moment of silence, as if to recreate on a lesser scale the miraculous quiet that descended on the Western Front on the eleventh hour of the eleventh day of the eleventh month in the eighteenth year of our century and brought surcease to a world that thought the noise of Maxim guns and Whizbangs and *Minnenwefers* and French 75s would go on literally forever.

Four years of killing. Enough money spent on artillery shells alone that the cost extinguished three empires and left two others permanently crippled. Nine million combatants dead, twenty-one million wounded, 12 percent of the entire male population of Britain turned into casualties, fifty-seven thousand of these (or the same number as there are names on the Vietnam Memorial) occurring in one day's fighting on the Somme, the majority shot in its first ten minutes. All this, the wretched statistics, the heartbreak they mask—and then with no warning the following order was received by commanding officers all up and down the front line: *Hostilities will stop on the entire front beginning November 11 at 11 o'clock French time. Signed: Marshal Foch.*

It was over. "In the line there were no cheers," one of the history books puts it. "The infantry stopped in its tracks, the roar of the artillery died away and men gazed stupidly about them. Dumb with fatigue they were unable to comprehend the significance of this sudden unwonted silence."

What was the war about? Well, no one knew then, no one knows now, read all you want to on the subject, no one really knows. Looking back it's hard not to decide all the slaughter had as its purpose the deliberate erection of a wall of corpses to block off everything that happened after the war from everything that happened before. "In 1914," as Leonard Woolf put it, "in the background of one's life and one's mind there was light and hope; by 1918, one had accepted a perpetual public menace and darkness, and had admitted into the privacy of one's soul an acquiescence in insecurity and barbarism."

Armistice Day, the actual day itself, had been the signal for wild rejoicing, not only in London and Paris, but in Toronto and Sydney and New York. All this was soon over, the century-long hangover about to begin. November 11 became the one date on the calendar where it was everyone's civic duty to remember and, remembering, to be sad. Placing it in November—and it seems deliberately placed there—ensured that the somber, autumnal note would find its resonance in weather that matched.

In the U.S., of course, the Great War didn't last long enough, didn't kill enough doughboys, to make much impression on a collective memory that's a bit haphazard even in the most intense of historical circumstances. In other countries it's still remembered with at least some passion, as any visitor to Western Europe in November will quickly discover. In London, dignitaries gather at the Cenotaph in Whitehall as they have for eighty years; grave words are spoken, and then comes the two minutes of silence that has always been the most eloquent part. In Paris, there are similar ceremonies—the graves in the war cemeteries get fresh flowers, and there are always articles in the papers by someone rediscovering the overwhelming loneliness of Verdun. In Italy, up in the north where the hills rise toward the Alps, each village square will have its wreath of red, white, and green, remembering the war in which Grandfather fell, or Uncle Umberto, the handsome brother Grandmother never knew.

Twenty years ago I spent a November in Edinburgh, where on street corners and in shops they were selling those papery red poppies that support the Haig Fund, help veterans in distress. In Britain, Armistice Day is celebrated on the nearest Sunday, Remembrance Sunday, and on that morning, without having any fixed destination in mind, I got up early and walked past Waverly Station and on up to the dark winding streets of Old Town.

Plunk into the middle of a celebration. A celebration, that is, if you define it as my dictionary does, "to perform a sacrament or ceremony publicly and with appropriate rites." There in the square outside St. Giles Cathedral, the historic center of the Scots' world, a vast congregation was assembled, one that was composed largely of the same aging men and women who I had noticed walking up from the New Town beside me, many with decorations and campaign ribbons on their lapels. They were formed in three long ranks on the north side of the square; on my side, troops were lined up at parade rest, staring with fixed attention toward the distant cathedral steps where men in black and scarlet robes were moving around in ways that made no sense to me, but obviously had something to do with the flags and battle flags gathered there, the honor guard of young soldiers, sailors, and cadets who now, at a single barked command, went rigidly to attention.

A bit slow on the uptake, it took me a while to realize this was connected to those poppies, the fixed concentration in the faces of those aging men. Remembrance Sunday—well, here was the remembrance all right, the Brits at their ceremonial best, complete with an army band playing the slow march from Holst's *The Planets,* than which no more poignant, bittersweet music, given the echoes it had there, has ever been composed.

Just before the music became unbearable in that mingled note of victory and sorrow it so perfectly conveyed, it stopped and in the silence where it had been came the high, lonely toll of the cathedral's bell striking off the hour. Eleven o'clock. Again came that hoarse shouted command, again the heels drumming in two separate raps against the paving stones, the rifle butts slamming down with them as every soldier in the square came to attention. The old soldiers stood at attention, too, trembling they stood so still, trembling with the effort of rigidity, trembling with what they remembered. Men in their sixties most of them, but at least a dozen were much older—men who remembered being boys, not in the Western Desert or Dunkirk, but on the Somme, Mons, or Cambrai. Watching them, scanning their faces, I realized it wasn't something old and vanished that was being commemorated here, not the memory of war, not history, but the actual event still in progress—that war's pain and sorrow and pride were right here in the square, as tangible and solid and alive as it's possible for anything to be.

Silence—and then, like a deliberately planned overflight, three gulls swooped in off the Forth, cutting through the gray square with their high-pitched calls, which, trapped by those ancient walls, echoing wildly in that silence, became like the pitying keen (there is no other phrase) of the earth itself.

The eleventh hour of the eleventh day of the eleventh month. Two minutes of silence. A last command, the music starting up again, the old men—so tightly aligned—breaking apart into the morning, smiling bashfully, waving to their grandchildren, walking, holding each other's arms the oldest ones, to the tea shops and pubs.

∽

I've been thinking about this more than usual lately, not just because of the eleventh and my own stubborn celebration, but because of a curiosity I found earlier this fall on the dusty bottom shelf of a poorly lit secondhand bookstore in a remote, forgotten village across the river in Vermont.

It's a book, an odd and moving one, with "$2.00" penciled in on the flyleaf, but otherwise as immaculate and firm as the day it was published. There couldn't have been many places in 1918 as far removed from the chaos of Passchendaele or Verdun as the state of Vermont, and yet here too the war had its effects, some 16,000 Vermonters having served in the armed forces, a not inconsiderable number given the fact that this was the time of an already small state's greatest depopulation. After the Armistice, an official history was deemed a fitting memorial to these men—the book that, bound in the pastoral green of her mountains, now rests beside me on the desk: *Vermont in the World War.*

The book, some 800 pages long, covers all aspects of the state's involvement, with chapters entitled "The First Vermont Infantry," "The Yankees at St. Mihiel," "How Food Helped Win the War," "The Industrial Situation," "Patriotism of Those in the Department of Institutions" ("It might be an interesting fact to mention that in the year 1917, $47 was raised in the Windsor Prison for the Belgian Relief Fund"), and "The Churches in the World War."

Having surprised myself by reading every word (the first person to do so in how many years?), I'm struck not by the overall futility of such a monument, the jingoism and pompous sloganeering that occasionally mar it, but at how much of the real pain and heartbreak of those years comes through.

"The Vermonters," it explains in the introduction, "proved to be tractable soldiers, obedient and courteous to their officers, but without losing any portion of that self-respect and sense of individual quality which seemed to be an elemental part of their natures."

There is much in a similar vein, but then the first Vermonters are sent overseas to the trenches, and the tone changes.

A faint, far away rustle, such as can be reproduced by holding two or three sheets of thin paper between thumb and finger and shaking them slightly would announce the departure of the missile from the enemy's battery pit, and all ears instantly attuned themselves to that malicious whisper which gossiped of death. . . . Caught in the swish of this merciless steel broom, a healthy, sturdy specimen of intelligent young manhood becomes, in the wink of an eye, a mere bloody mist, a torn and tattered ball of fleshy rags, or a hopeless, shaking, lopped cripple for the rest of his days.

A mere bloody mist? A lopped cripple? This is a long way from Pownal and Brattleboro and Highgate Springs. Worse was yet to come, the hated poison gas.

> Within fourteen seconds from the flash of the pro-jectile batteries the congested trenches would be flooded with a pall of deadly poison so concentrated that a single breath was fatal to the unfortunates who failed to sense the significance of the flash. . . . The Vermonters on European battlefields had to endure all these things and more. . . . *He was denied even the meagre relief of confiding his impressions to others, for the science which had perfected the savagery of human destruction had neglected to provide a vocabulary fit for the description of its nightmares.*

As in the Civil War, when farm boys fresh out of the hills, lacking any immunity, had been mowed down by measles and whooping cough, the Vermonters in France suffered even more deaths from disease than from bullets, including the final ironic scourge of the Spanish flu.

> During its prevalence no man at morning knew whether nightfall would find him still among the living. Men died like flies, and the hospitals became places of horror even as the barrack room became places of dread. . . . Death as prodigal as that from the muzzles of enemy machine guns swept through the crowded decks of the transports, and struck where it willed. . . . Many lost their courage in the presence of the malignant passengers, and committed suicide, pre-ferring death by the pistol or drowning to the mocking uncertainties of the plague.

On November 11, with the war's end only seconds away, the 101st Infantry, many of them Vermonters, was ordered to attack "Hill 265" near the village of Maucourt in the Meuse-

Argonne—the reason given being "that the enemy must not be allowed to discern any slightest sign of weakness in the armies which menaced him." The attack was called off, but then reinstated, and the troops advanced as they were told. "Nearly 200 of the regiment are buried in the American cemetery at Lambezellec. The cemetery is well located on a hill, from which, looking to the west, one gets a beautiful view in the distance of the great ocean separating the sleepers from their homeland."

What comes off the page with the greatest force is the list of casualties that occupies forty-three single-spaced pages in the center of the book. Linked together, unadorned, they are moving in the same way the names on the Vietnam Memorial are moving. Andrew Armington is there, a private from the market town of Waterbury, who died of disease on October 2, 1918. Leonard Lord is also there, a corporal from Swanton in the Champlain Valley, the first Vermonter killed in action, April 12, 1918. Listed too are those for whom the Armistice came a few days too late. Morton Stiles, killed in action November 1, 1918. Harold Holmes, private from Essex, died of wounds November 10. Some entries, with brutal honesty, spell out another cause of death. "Joe Smith, private, Lyndonville, suicide, December 15, 1918."

Along with these are the names of the wounded, broken down into three categories: "Severely," "Slightly," and "?" These include Flavien Rousseau of Rutland (a stonecutter? a laborer in the mills? his hand cut away, his living?), who falls into the "Severely" category; Perry Rogers of Northfield under the "?" (flesh wound from shrapnel?); and Lyman Prim of Winooski, "Slightly" (a Blighty wound that got him home in one piece?).

Immersed in reading, it comes with perhaps more of a shock than it should that some of these men may very well still be alive. There were seventeen-year-olds in France, men born in 1901, which would make them ninety-seven today. Not many of course, but some.

When the leaves fall here, like a curtain parting, Vermont becomes visible across the river, four miles of it anyway, rising in a long esker-like ridge from Thetford Hill in the south to Potato Hill directly opposite. There are old farms in that stretch, old houses in the village. Are any "ancient worthies" living there now, helped to the window by a willing granddaughter or great-grandson, remembering, remembering hard? The last Civil War veteran died in 1959, John B. Salling of Tennessee, age 113. Using the same scale, the last Great War veteran, the last to know the trenches, won't die until well into the twenty-first century's second decade, a miracle of survival that beggars comprehension. People who knew him, boys and girls who listened to his stories, will still be alive in the twenty-second century, and perhaps it's only when they too are gone that the last living link to the 1914–18 war will be totally extinguished.

A novelist, of course, is someone on whom nothing is lost (or rather, in this age of extinction, a person to whom the lost is not nothing), and that includes the contents of a dusty book in a secondhand bookstore that has gone unread for decades. The temptation to fashion this somehow into fiction is a strong one . . . writers, faced with this sort of challenge, like to remember that Tolstoy waited fifty years after the event to write the great novel of the Napoleonic Wars . . . but then thinking of the names listed in *Vermont in the World War,* the families slogging through the mud of Passchendaele the moment the war ended trying to make some communion with the agony of their sons, the soldiers lined up there outside St. Giles, the veteran who, at a farmstand once in Maine, rolled up his pants to show me the bullet hole he'd gotten at the Chemin des Dames . . . thinking even of my own case, a remembering sort of guy trying to understand where the gene comes from that in the middle of a happy life causes me to see nothing but disaster in the events of the larger world . . . I feel only the overwhelming helplessness of ever doing all this justice. *"He was denied even the meagre relief of confiding his impressions to others, for the science which had perfected the savagery of human destruction had neglected to provide a vocabulary fit for the description of its nightmares."*

So what can I do about all this? I can spend two minutes each November thinking about this, that's what I can do, stand out here on the edge of our meadow until my kids are old enough to ask me why I'm standing out here, and then continue to stand out here after everyone quits asking, and my little ritual becomes as quaint and harmless as someone celebrating the relief of Ladysmith or the victory at Saratoga.

But that's all right. A breath of air in November never hurt anyone. To the east the meadow descends in brown slanted grass to the first white pines; to my left, a stone wall topped with rusty barbed wire makes the same declination. Around me are wrapped the clouds, not exaggerating the background noise as they often do, but muffling it, so the only sounds that come through are the ones that seem to travel from the past, as if that's the only conduit open. A train over in Vermont, following the river. Bernard Tullar calling in his cows. The remote echo of a deer hunter's gun. These things only enhance the silence, so that for a moment, a long moment, it's perfectly poised over the meadow, and then fifty yards to my right, with the suddenness of church bells, comes a happy cascade of shouts as the son I've forgotten was there releases a butterfly from his net and waves it in joyous emulation away.

November 16:

On a whim, lured by nothing more substantial than a softness in the air, I took the canoe down from the sawhorses, packed a quick lunch, and ten minutes later was drifting down the Connecticut past the abutments of an old stone bridge.

Odd to be out here this late in the year. Odder still not to have a fly rod in the bow, not to be asking the river for favors. With the leaves gone (except for a substratum of sharp oak leaves that form waterlogged rafts just below the surface) the river seems wider, wilder. In the backwaters the cattails have turned the burnished wheat color so typical of salt marshes, estuaries, and bays— that kind of expanse, though the nearest salt water is three hundred miles downstream. I've got my binoculars with me, but with the front stalled overhead, a breeze blowing from the south, what migrants are around are enjoying the warmth, sitting tight.

Upstream? Down? Down—the wind will be on my back coming home. The banks were once connected here, but the bridge has been out ever since the 1936 flood, and the little collection of houses on the Vermont side seems like it should be joined to the even smaller assemblage of houses on the New Hampshire side; the effect is of a sudden geological parting, village drift.

I'm alone of course. Six billion people on this planet and only one decides to go canoeing on this stretch of river on a perfect November day. Where the banks grow steeper comes a band of white pine; some of the largest are in the river perpendicular to the bank—black, alligator-scaled victims of spring's high water—and a certain watchfulness and care is needed in navigating past them. The water, so soft in its grayness, is somewhere in the forties, and it's not a day to capsize. I pull a little on the left, back water a bit on the right, and— there. The canoe is parked in the springy top of the largest sweeper, held there comfortably, a perfect place to scan the river and eat my lunch.

Fifty yards downstream, out in the middle where the light is strongest, a beaver the color of wet chocolate barges through the water in that purposeful, reproachful way beavers have, as if they're driven by a Puritan work ethic ten times stronger than yours. Further below is a bright splashing commotion that won't come into definition even through the glasses, but very well may be a family of otters caught up in a different philosophy altogether, enjoying the sun. Meregansers? Another possibility—they're splashers, too—though I haven't seen one in several weeks.

When I put my binoculars down the better to chomp into my sandwich something catches my eye up over the Vermont bank—something that at first seems like a floating lollipop (such images are not uncommon when you have children the age of mine), but which turns out to be our local hot air balloon, all pink, black, and green.

We see it frequently here, floating down from the landing strip at Post Mills, but each time it hovers into sight it still makes me feel like an unabashed rube, and as usual I gawk up at it in wonder and delight. My red canoe against the gray river must make a pretty sight in return; through binoculars, with a saluting kind of motion from their foreheads down, I can see its occupants wave.

A gift, summer weather like this. Even the most laconic, that's the term they're using when you meet them in town. "Hey, what a gift!" But as warm as the wind is, as much as I'm tempted to follow it to its source, canoe forever in a perpetual southing, there are chores and obligations waiting for me at home. Not resisting as the breeze swings around the bow, the paddle resting on my lap, I let the river nudge me back toward winter, where I belong.

Scan the newspapers, listen to the radio while shaving, and you'd think there's lots happening lately on the remembrance front. Holocaust survivors strive desperately to make sure the memory doesn't die with their own passing. Historians bury their heads in computers while ideologues battle over textbooks. The nation goes through another of its periodic rediscoveries of the Civil War while theme parks threaten to bury the unspoiled inheritance of that era under pavement. All this fuss, and yet it doesn't hide the simple fact that most Americans don't remember a blessed thing. Not the candidate they voted for last time, not whose fifteen minutes of celebrity was celebrated fifteen minutes ago, not which fad or fancy had dominion over us before the fads and fancies that enthrall us now.

Of course people have commented for years on America's amnesiac habits, most deciding that all in all it's a good thing. Europe remembers—in Ireland and the Balkans they remember too well. Better, the argument goes, a historical amnesia than the historical grudge.

But for individuals, amnesia is a different story. Just as a sense of the past, some feeling for it, can deepen a personality, temper it, give it interest, so too *no* feeling for the past can make a person seem foreshortened and shallow. Too many adults these days have a look of perpetual loneliness on their faces, and why not, since so many are stuck in one dimension in time, racing furiously just to stay there, drawing no solace from that greatest of human resources: that which has come before.

There's someone in particular I think about here—a story, but one I'll keep short. As a young man trying to buy writing time, I had all sorts of odd jobs, but among the strangest was as a tour guide taking people through the enormous Gilded Age mansions of Newport, Rhode Island. One thing I noticed right away was that my tourists, as they roamed the baronial homes of the Astors and the Belmonts and their kin, observed a lot more silence than they did in any church we visited, the only sounds being their appreciative oohs and ahhs as they stared. I took a lot of people through those mansions and it was rare to have anyone not share this worshipful mood.

Which is why I remember a small, round-shouldered man in his sixties named Henry Shapiro who worked selling tokens in the New York City subway. He'd enjoyed the tour so far, was the life of the party with his expressive, rubbery face, his store of jokes, so, seeing him standing alone by the bus while the rest of my people filed in to the next stop on the tour, the Vanderbilts' "The Breakers," I went over to see what was wrong.

"What's up, Mr. Shapiro?" I asked, bracing myself for the usual: a complaint about the hotel; something with the food.

"Those b-b-bastards," he finally managed. "Those goddam bastards!"

I still didn't get it. "Who?"

He jerked his thumb toward the Breakers. "Those bastards made their money with the sweat and blood of my parents! With their blood!"

His anger overcoming him, he turned and spat contemptuously toward the pillared entrance—and with that seemed to rise a good ten inches in height, taking on the one quality you wouldn't think he could ever assume, not with that kind of gesture. Dignity. It was human dignity I was watching as Henry

Shapiro raved, as far removed from the fawning worship of the bulk of mankind as a flower is from a chunk of pavement.

A man that could spit on the grave of the Vanderbilts! That's remembrance for you, and that's what it can do, turn the meek into giants, fill the air with curses, pay tribute to the kind of truth a thousand years of forgetting can never totally erase.

PLAY

Soccer-base we called it—baseball played with a soccer ball, the ball kicked rather than batted, outs made by hitting the runner with your throw or beating him to the bag. We played it all the time as kids, before school, at recess, after lunch. It was the suburban version of stickball, and I was regarded as among the top players in sixth grade, it being the one sport where my long-muscled legs and weak-muscled eyes managed not only to coexist, but to team up in a happy symbiosis that resulted in some heroically long kicks.

Were it a professional sport I'd probably just be retiring now, after a long and glorious career full of every soccer-base honor it's possible to receive. Generous in granting interviews, willing to pose long hours as a sculptor cast a bronze replica of my right leg (pro athletes being the only Americans who are commemorated in civic statutory anymore), I'd be especially gracious in my remarks when it came time to be inducted into the hall of fame, thanking people like Roddy Manning and Steve Chu for their support in the outfield, Mike Scheffler for pitching so brilliantly under pressure, and, most important of all, the coaches and parents and teachers who, in what already seems the halcyon days of 1959, left us remarkably absolutely blissfully alone.

I don't think they even knew we played soccer-base, half of them. It was a pickup game in school, a street game on weekends, nothing that was organized or had sponsored teams. Which is why we loved it of course—loved the anarchism, the fact we put bounds on it as our own umpires, managers, coaches, thrashed things out by ourselves. Already in those days Little League was the big thing, and we all hated it, even the ones who had real skills. When you're eleven you *know* you're eleven, and you can't help feeling the injustice of it when a man three times your age stands there screaming at you because a much bigger kid has just thrown a ball too fast for you to hit.

So it was prime time for a sport like soccer-base, one that grafted onto the savagely exuberant instinct for play we were all blessed with just enough structure and form to make it fun. Kicking the ball was relatively easy, so even the most uncoordinated could get in on the fun. True, we all lived in mortal fear of "spinners"—"No spinners!" we would shout when it was our turn up—though none of us had ever actually *seen* a spinner, much less knew how to throw one. The soccer balls in those days weren't waterproof either, so on soggy days it was a feat for even a slugger like me to get one out of the infield. And, playing in mud, sliding desperately to avoid a ball that was thrown *at* you, we often sat through the rest of the school day soaked and muddied to the skin—but all this, of course, only added to the game's allure.

Each boy in my class had a different style. John Adams running in short mincing steps, then, with a good try, managing to kick it all of three yards. Roddy Manning begging for one of those beautifully sweet "bouncers" that enabled you to get your foot under it, send it flying. Billy Bartlett, elegant already even at eleven, his pant leg rolled high to show he meant business, rocking in a lazy crouch as he waited for the ball to roll in—Billy Bartlett, who totaled his Schwinn in a collision with a school bus, then came back the next day to play in a cast.

Me, I had my own style: power, naked and unadorned. After a lifetime in and around sports I still recall with the greatest satisfaction the sight of outfielders hightailing it back toward the chain-link fence when it was my turn up. None of us had ever kicked one over this fence, but then on one memorable March day I managed to do just that, getting under one of Mike Scheffler's bouncers and lofting it out into the busy traffic on Stewart Avenue. Our home runs were usually accompanied by a lot of mad scrambling—they were all inside-the-park jobs—so none of us knew what it was to have a home-run trot, but I developed one in a hurry. No high fives in those days either. As I rounded the bases, players from both teams waited to shake my hand, so gravely and solemnly, with such respect, that even now, writing about this, I can feel the pride of that occasion, feel those hands reaching out, grabbing, fastening hard—welcoming me, with no men present, into the world of men.

❧

Jump ahead thirty-five years. It's a cold December day in the New Hampshire hills, and with Mom not due home until eight o'clock, there are four hours of darkness to fill in as best we can. Matthew, age four, is playing with his Brio trains downstairs; Erin, age eight, is upstairs reading. Dad, old enough now, shuttles between various tasks too commonplace to mention. Eventually, growing bored on our own, we all converge on the staircase to see if we can manage some collective fun.

Erin has a pink ball in her hands—the cheap plastic kind you can buy in any drugstore. Why, I'm not sure, but she decides to throw it past me downstairs. Quicker than that, with an instinct drilled into me by countless coaches (who thought they were wasting their time!), I put my arm up and neatly block it, so it bounces off a startled Matthew's chest.

Matthew crumples over in laughter, grabbing at the ball as his sister, giggling herself now, grabs for it, too.

"Matt's turn!" I shout—and as quickly as that is born "the ball game," which immediately becomes a Wetherell family favorite.

Rules? I have to sit on the *second* step down from the landing, so as to create a zone where if they throw it just right it's too high to block. Get it past me downstairs and they score a point. When they carry it back upstairs I'm allowed to try to knock it out of their hands—unless they have their fingers crossed, in which case I'm *not* allowed to do this. One ball not being adequate, they each get a ball now, and have learned to wait until I'm blocking the other's shot to slip theirs past me.

We've tried some variations on this, but none have taken hold. For instance, to spice things up I offered them a penny for each point scored, but neither bothered asking to collect after-ward, disdaining even this modest form of professionalism. We've tried playing it when Mom *is* home, but for some reason it's much more enjoyable when she isn't. Erin's figured out how to fake me one way, then throw it the other; Matthew's favorite tactic is to giggle so hard he gets me giggling, too, then, jump-ing his monkey jumps, throws it past me when I'm helpless.

It's not hard to understand the fascination all this holds. No other object in the world is as interesting in its physics as a per-fectly round ball—the satisfying feel its symmetry leaves in the hands, the unexpected directions it can take when released, the resiliency that makes it bounce, its capacity to roll great dis-tances with the application of very little force.

Then, too, getting it past me is just difficult enough to be a challenge, requiring just the right amount of skill; in this respect, it's not all that different from the satisfaction of doing a puzzle. Physical effort counts, too; our wild stretching locomo-tions *feel* good in the muscles and joints. Most important of all, our improvised rules give just enough form to the inherent human instinct for play that the instinct becomes communi-cated, a social experience, a shared form of delight. Play like this is largely pointless—which in our goal-oriented, overachieving world, is exactly the point.

∽

It's astonishing, now that I think about it, how much time and creative energy was given over during my youth to play-ing such games—either games we invented ourselves, or variations of the standard games that under a lot of impro-vised shaping then became ours. At the same time, on parallel tracks that never quite touched, we were caught up in the "official" sports world. Little League and Pop Warner, inter-scholastic sports, the crazy thralldom of being a fan (for me, the New York Rangers circa 1961, with heroes like Gump Worsley, Leapin' Lou Fontinato, the graceful Andy Bathgate, and, favorite of all, little Camille Henry—"Camille the Eel"). There's little about this world I don't know about firsthand. I'm a whiz at sports trivia, have played almost every organized game known to man, and have two bad knees and a wretched back as permanent souvenirs.

But this official world of sports was nowhere near as enjoyable or valuable as the unofficial world, and I can dismiss it here in a few sentences. To us, coaches were figures of fun and/or contempt. Star athletes were looked upon with a certain amount of respect, but with a suspicion that their talent rested on genetics and so was essentially freakish (a six-three center who was far too short to ever stand much chance of success, I agreed with the famous sportswriter Red Smith, who referred to basketball as "goonball" to his dying day). We knew sports were meant to teach us various good things, but what most of us learned from them was anxiety, fear of failure, how to curry favor with adults.

Our own sports world, our underground sports world, was totally different, and I took away from it nothing except a delight so keen it can still make me laugh out loud forty years later. Once we started to outgrow soccer-base, we turned to stickball—not the city version where "three sewers" was a heroic shot, traffic a natural part of the fun, but a suburban, much plusher version, using the wall that ran along the back of our school, the twenty-yard-wide band of pavement that stretched away from it, and, backing up this infield, a limitless expanse of perfectly manicured grass.

We played a luxury game in all respects. Our bats weren't homemade broom handles, but tape-wound bats we bought in the candy store for eighty-nine cents. Our balls weren't the pinkies or Spaldeens of the city game, but real tennis balls, fuzzy Wilsons or McGregors we cadged from our parents. Our wall, perfect as it was in most respects, had as part of its weirdly Gothic design a buttress running along the smooth bricks about four feet off the ground—right on top of the boxes we chalked in for strike zones.

A problem—but as anyone who ever played stickball knows, ground rules and home-field quirks are at the heart of its fascination, and we soon incorporated the flying buttress into play. When a ball struck it, it would bounce, not back to the pitcher, but straight up in the air. When this happened the batter would have to drop his bat and race pell-mell toward the edge of the pavement, while the pitcher raced in past him to field it on one bounce and throw it against the wall into the strike zone. Depending on who accomplished what first, the batter was on base with a single or an out—and to this day there must be dozens of adult men scattered about this country, my one-time opponents, who carry scars where they slid in on their kneecaps to make this play.

When autumn came we switched to touch football, though our version was more like rugby, wide looping laterals being the play of choice. We played on a vacant lot adjacent to Doubleday's Country Life Press (already with a literary bent at thirteen, I pictured Joseph Conrad coming out to watch us play); again, we were left entirely on our own there—indeed, were all but invisible in the smoke of burning leaves, cinnamon in its sweetness, that drifted in from the neighborhoods on either side.

Success in these games often went to the team that could choreograph the wildest plays. I remember something called the Ovaltine Offense, which consisted of our entire five-man backfield running in counter-clockwise circles around the quarterback, who was meanwhile spinning around in the opposite direction, the better to confuse the rushing linesmen on the other side. Gamesmanship was part of this, too, if not outright cheating. I remember a game, tied going into darkness, when the play that won it for us consisted of having our two wide receivers pretend to get in a fight, actually punching at each other, stomping off the field in disgust as the ball was snapped, then suddenly swerving back again, the one to take out the opposing team's safety, the other to catch the ball in the end zone for a touchdown.

But that was the anarchist part—the stubborn refusal to believe sports had anything to do with virtue; that they should be anything else but fun.

After our games were over we would go home and shoot baskets under the spotlights in our driveways, work in a quick game of Ping-Pong before dinner, follow that up with some hard-played Monopoly with our sisters, then—on our way to bed—start shooting crumpled up Kleenex into the bathroom trash basket, keeping score. We played tennis by knocking old balls up against the siding of the porch; our golf was played with our parents' drivers and plastic Wiffle balls, the object being to drive them over the neighbor's garage. And that's just the start of it. Checkers, chess, dominoes; caroms and Knoc-hockey (a particularly aggressive kind that would bloody up the knuckles, leave someone howling); darts downstairs in the cellar; miniature pool; electric football, the field vibrating under our fingers; shuffleboard when we went on vacation; pinball when we had dimes for it; an improvised kind of handball called *Zerch* we played in school with a ball made out of wadded-up aluminum foil off our sandwiches; two-handed canasta with our grandfathers; Duncan yo-yos (around the world!); miniature golf played our favorite way, using the putters as cue sticks, laying flat on our stomachs to line up a shot; fetching every kind of ball ever created from underneath every kind of car (a sport all its own); guns, the kind where we supplied our own sound effects, went *ka-pow ka-pow* all up and down the block (the heyday of the politically incorrect toy!); table hockey where you had to twist and spin the control rods like mad; snowballs launched at anything and everything; elimination dodge; hula hoops; the old reliable hide-and-seek.... Well, I get winded even making a partial list, looking back on those days with some astonishment. Where did the time come from for all this? I was reading all the time, too, playing official sports, rooting for the Rangers, being a Boy Scout, going to school. It's as if childhood were bigger then, had more time in it, more empty spaces left to marvelously fill.

There was a kind of genius behind all this, or at least a patron saint: my father. If any man was ever put on this earth to have fun playing, he's the man. A successful businessman, a man who fought hard to overcome a severe handicap, he was splendidly mature and grown-up—and yet an essential part of this maturity was his boyishness, the fact he never lost touch with it, was never too busy that he wouldn't drop his briefcase, pick up a basketball, launch an old-fashioned two-hander toward the garage.

Of course he never knew where the ball would end up—
that was part of it with Dad. A good athlete as a youngster, he'd
lost most of his eyesight while in the service, could hardly see a
thing—and so improvisation, when it came time to playing
with his kids, was all but a necessity. He couldn't read the rules
of our board games, couldn't see balls well enough to hit them
out to us, couldn't put any of our toys together, couldn't make
out the backboard more than fifteen or twenty feet away—but
what he *could* do was harness his imagination, invent his own
games, remain always willing to clown it up.

This was the era when dads still went outside after dinner
to play catch with their sons, but it was different with us: *I* was
the one who had to throw gently, aiming the ball—the softball,
the tennis ball, the baseball, the football—in a high looping arc
that would give his eyes time to pick it up, and then . . . with a
clapping gesture that could never help being startled . . . make
the catch.

"Good toss!" he would shout, then, with a double pump,
triple pump, *crazy* pump, throw it back.

Almost eighty now, he still retains this boyish capacity in
full strength; if anything, having grandchildren has given it new
life. Their favorite is something called "the hall game." He sits in
the rocker in the living room, and challenges the kids to circle
around the hall *backward*—or patting their bellies, or patting
their bellies and singing at the same time, and so on, him acting
as the referee to see they do this properly, then inventing a new
variation they have to try next—such a good game, such a
simple game, that when my mother, after her last long stint in
the hospital, had doctor's orders to walk as much as she could,
Dad made her play "the hall game," too, him sitting there
applauding when, with courageous and painfully slow steps, she
at last made it around.

༄

There was never a real stoppage in our play (to fall into
sportswriterspeak) . . . I could easily extend the above list
through crazy improvised games we played in college, drunken
nights on Cape Cod in my twenties when I played soccer with a

beachball, blasted it toward the stars, lonely afternoons God-
knows-where when I took my bitterness out on a basketball,
shot foul shots and jumpers for hours on end . . . but there was
definitely a slackening, and I can pinpoint exactly where and
when this happened.

November 22–25, 1963.

A long weekend. The longest weekend any of us had ever
known. Not knowing what else to do, longing for distraction,
one another's support, we played touch football just as though
things were normal, only it was an endless game this time, a
marathon session that extended from the first afternoon of wild
disbelief through the moment Ruby shot Oswald to the solemn
mourning of that unexpected Monday off. Doubleday having
turned our field into a parking lot, we played on a patch of grass
near the Rainbow Division monument on the other side of
town—a smaller field, covered with dog-doo and wet leaves
that made the footing treacherous.

We played for hours, but there was no fun in it. The plays
were routine—no one could think of any brilliant ones—and
people kept leaving to go home and watch TV. And it wasn't
just that Kennedy was dead either. We were fourteen now, some
of us fifteen. Girls, the demands of school, the ruthless division
that had become apparent between those who would go on
to college and those who wouldn't (and for the latter, the
inevitability of the draft), the way the future seemed with all its
uncertainties and perils close enough now that we couldn't
ignore it. A lot of my friends, often the same ones that took part
in these games with the greatest exuberance and skill, seemed
to perceptibly age between one day and the next, as if they had
forgotten something, forgotten how to play, and thereby abandoned the youth that was otherwise still theirs. . . . Or perhaps,
TV having gotten our attention in such dramatic fashion, it now
became easier to watch it all the time, let the Packers and the
Giants do our playing for us.

But I didn't have a name for any of this, was hardly aware of
it other than being generally pissed. We were all pissed for that
matter. I remember Paul Bradley running out for a pass in the

crazy zigzags he was famous for, breaking free in the open, one arm raised, and then the play just collapsing around him, no one bothering to shadow him, no one bothering to throw the ball—it all just collapsed . . . and Paul standing red-faced in the end zone marked with our jackets, screaming at the rest of us: "Get in the game! Get in the game goddammit!" . . . then someone, I forget just who, spitting sideways in disgust, throwing at him not the football, but what in our sports world was the cruelest putdown of all.

"Aw shut up," he said. "You sound like a fucking coach."

December 22:

We often have our first snow before Thanksgiving, and if it waits much longer than this, as it has this year, people grow restless. A bare winter is one of the worst calamities nature can lay on these hills. The frost, driven deep without the insulating layer of snow, can snap pipes in half, freeze springs, crack foundations, kill trees and plants that have weathered previous winters with ease. A bare winter looks wrong, too; winter needs white the way spring needs green, the starkness of late fall being bearable only if it blossoms into sunshine on snow, cold blue shadows, mica-like gleamings—the whole winter bag of reflective tricks.

But it doesn't snow. The clouds hang in, the cold is there, but some invisible command or trigger seems missing, as if, when it comes to snow, nature has simply forgotten how.

I'm restless anyway this time of year. Living in the country it's hard not to feel the atavistic yearning toward readiness that must have driven our ancestors wild. At night this instinct is at its purest and most distracting. Countless trips outside to the woodpile, endless fussing with the stove, three laps around the circumference of the house checking windows and doors for drafts, snack after snack—getting the cave ready, on the lookout for carnivores, adding on the body fat . . . man at work.

We're not the only ones worried by this snowless December. Last night there was an unholy chorus of yipping right out the window that woke us all up. Coyotes. This morning as soon as it was light I grabbed a jacket and my boots and followed their tracks in the frost down to the small pond below the house, trying to discover what the commotion had been all about.

And immediately ran into our neighbor Trina embarked on the same mission. Her cat hasn't come home from its nocturnal wanderings, and she has some suspicion that what those coyotes were doing last night was celebrating in fiendish revels its demise.

Trina knows about fiends and demons and such. She's one of the country's best children's illustrators, has the talent for making the ghoulies, dragons, and witches that inhabit her work seem possessed of real malevolence—a malevolence, such is her art, that might be won over to your side if they sense you're good and sincere and mean them no harm.

She's something of a force of nature in her own right. Small, bifocaled, cigarette-smoking and at first glance tough, she has the fierce independence of someone who even in this age still manages to live by her wits—someone whose rough edges haven't been smoothed out by having to be a team player, work with committees, suffer workshops. Our kids idolize her. On her twenty-year-old Toyota is a bumper sticker that reads MEAN PEOPLE SUCK.

There's no problem with the cat. He struts into view through the bristle of old aster, a cocky look on his mug, as if he's taken care of those coyotes without working up a sweat. Our conversation turns to Trina's latest project: illustrating an anthology of poems about winter. Without snow, it's been impossible for her; she depends heavily on local scenery for inspiration.

"Snow, dammit!" she says, cocking back her head, staring skyward. "Snow!"

After wishing her well, exchanging last pleasantries, I
start up the hill toward the house, only to be touched
lightly on the forehead by something wet and warm, then
again by something wet and colder that gets caught in
my eyelash and makes me blink. Snow—and then
quickly lots of it, so when I look back toward Trina to
wave and laugh, her small shape is already blending out
against the pond, spreading apart into atoms, becoming
particulate, then dreamy, then—gone.

Is play on its way out? There's plenty of evidence to think so.
Walk the same suburban neighborhood I grew up in and you
won't hear any basketballs bouncing off any garage backboards,
won't see anyone tossing a football in the streets—the streets
that are eerily deserted now no matter what time of day, except
for teams of recent immigrants who soberly cut the lawns. Kids
are woken up at five A.M. to be hauled off to the hockey rink for
ice time; sports camps and clinics are now *de rigueur* for even
the unwilling; video games tell us what to do, flashing lights in
our eyes, forever beating us—all this and the cesspool of big-
time sports, the way we've contracted out our "playing" to
millionaires who we watch "play" for us (and the essayist
Roderick Haig-Brown, considering this last phenomenon, calls
it "the greatest loss of positive pleasure in the history of the
world"). Ironically enough, we seem to be losing our taste for
play, the knack, at the very moment wildlife biologists are at last
willing to admit the fact that many animals *play*, and that it's an
important, even essential part of life.

My wife, Celeste, could add something here. Two years ago,
disgusted at the rundown condition of what passed for a playground behind our school, she decided to organize parents to
build a new one. The money would be privately raised, of no
cost to taxpayers, available free to every kid in town.

Great idea, right? How can anyone argue with a free playground? And yet it turned out to be a hard two-year fight to get
it built, since it became obvious right away that a substantial
number of people in town did not want a new playground.

Reasons? The old equipment was good enough for us, by God. Free, yeah, but what about insurance? It's a lot of money—shouldn't we spend it on, you know, computers? All these complaints and more; she was even hauled before a special meeting to defend her efforts (there's a certain kind of person, especially common in New Hampshire, who not only likes to look a gift horse in the mouth, but insists on shoving a flashlight down its throat). None of these objections made much sense, until you stopped and considered them from another angle, realized that many people no longer see any sense in play (which my dictionary defines as "the spontaneous activity of children"), and are even actively hostile to the idea.

In the upshot, the kids got their playground, thanks to the devotion of a small group of volunteers. We put it in last week, a hundred of us working hard to beat the darkness that comes early this time of year. There was some thought we should wait until spring, but eagerness overcame prudence, and—fortune favoring the bold—the day turned out to be one of those miraculous soft ones you can sometimes get here in December, warm enough that almost everyone worked without gloves or even jackets.

Put it down as one of the two or three really special occasions in the fifteen years I've lived here. A supervisor came from the playground company to help us with any problems, but as with any large group of Americans, there was a plethora of engineering talent on hand, carpenters, mechanics, the generally handy (the only sign of the times being that a good many of these turned out to be women), so construction moved right along. One group assembled the climbing wall, another group—not without some head-scratching—got the zip line going, while yet another, the heavy hitters, manhandled the slides into place. We all broke for lunch . . . hot meatloaf sandwiches cooked by a volunteer crew, served by the Boy Scouts . . . then went back to work.

By five, just as it was getting too dark to work, the last bolt was hammered in, to the kind of cheers that must have accompanied the driving of the last spike on the Union Pacific.

Celeste, carried on everyone's shoulders, blushing furiously, got the first slide down, but then all the kids that had been hovering around the edges all day, chomping at the bit, poured over the timbers in a happy wave of motion . . . and then the adults joined in, until everyone—toddlers, kindergartners, school kids, teenagers, farmers, accountants, lawyers, teachers, nurses, grandparents, *everyone*—was sliding and jumping and swinging and shouting from sheer exuberance, so loud the very hills rang with it, a rich and solid joy to the world.

I*nfinity* is an easy word to fling at stars, especially by someone starting out to celebrate his love for the night sky. Like a certain kind of poet who must plunge right into profundity, the daily, homely texture of life be damned, there's a certain kind of essayist, often the most learned, who can't go three sentences without using a big I-term, cosmologists having long since decided what the philosophically correct attitude toward stars should be. Wonder, amazement, a metaphoric shriveling up as we realize how puny we are faced with such, well, *immensity.* You don't have to read much in the poetics of astronomy to see what I mean.

But immensity, like the harmonic depths in Bach's music, doesn't necessarily come at first exposure. When I go outside of a dark and clear winter evening, high-step through the snowy drifts in our meadow to stare up at the sky, what I'm aware of first is a happy play of light, a bright intimacy, a cozy flashing. Orion rising sideways over our local mountain, slowly straightening. Cassiopeia back behind me, spelling out in delicate tracing the first letter of my name. Cygnus, the bright northern swan, still visible in the west, a survivor of summer that is stubborn to quit the sky. At first there is nothing cold and infinite about these at all. Planted there in that twenty-degree-below-zero night, my feet numb even in boots, my forehead feeling encircled by a tight crown of ice, I'm aware most of all that these are *suns* I'm standing under, not so distant they can't transform their warmth into beauty, focus it down to the spot where I'm standing, send a comforting surge from my eyes to my heart.

Sometimes I play a game with all this, try imagining how all this would appear to someone who had never seen stars before, had no inkling of what they were—a person who had lived forty years in a cave, or a blind person just recovering their sight. Wouldn't their first reaction be to throw their hands over their head and cower, wincing from the expected impact as this bright chandelier crashed? Reaction two, upon realizing it wasn't going to fall, might be to laugh—laugh like a child waking up to find a wonderful mobile had been hung over their crib?

I often try to see stars this way, as a visual phenomenon worthy of admiration on its own, never mind the physics, the stellar intricacies and laws that hang them in place. Around me is a dome of blackness arcing above the horizon, its base decorated with the silhouettes of hemlock trees, the swelling anticline of a distant mountain, the wide upside-down V of a barn. Sparsely just above these, increasing as I look higher, thickest two-thirds of the way overhead, are crystalline pinpoints of light that seem to shine with an active sharpness; their distribution suggests a blossom, the kind that comes when fireworks spread open—the whiteness intense toward the center of the blossom; more delicate, even wispy toward the sides, where the shape crests apart. Some of these pinpoints are much brighter than others; as you stare at them, their crystal seems to meet you halfway. One of these is low in the western sky; two a little higher to the northeast, trailing some fainter ones; a band of three cuts straight across the sky toward the south. Scattered as these are, there seems to be a logic to the various groupings (*asterism* turns out to be the beautiful word for these), and not necessarily a difficult one; their brightness seems to be pointing you where to look, asking you to connect the lines, make of them familiar shapes.

Stare long enough and it becomes apparent that not all these pinpoints are white after all. Some have a definite reddish cast, while others suggest a vivid yellow or blue. Other points are smudged, enough to make you rub your eyes trying to clear them. But no, the smudge is in the sky, and here and there shines with beautiful luminosity, like stellar webs drying after an early-morning rain. Between the colors and the various degrees of brilliance—our perception that makes the brightest ones look closest, the fainter ones more remote—the impression is soon conveyed of dimensionality and great depth. That first instinctive sweep made of these pinpoints a ceiling, but the longer they're stared at the more that ceiling lifts, revealing higher ceilings, ceilings upon ceilings, coming so fast, so thick, that the word *ceiling* soon loses all meaning, and you realize what you're staring at literally has no top.

Infinity. Even on that first naive, primitive glance, the evidence is there. And by much the same process it soon becomes apparent that these points that seem so static are actually moving, not only relative to you, but relative to the sky. Many of them, the thickest collection, seem grouped in an actual band, or rather a great river—a river running from the lighter darkness in the northeast up to where the sky is blackest, replenished there by other faint swarmings, then continuing on in a great milky unrolling toward the west.

And that's not all. On some nights the stars, spectacular as they are, seem merely to act as the painted backdrop to the sky's main events. A burnished sliver of orange that appears where the sunset blends toward black and yet hangs separate from it, a different substance—a sliver that widens each night, climbs higher, takes on more white, until it becomes huge and dominant, soaking up the light of all but the brightest pinpoints, then, like an ivory mirror, casting it back. Pale streamers that pulse skyward in the north, take on a metallic green-blue shade at their apogees, restlessly shimmer. Sudden match-like flarings that quickly burn out, creating a flash of gladness in whoever sees them. A pinpoint that doesn't flicker like the others, but shines in a steadier beaming that suggests a lighthouse set in an immense and lonely sea. . . . All this activity, as if the wonder hasn't been created in dabs or even brush strokes, but been tossed at the canvas in extravagant heaps.

The stars are the wilderness overhead, the nearest any of us will ever come to glimpsing the heavens, the great elemental sight. Like sunlight on ocean, the pattern of wind moving through a grassy field, the high sweep of distant mountains, it demands the kind of seeing that takes us out of ourselves, diminishing us and exalting us all in that same glimpse—the sky's catharsis, the night's art.

"Learn to reverence stars," the great American naturalist Henry Beston once wrote. "When the great earth, abandoning day, rolls up the deeps of the heavens, a new door opens for the human spirit, and there are few so clownish that some awareness of the mystery of being does not touch them as they gaze. For a moment of night we have a glimpse of our world islanded in its stream of stars—pilgrims of mortality, voyaging between horizons across eternal seas of space and time."

⁓

For many years, when it came to stars, I was content with these two extremes—with enjoying their happy, naive play of light on one hand, and taking from them the occasional shot of metaphysical reverence on the other. I knew some astronomy, of course, had often wanted to learn more, but had never found the impetus to begin. And then my daughter, Erin, was born—in 1986, the year Halley's Comet fizzled out against the sky—and it became simply intolerable to think she would ever ask me a constellation's name and me not know it.

So I set out to learn.

We were living higher up in the hills those years, in a very old, very rickety house set within a village that hadn't changed its outward appearance in well over a hundred years. On the little rise back off the road is the "Academy"—a two-room schoolhouse built in 1839. Past the slides and swings is a large open field—smooth grass in close to the academy; rougher meadow where it begins its gradual slope up to the woods. It was a two-minute walk from our house; with its view toward the horizon on three sides, a perfect place to begin my explorations.

This was in January, the heart of winter. Feeling a little conspicuous . . . a man walking past his neighbors' windows to stand alone in a field at night . . . I brought along some props. Cider, our golden (no one questions you if you're with a dog), a small flashlight (which I seldom used), a thermos of hot tea (which I used a lot), a child's guide to the constellations (figuring the simpler I started the better). There was a picnic table on the marge where the grass slanted up to the meadow proper, and even though it was covered in snow, I found it useful as a base camp and point of reference.

I didn't look up at the sky right away, though it was a dark, perfect night; if anything, I felt that odd shyness that comes before the start of any new venture, and it made me want to ground myself in the terrestrial before starting, as it were, to fly.

There, fifty yards to my right, was the Academy building, blocky and dignified, even whiter than the snow, smoke rising from the chimney pipe to split around the bell tower and reform above. To the east, a hundred yards across the meadow, was the weathered house of Jeannette and Jasper Day, the lights from their window breaking across the snow in slanted bars. Above them in a dark semi-circle was the first band of softwoods, out of which the occasional moose would appear, wandering down into the village to eat people's flowers. Closer in was the gabled Victorian house of Pearl Dimick, age one hundred—for many years the town clerk, our oldest inhabitant. Behind me, just barely visible over the bulky lines of the old parsonage, was a warm rectangle of yellow light on the back side of my house—and somewhere within this, though I couldn't see her, my wife putting our baby daughter to bed.

All this taken in by way of preparation, feeling as firmly planted on this earth as it's possible to be, I pushed back the watch cap from the top of my forehead, blinked to get the cold out of my eyes, craned my head back, stared straight up into the sky . . .

And knew right away I was in for trouble.

To say there were lots of stars in that sky is like saying there are a few grains of sand on Cape Hatteras. They were everywhere, so thick their whiteness crowded aside the black, so it was as if everything had flip-flopped, the snowfield become snowy sky—and me faced with the task of separating out the individual flakes, guessing their names. Always before I had wanted to be lost in the stars when I looked at them, but now it was different: I wanted signposts, directional signals, maps, and here if anything there were too many of them, they pointed every which way, so I hardly knew where to begin.

I'd made up my mind that the circumpolar stars would be the ones to look for first—those constellations that are visible above the horizon every night of the year. Almost immediately, though, I encountered the two basic problems beginners stumble up against. First, that any printed chart of the heavens suffers from its flat dimensionality, so it takes real visual imagination to lift it off the page, drape it on the right axis, apply it to the sky. Second, that few constellations look like what they're supposed to look like, and preconceived notions of a "bear" or a "queen sitting in a chair" are often more confusing than they are helpful.

But after a while, staring and squinting, I began to see a few things that made sense. The first of these was Polaris, the North Star—the fixed point around which the heavens seem to spin. Knowing that it formed part of Ursa Minor—that it was at the tip of the Little Dipper's handle—hardly helped at all, since only very faint fourth-magnitude stars connect the handle to the dipper part, so beginners get lost trying to make the connection. More helpful was learning that Polaris can be found in the north (I meant it when I talked about keeping things simple!) the same number of degrees above the horizon as the latitude you're standing on ... in this neck of the woods, the 45th ... and that—a splendid trick!—ten degrees of sky can be measured up from the horizon by extending your arm and sighting along your clenched fist, the portion it obscures being approximately ten degrees.

I faced north. I extended my arm. I squinted. I "climbed" four fists, added a knuckle or two more—and there it was. Not the brightest star in the sky, not the most beautiful, but the best behaved in its medium whiteness, remote like the pole is remote, utterly reliable. . . . And armed with that small beginning, centered in the sky just like I was centered on the planet, I felt ready for more.

The next constellation was easy. Ursa Major is the one everyone knows, its Big Dipper asterism—the slaves' "Drinking

Gourd," the "Plough" of ancient Britain—so square and unmistakable overhead. In January, it's still relatively low in its
clockwise progression, so the Dipper looked more like a snow
shovel than anything else, ready to bite off the drifts on the hill
at my back. My star guide (which I consulted every now and
then with the penlight) delineated each individual star. Merak
and Dubhe, Phecda and Megrez, Alioth, Alkaid, Alcor, and
Mizar; in their happy confusion of letters and sounds they
made me remember the delight I took as a boy finding out the
Three Wise Men had actual names.

I came away with two more constellations before I went
home: Cassiopeia a definite; Cepheus—house-shaped but
faint—a maybe. One of the hardest things about identifying
constellations is knowing where they start and where they end,
how much sky to focus on, the space they occupy. Are you looking for a big house or a small house? Which ones of the faint
background stars toward Polaris is really Cepheus's peak? If
anything, the clearer the sky, the harder it is to separate out the
patterns, so the process becomes similar to a child trying to
learn to read—to see letters as distinct entities in a world full of
competing squiggles and swirls.

It snowed hard the next night, and when I went back on
Thursday it took a real effort to reach the picnic table, set up
shop. On winter nights in these hills you can feel the clearness
as a firm centered ring around the outside of your heart, so—
feeling this, taking for granted the sky was clear—it was with
some surprise that I looked up into a thick layer of stratus. No
stargazing tonight. Disappointed, I'd called Cider in from her
bunny-hopping up-and-down circuit through the drifts, started
toward home, when some vague pulse of energy, a premonition
so faint it hardly deserves the name, made me look back over my
shoulder . . . in time to see the largest cloud thin, shred, part
entirely, and there beyond it, in all its splendor, appeared Orion,
winter's hunter, the greatest constellation in the sky.

Orion of the famous belt. Orion of Betelgeuse and Rigel, the
supergiants yellow and blue. Orion of Bellatrix. Orion with the
sword, the nebula that shines in its middle with an iridescent

smoke. The hunter is the key to the winter sky, the stargazer's friend, for once understood it serves as the guide to a good half of the heavens, its geometry managing to be remarkably impressionistic on one hand, and, when it comes to pointing the way toward other stars, reliably precise on the other.

It wasn't long before the rest of the clouds were gone. So crisp and clear was the sky that night, even with the understory of a snowy planet, that the constellations seemed to fall into place like puzzles whose pieces had all turned magnetic. There above Orion's high shoulder was the bright V of Taurus, just the way my book plotted it, with the Pleiades a hazy sheen higher still. Look the other way back from Betelgeuse and there were the twins of Gemini, Castor and Pollux, fraternally spaced, unmistakable. . . . And right below them Procyon in Canis Minor. . . . And wait a little more, following Orion up the sky, appeared Sirius, the brightest star of all, Frost's "great heavenly beast" who "gives a leap in the east." . . . And then even Lepus the Hare, faint but discernible there in the southeast, testing my eyes' acuity, drawing me further, deeper, into the sky.

I felt like a child who, between one moment and the next, understands algebra, how to read, how to *see*. There was a long way to go yet, but at least I understood now the dimensions I was dealing with, the scope and magnitude; before, a puny terrestrial, I was looking at chunks of sky that were far too small. Focusing back was the key, seeing the larger pattern—not only bright Capella straight overhead, but the huge pentangle of lesser stars that, as Auriga, accompanies it through the night.

I went out again the next night, and the night after that, and every night the clouds permitted right through spring. Gradually I began to realize northeast was the crucial direction—that in the slow turn of earth through the heavens this is where most of the major constellations appear first, their westernmost stars peeking up over the horizon as if out on a reconnaissance well ahead of the timid main body. The best star guide I found had you face that direction every night of the year, identifying the stars when they were most isolated and vulnerable. Using this principle, keeping my eye on the corner of the sky there above Jasper Day's old barn, I was able to find not only Leo (which to my eyes looked remarkably like the lion it's supposed to look like), but faint Cancer and Corvus and the delicate flying arc of the beautifully named Corona Borealis.

Favorites? I soon had some, as my seeing improved. The long line of Andromeda, the exuberant stretch of its stars across the sky ("living hearts of companionable fire" astronomer Fred Scharf calls them). Little Sagitta, the third-smallest constellation, arrow-like, faint. The Pleiades, if for no other reason than every time I look at them I hear Jon Vickers singing the haunting tenor aria from *Peter Grimes:* "Now the Great Bear and the Pleiades." Scorpius, looking at times like a scorpion, at other times, watching in different moods, like an upraised arm shaking defiantly at fate. Orion—the stars in the heavens I always look for first, even late in the spring as it sinks greatly diminished in the west. These are the constellations I fell in love with that first year; these are the friends I come back to again and again.

⁓

You can get hooked on expanse just like you can get hooked on anything. Nights I can't go out and watch the stars I feel a clenching kind of disappointment, as if whatever else the day has brought me, an essential part of the fabric is still missing. When we were looking to move down from the hills closer to the river, found at last the house we were searching for, not least in the deciding factors was the fact it sits within a large meadow, allowing views in all directions—so perfect in this respect it even comes with a slight hillock in the center that serves as a comfortable backrest facing the northeast sky.

Ten years a stargazer, armed with this view, I'm beginning to have a modest résumé of spectacular sights. Two lunar eclipses, one in summer, the other late in fall—the moon striped by the branches of our solitary elm, then rising clear, only to get caught up in what seemed a gray slice of cloud, then quickly a shadow more adamantine and ruthless than any cloud's. A solar eclipse that, while not total, still gave a warm spring afternoon the burnished feel of late October. A rare and beautiful conjunction of three planets, Mars, Jupiter, and Venus, that flirted with one another the entire month of June, moving around in various combinations like peas in a shell game, until at last they stood posed within the diameter of a transparent quarter in the evening sky to the west. A frigid winter when the Northern Lights were at their brightest, including a night just before the Gulf War when they pulsed in a color that can only be described as "blood" red—shined intensely enough to actually shake me, convince me as nothing before ever had that our "primitive" ancestors were speaking quite literally when they talked of portents and warnings and omens in the sky. And, most memorably of all, two comets: Hyakutake, sloppy and low, an angel in a star-blown granny skirt; Hale-Bopp, higher, tighter, a well-packed snowball hurled toward the sun.

There have been disappointments, too. I've yet to see meteorites really *shower;* the Perseids in these years have been more of a sprinkle. But the point is that the night sky is far from the static, unchanged immovable landscape it seems at first sight to be. When I go out at night, it's not just to renew acquaintance with a featureless map, but with every expectation of seeing something happen.

And of course I know more about stars now than I did those early nights behind the school. Named, linked, the stage is set for mythology and astronomy and physics and the whole superstructure of knowledge our understanding seeks to weave upon that flimsy and delicate fabric of light. Just as the night sky is filled with an infinite amount of shinings, there is an infinite amount of things to know about these shinings—and an infinite amount of things *not* to know, stars being the one place where our ignorance and knowledge are on display simultaneously. More than in most activities, a decision has to be made, on the part of the interested amateur, as to how much knowing is enough.

How much? Along with the names of the constellations, it seems important to know something of their stories—important to know that Perseus, on his way home from slaying Medusa, found time to rescue Andromeda from a salacious sea serpent. It's even more important to know that other cultures beside the Western have embroidered their own stories across the sky, some even more compelling and suggestive than those from classical antiquity that have stuck. Aquila is not only the thunderbolt-carrying eagle of Zeus but, in Indian mythology, the footprints of the god Vishnu. Corona Borealis is not only the crown of Ariadne but the Celestial Sisters in the tales of the Shawnee Indians, a boomerang to the eyes of the aborigines. More beautiful and telling than the stories themselves is the impulse that made man *want* to name them, find in their patterns a humanity that is and is not of the earth. Mythology was man's early attempt to understand the stars, give them motivation and logic, make their motion, their placement in the sky, comprehensible.

Science picks up the story next—and again, the amateur has to decide how much of this he or she wants to delve into. Certainly it's important to know some of it—important to know that the characteristic twinkle of Sirius is caused by its appearing so low in the sky, where the earth's atmosphere can play with its light; that the hazy iridescence in Orion's sword (astronomer Sir John Herschel described it as a "curdling liquid") is in reality a vast nebula made up of gas, dust, and some of the youngest stars in our galaxy. Reading about stars, studying them even semi-formally, reinforces the message that comes with mere looking. Understanding that the light of Fomalhaut, the solitary autumn star, took eight years to reach the earth, the light of the faintest star in Auriga 520 years, the fuzzy glow of the Orion Nebula 1,500 years (the light we see "happening" simultaneously with the fall of the Roman Empire) makes that light, as you turn your eyes toward it, even more precious and mysterious than it would otherwise be.

And there's another crucial lesson to learn here, in many ways the hardest. The naked eye, trying to make sense of the heavens, swallows instinctively the cosmology of, say, 1595, taking for granted that the sun, the planets, the stars all revolve around the fixed center of our planet. The very notion of stars "rising" in the east falls into this totally naive, perfectly natural assumption; it's not the stars that are rising at all, but the earth in its triple revolutions that make them seem so—the daily spin along the equator, the seasonal wobble about the poles, the yearly circuit around the sun. The motion we see in the sky is largely ours through the heavens, and realizing this, understanding this, *seeing* with this, is the very key to understanding the night sky in its fullest majesty. Never mind science fiction, day-dreaming about interstellar travel on satellites or spaceships. We already journey there, even the dullest, most insignificant person on this planet who on whatever impulse glances up toward the night sky; with our baggage of hopes, fears, and dreams we journey nightly through the galaxy, our faces at the portholes, our eyes illuminated and enchanted by the happy light of dying suns.

⌒

January again, and after writing late into the night, I've walked down to our meadow on the path my boots have on previous nights worn through the drifts. As cold as it is, the stars seem to be shining all that much brighter, as if whoever is in charge of celestial stokings, in pity at my shivering, has generously turned up the heat. The great pattern of winter spreads across the sky, from Capella high behind me to Sirius there in the south. On this kind of night stars are so brilliant their light seems to become aural, the stars actually to chime—and then the sound descends, becomes rounder, turning itself into the familiar ring of the church bell across the frozen river in Vermont. A great horned owl, disturbed by this or pleased, hoots in the woods below the field's edge—one long sound, then, hesitating, a quicker second and third. Lower, fainter than any of these, comes music from the stereo inside the house . . . pedal of harpsichord, bowing of violins . . . making the walls throb with the same kind of harmonic aura that drops from the stars.

As dark as it is here, there are other lights beside starlight. On the high esker over the river are the steamy lights of a working barn; closer, the lights from our neighbor's house caught and broken in the bare trees of the hedgerow. Closer still is the reading lamp in my daughter's room—yellow enough it can churn to cream the snow that slants from the siding outside.

Facing these, considering them, immersed deep in that wintery kind of lofty appraisal, I come to the decision almost everyone has to reach at least once in their lives. Push off heedless for the distant promise of those stars? Cling, however helplessly, to the familiar limitations of our earth? The two extremes of our predicament, our opportunity, and it seems fitting, standing under this wilderness of comprehensible pockets set within the much larger unknown, to remain poised perfectly in between . . . and then the cold finally getting to me, to turn back toward the warm promise of our house and the picture window where, in silhouettes of ascending diameter, my family squints outside to see where in all this immensity Dad has gone.

January 9:

Three lines into a new short story and my e began to spasm, hitting the page again and again and again in a vowelish ecstasy I was powerless to stop. As usual, any interruption of smooth mechanical functioning makes me furious. Disregarding the twenty-degree-below-zero weather, the glaze of ice created by last night's snow, I bundled the machine up in a blanket, drove thirteen treacherous miles to the nearest office-machine shop, plunked it down on the counter, went out for an impatient cup of coffee, came back to hear the repairman render his verdict.

"It's broken," he said. Then, seeing me frown: "Not too many use typewriters anymore, not in your line of work. Hard to get parts. Good time for a computer, seeing how we're having this sale."

I knew what was coming next: "Once you try one you'll never go back." Too boringly familiar is that phrase, the look that comes over people's faces when you explain that you're not up to date on the newest technology, whether that be a fax or a microwave or the miraculous labor-saving device that doesn't exist as I write, but will by the time this is published.

I'm braced for it now. At the rare conference I attend, from the occasional interviewer that finds his or her way up our quiet dirt road. Questions about my latest novel? Some intricate explanation re characterization or plot? Nope, very first question, glancing toward my desk. "Don't you use a computer?"

I have a variety of answers, pick which to use depending on my assessment of the person asking, whether they're polite enough to be content with a polite answer, or whether they're the kind that ask like inquisitioners probing for heresy.

1. NO.
2. NOT YET.
3. CAN'T AFFORD ONE.
4. I PREFER NOT TO.
5. TEND ENOUGH TECHNOLOGY AS IT IS.
6. DON'T WANT TO WORK FOR THE PHARAOH, DON'T THINK WE NEED MORE PYRAMIDS, THANKS JUST THE SAME.

The serious side of all this is that at times I feel like the old-fashioned tools I use are literally being yanked from my hands, sense the existence of a large body of people who, not to mince words, hate/fear/detest me (or rather, my type) because I won't go along—and a somewhat larger group of people who, seeing my stubbornness, are bemused/bewildered/bothered, feel a missionary zeal to make me see the light.

If anything, I only regret having given up a manual typewriter for this electronic job. That was typing! The reassuringly solid weight of the carriage under the hands—how after a vigorous passage written with passion the whole typewriter would slide a good six inches to the right. The way the bell rang when you neared the margin—a real ring, too, not the wimpy beeping the world has substituted in its place. How when you put a

*new ribbon in you could sometimes smell the ink, so it
seemed you weren't just the writer but the compositor as
well, begrimed in your own creation. The delightful feel
of the return lever quick against your palm—the solid
thunk as you shoved it back. The stubborn resiliency of
the keys that made typing real work, so you could feel
the tension in your fingers, feel your thoughts flow from
brain to muscle, that old human current, the re-estab-
lishment of which is half the satisfaction in any craft....
And then the busy rat-tat-tat-tat thump, rat-tat-tat-tat
thump, rat-tat-tat-tat rat-tat-tat-tat bing! that on a day
when the writing went well sounded like a happy and
effortless sonata, to the point where, like a pianist, you
would lift your elbows up to gain more speed, get some
shoulder action, dip and bob your head like a Rubinstein
playing Chopin.... And how occasionally all this—the
bells, the pushing, the swiping, the wild play of fingers—
would all come together in that most beautiful and
miraculous of creations: a sentence that took on a grace
independent of the clumsy fingers that gave it birth.*

Drive from the vicinity of Portland, Maine, to well below
Miami; Chicago to Dallas; Seattle to San Diego ... drive, that
is, through the urban and suburban heart of this continent,
and you would have a hard time finding anything dark enough
for a time traveler from the past to recognize as *night,* let alone
stars visible within that night. Sodium street lamps (with their
harsh blue glare reminiscent of penitentiaries), the neon stain
of malls, highways with their arc lights, the millions of backyards lit by floodlights to keep prowlers at bay. Throw in some
smog, the acidic atmosphere, and you end up with a night sky
that is hideously purple, through which only on the odd freakish occasion become visible what no less an authority than Dr.
Seuss, with a sad shake of the head, termed the "smoke smug-
gered stars."

Even here, two hundred miles from the nearest big city, the
effect is obvious, the sky light enough in the south that I've

taught myself not to look that way, since there are no stars visible in that glow. Astronomers, not a particularly pessimistic bunch, tell us that if light pollution continues to increase at its present rate not one child in ten born in the U.S. will ever really *see* a star. In my grandfather's day it was possible, for a Manhattanite so inclined, to saunter over to the North River piers at twilight and watch the stars appear in all their glory over the distant Jersey shore; by my father's day, the nearest stargazing to New York was in the suburbs, or at least out on the beaches. Now even this is gone, washed out in the flood of vapor lights designed to protect us from each other.

To the astute eye, all this was apparent a good many years ago. Here is Henry Beston writing in 1927 from his "Outermost House" on Cape Cod.

> Our fantastic civilization has fallen out of touch with many aspects of nature, and with none more completely than night. Primitive folk, gathered at a cave mouth round a fire, do not fear night; they fear, rather, the energies and creatures to whom night gave power; we of the age of the machine, having delivered ourselves of nocturnal enemies, now have a dislike of night itself. With lights and ever more lights, we drive the holiness and beauty of night back to the forests and the sea; the little village, the crossroads even, will have none of it. Are modern folk perhaps afraid of night? Do they fear that vast serenity, the mysteries of infinite space, the austerity of stars? Having made themselves at home in a civilization of energy, do they fear at night for their dull acquiescence and the pattern of their beliefs?

Of course, even this gloomy assessment reads, in retrospect, like the idyll of a golden age. Fine for Beston to say we no longer fear the energies and creatures to whom night gives power. They're back, in full force, and it's no coincidence that one of the largest organized groups against crime and violence calls itself Take Back the Night, as if the night alone were to blame, and not our nocturnal enemies, that is, ourselves.

The upshot for someone who still worships night, the great stars? Look and take your fill, for that wilderness may soon be as extinct as any wilderness, or as good as for those of us who can't afford the fare to the high Andes. Take your kids out, too, so perhaps one day they'll remember in the deepest recess of memory a bright pinpoint surrounded by gladness that, even from such distance, can still warm the inner fiber of their hearts.

 On a bright winter day in 1982, having found by a lucky miracle the perfect woman, I went looking for the perfect town.

This was in the hills of western New Hampshire, though it could just as easily have been somewhere in the matching landscape of rural Vermont. Only the narrow Connecticut separates the two here, and in its achingly beautiful valley the pastoral feel is much the same no matter which side of the river you happen to live on. Socially, politically, it's a different story; indeed, there are many in town who feel rejoining New Hampshire in 1777, after the town briefly "seceded" to Vermont, was by far the worst mistake it ever made.

But here I'm already wandering from my main theme. On that January morning, driving north along the river, the white pines on my left intermittent enough I could see the wind-ribboned drifts on the snowy ice, I had not only a pretty good idea of what I was searching for, but the fixed conviction I would know it the moment it hovered into view.

My criteria were these, in descending order of what I could with any realism expect to find. A small rural village of less than two thousand souls. A village in the hills where the fishing was good. A village within reach of a hospital where Celeste could work. A village where the life I had read about, worshiped from afar—the old rural life of the nineteenth century—was still at least partially intact. A village tourists didn't know about. A village cosmopolitan enough to tolerate what I did for a living. A village where we could live for the rest of our lives.

In short, as I passed the inconspicuous road sign that marked the neighboring town to the south from what I didn't know yet was *my* town, I was still haunted and vexed by what was undoubtedly the most characteristically American trait in my arsenal: a geographic restlessness that had tormented me for years. Just over the horizon/rainbow/divide lay that great good place where at last I would feel at home ... or as the poet Sydney Lea puts it, embarked himself on such a quest: "I thought of how, from an astonishingly early age, I'd vowed to find a region—some beautiful and intriguing country, home to fleet wild things—and marry it."

So into town I drove, very much the anxious suitor, and knew within the first three minutes, with an instinct that raced ahead of the evidence out the windows, that my search was over, my great good place had been found.

What I was looking at as I slowed down past an icy trout stream was a village of twenty houses banked to their lower windows in snow, the vivid white of the drifts serving to accentuate the even whiter siding, so it was impossible to look at any of them without squinting. These were mostly Greek Revival houses, or at least showing that influence, and on a clear day like that one they had something of Greek purity of stance and form, the banked snow acting as their pedestals ... and then further along came a Victorian updating, with a high monitor roof of mirror-like glass ... and then in the open space beyond it, a farmhouse fronting a field solemnized by rusting tractors and holsteins nuzzling the muddy intervals between drifts. To the left, closer, was a school in two parts: an old red building of scalloped wooden shakes and a more modern wing of utilitarian brick, the windows decorated with construction-paper valentines. Past this was the town common, around which the road divided, coming together again near a traditional Congregational church at the east end, an old cemetery on one side and on the other a long red horse shed, the kind where worshipers once left their sleds.

There wasn't much besides this. A hardware store as simple and classic as any of the houses. An inn of shabby gentility. A general store. That late in the morning, on a cold winter day, the only signs of life were the straight, sun-bleached columns of smoke rising from the chimneys, and the grayer, horizontal puffs coming from the idling pickups by the post office and store.

On the wall of the latter various notes were posted, including one advertising a house for rent just off the common. An hour later, after a quick inspection, I had signed a lease, and on Friday of that week Celeste and I moved in with all our worldly possessions: a colander, two stereos, three typewriters, eighteen cartons of books, and more fishing rods than I care to remember.

But it was a lucky house for us right from the start. Built in the 1830s during the town's heyday as a sheep-raising center, it was now owned by the couple who lived next door: old Doctor Adams and his wife, Helen. He'd been town doctor for well over forty years, and was the hero and anti-hero of all kinds of stories (his angry, accusatory tone when someone hurt themselves doing something dumb; his wild driving on icy back roads; his teaching Greek at the local high school; his being the only doctor willing to go back up into the communes of the '60s, help out with a birth). I'd read enough about country doctors to know they were supposed to be generally beloved, but, as we began hearing people talk, it was obvious Dr. Adams wasn't, and there was some mystery as to why.

Certainly he was a tragic enough figure now, bent over with Parkinson's, going unshaved for days, his eyes shorn of everything except the embers of his intelligence, managing nothing longer than walks to the post office, orange reflective patterns sewn on his threadbare coat. His wife accompanied him on all these little expeditions; she was a remarkable woman herself, with a dignity that veered toward aloofness and a self-discipline that at first glance seemed ice. A typical New England iciness, the kind that's rarer these days, and it took us a long while to gain her favor ... but once gained it resulted in a spell of friendship I remember with gratitude, since she was a great compiler of local history and lore.

But here, just as I knew I would, I begin once again to stray. So many people to write about here, or rather, just enough it's conceivably possible to do them all in one chapter! Before that first month was over we were launched on an exploration that is far from done yet, installed smack in the middle of a place that was comprehensibly sized, comprehensibly peopled . . . the kind of place where, knowing something about the world, I could at last devote myself to learning something of the parish . . . a place where, as I do nowhere else, I have the conviction that anything that happens here is interesting because is happens *here*. When I leave on a trip, go away for a short stint teaching, I always feel, upon coming back again, like a baseball player who after an exhausting circuit of the bases, a desperate slide toward the plate, looks up to see the umpire spreading his arms apart and yelling *"SAFE!"* I can even foresee a time not too far in the future when, like many old-timers here, I pride myself on not leaving town at all, and while I hope I never go quite that far, it's a measure of my love for these hills that it doesn't seem the worst of fates.

∾

All this goes to explain why I enjoy showing visitors around—to recapture some of my first excitement; to see things fresh through their eyes. I have a little circuit I've worked out, a regular tour, but here I'd like to take advantage of the miracle of prose (the miracle it still survives!) and conduct an even better tour, one that might be hard to duplicate in the real world, where constraints of time and weather come into play. In January our local mountain can be a bastard to climb; the lower slopes are easy enough for those on snowshoes or skis, but past the halfway point the grade steepens, the trail turns to ice, and unless you're lucky with the weather it can be a real haul . . . and yet thanks to the elevation, the outlook, there's no better place to start sizing things up.

The mountain I'm referring to is called October Mountain, all 3,238 proud feet of it, the mountain that gives what would otherwise be a gentle valley town its hard wild backbone in the east. High enough to generate its own weather, fringed near the top with a wind-bent band of boreal spruce, graced but not cluttered with trails, haunted with cellar holes and old walls,

October is the central geographic fact for most of the citizens in town, not only those who hike or hunt it, but those lucky enough with topography to have an unobstructed view of its summit from their homes.

I'm in this last group, solidly. If I take my eyes off this type-writer between sentences, I can glance out the window and see October in profile, the long domed summit rising above lower Lambert Ridge. In March from this angle the sun rises directly above the summit, making it seem as if some prehistoric and vanished race through unimaginable labor erected the moun-tain to mark off the equinox, give the returning sunlight an axle on which to spin. Now, writing in winter, the sun rises a good twenty degrees to its south, but still manages to illumine the summit before coloring anything lower. It's the first thing I see in the morning, the first fact that registers, the undeniable bulk of it slapping me awake in a way the morning news, the first cup of coffee, can't even begin to emulate. How fares it with October this morning? What lenticular cloud smudges and enlarges its silhouette? What birds soar across it? What will the morning light do to its shape?

Its shape? I happen to love it, but honesty compels me to admit that shape is not October's aesthetic strong point. No perfect cone here, no rectangular symmetry. The terms that come to mind in describing October's silhouette tend toward embarrassing rhymes: lump/bump/rump/hump. It's all these (and while we're being honest, the mountain was named by a poacher who stole pelts from Indian traps), but after you know it for a while, the long anticlinal line tends to become softer, more fluid, suggesting the flattened breast of a reclining Modigliani nude or, in summer, a green whale breaching north-ward through the mist.

There's an old fire tower on top, ice-encrusted this time of year, and when the sun sets just the right way it shines like a silver match. From the top—climbing the mountain now, no longer admiring it from our rockers—the view is expansive, taking in a good portion of western New Hampshire and east-ern Vermont. Toward the northeast the views are bounded by the Whites, including Mount Washington; to the west, the long line of the Green Mountains, topping off in Killington's raped and battered slopes. The town's location between these two tourist magnets ensures a somewhat forgotten status; no one here wishes those mountains and crowds were any closer.

But it's the local panorama we've come to study. Directly below the broad summit is Reservoir Pond and the cluster of beaver ponds that feed it, showing up as doglegged white intervals in the shaggier white carpet. To the south, the trails of our modest little ski area, leading up to a chevroned zigzag of gray cliffs. To the east, one of the largest, roughest tracks of woods in the state—so rough there is no through-road to our neighboring town in that direction, and anyone asking directions can be told with absolute honesty that old Yankee one-liner *You can't get there from here!* To the west, seemingly flatter than it really is because of the terrain that rises from its edges, the narrow plain on which the village rests.

Two lessons are at work here: the stunning beauty of the town's natural setting; the perfect way its political boundaries nestle into its geographic ones. The town ends on the Connecticut—not harshly, abruptly, but in a natural and relaxed draping, as if everything about the terrain had as its logical westward conclusion this sinuous white line. To the east, the town ends more abruptly but with equal logic on the height-of-land that separates the Connecticut watershed from that of the Baker River one valley over (*"I Joseph Blanchard testify and say that in the winter of the year one thousand seven hundred and sixty-one I was employed by his Excellency Benning Wentworth, the Governor of then Province of New Hampshire, to survey and plan Connecticut River from Hanover to the upper end of Coos intervales, and make bounds on both sides of said river at the distance of six miles from each other so that the Grants of land lying on said River might be properly bounded."*) To the south, the town line crosses the sag below Deer Mountain; to the north, the sag below the aptly named Mount Sheer. Circumscribed and enhanced by all these limits is a patch of land roughly forty square miles in area; a patch that, grace it with ponds and swamps, streams and hillocks, pastures and fields, is enough for any man or woman to love intimately, not just in broad abstract sweeps, but in particular folds, crannies, and pockets, ones that were once important enough in everyday life to each have its name. *Dimick* Hill, *Plott* Hill, *Moody* Mountain, the *Pinnacle.*

The people who named all these are still very much a presence back in the woods, at least for those who know how to read the signs. Stone walls can be found up toward the 1,500-feet contour, testifying to the fact that most of this land was with backbreaking labor once cleared; slightly lower begin the briar-choked cellar holes, with their telltale apple trees set in front still tipping out in springtime blossoms, shading stumpy old lilacs turned now to black. On the road that runs along the mountain's base, set high and forgotten on a little rise, is a small cemetery the town still maintains, though the last ones buried here died in the 1820s. Nowhere else in town is the sense of those early inhabitants so palpable; nowhere else conveys to unmistakably the sense of land resting under a labor that was intense, desperate, and—so thin was the soil—doomed.

It's hard to be romantic about village life of that era, knowing the lonely lives theirs must have been, with a visit to town a great and rare occasion, neighbors giving up and clearing out in a steady drain, the early deaths from measles or whooping cough or fever. And yet so powerfully does that early dream of community still haunt us, so tormenting can our unrequited love affair for Utopia still be, that the hard simplicity of their lives seems heartbreakingly appealing, to the point where, looking down on those gray, lichen-scabbed headstones, staring up at the steep hill that robs the sun just as it begins to warm them, you don't feel the usual smugness of the present toward the past, but quite the opposite, as if the historical joke is strictly on us. Our anxious lives, our own brand of light-starved isolation. In few other places in America can this note of being within a vanished paradise, or at least the remains of a vanished paradise's possibility, be so pure and unmistakable, posing the question Americans have never been able to answer, not in four centuries of trying: *If not here, where?*

The mood colors the ride down; it's rare that anyone in the car says anything until the road swings in toward rushing Grant Brook, the notch widens, the sun returns in full force just as we approach the village center . . . and an explanation I hope does-n't sound too confused.

Here in these hills the town center is often not the same place as downtown; in fact, it's often quite the opposite, being the oldest, least populated part of town—the uphill part. The first settlers thought the hillsides offered the best land, being above the poorly drained, fever-breeding lowlands; often, in southern New England where they came from, this was true.

But winter can last a whole month longer up above 750 feet, and the original "Center" soon became the forgotten, déclassé part of town, as the tide of settlement moved downhill. Our Center remains in something of a time warp, since except for the black locust that replaced the elms toppled during the 1938 hurricane, it looks much as it did in the 1870s, the Center's center—nine or ten houses, a post office, a small white church and vestry, the old Academy two-room school—coming into view suddenly around a tight curve, emphasizing this lost-world, self-contained quality even more.

The old-timers still proudly stress what slight differences there are between Center and "plain," and, like hill dwellers everywhere, look upon the downhill inhabitants as vaguely cor-rupted and effete. The suspicion works the other way around, too. The Center has only recently outgrown its rock 'em, sock 'em reputation, caused in part by the Saturday-night fistfights that, forty years ago, regularly followed the dances held on the Academy's top floor. Until recently the Academy functioned, in its more pacific incarnation, as the town's kindergarten, but with a new school being built on the plain, it was decided to consolidate operations, and so the town's small rural schools, which earlier in this century numbered sixteen, are now down to one—and with this move, another piece of the Center's iden-tity has been chipped with the best of intentions away.

Sharing a driveway and grassy common with the church is the house we bought after two years' renting: a sagging red

gambrel with porches front and rear, a drafty and useless "L,"
and a connected barn so large it overwhelmed everything else.
Built in 1910, it hardly even qualified as middle-aged compared
to its neighbors, and yet it managed to inflict upon us every
misery old houses are capable of inflicting, including a leaky
roof, a crumbling foundation, an unreliable well, and eccentric-
ities and quirks too numerous to mention. In short, it was a
house we wrestled with for seven vexing years, losing on one
end where we gained on the other, the final indignity being that
it took us more than two years to sell it once we decided enough
was enough, the Great Recession having hit New Hampshire
with full economic force.

But this is an agonized story I'll save for another time.
Suffice it to say, I completed three books in this house—it was
the house where we brought our children as newborns—and
perhaps once all my failures there are forgotten my enduring
memory will be of pushing my two kids in their carriage down
from the barn, across the common, up the steep road that leads
out of the village to the south—steeper and steeper, really puff-
ing, onto dirt now, taking that carriage to places no carriage had
ever gone before, Erin prattling on about the goat farm or the
brook or the falling leaves, Matthew—full of formula—sound
asleep on her lap.

And it was a good place to get to know the locals—perhaps
too good a place, since the house's central location obliged us to
be more social and involved than a writer can afford to be. Still,
we had a remarkably varied assortment of neighbors those
years, a mix that could be repeated right through town.

Across the common was the old parsonage, mustard-
colored and homely, owned now by former commune members
in their forties who, unlike so many of their comrades, remained
true to their activist past, he being in charge of a center for
handicapped children, she going back to school to become a
nurse. On our west in a weathered old Cape lived the Pikes, one
of the oldest names in town, Charles a retired janitor at the college, his wife, Betty, a house cleaner who every autumn taught a
hunting-safety course in the church vestry. Renting next door

was their son, who worked in auto parts, and his chain-smoking wife, who was shy as an antelope, but always had her head stuck in a book (and so was a heroine in mine). Three doors down lived a young sculptor and his biologist wife; behind them and catty-corner to our yard, the proprietor of a trash service people called whenever they were doing spring cleaning; his wife worked double shifts as a nurse, finally saving enough money to replace their trailer with a real log house, complete with a separate shrine to her hero Elvis Presley.

I would be lying if I said all these types mixed perfectly— Celeste and I made friends with all of them, though some would walk past each other on the road without so much as a blink of recognition—but perhaps the important lesson here is that newcomers and locals mixed at all, were willing to let one another live in peace.

Read the town histories, talk to the old-timers, and you find out this wasn't always necessarily the case. Thirty years ago the population had been much more homogenous (in 1961, 75 percent of the town's residents were direct descendants of the original eighteenth-century settlers) and yet, as in any other small, isolated place, there were the fistfights, the feuds, the chronic drunkenness, the relatives who, living next door, didn't talk to each other for years on end. . . . And so while I can be as nostalgic as anyone when it comes to ruing the displacement of the old-time Yankee, the truth is the newcomers to the Center, at least that first pioneering influence, fixing up the dilapidated houses, caring for the land, cherishing the traditions already in place, had given the town a badly needed shot of vibrant new life.

After finishing my morning's writing, needing the exercise, it was my habit to get on my bike and ride down to the main village for the mail (or even ski on those mornings the plows were slow in getting out)—and such was the grade, I could get there in a fast ten minutes. One long easy glide along the brook, a furious piece of pumping near the old tannery site, then the exhilarating drop down to the plain where we began things back at the chapter's start.

Compared to the Center, the main village looks like a metropolis, though it still wears that chaste and beautiful clarity it displayed the first morning I saw it. Again, on a cold day there is little sign of life—and yet sixteen years into living here, I know this is an illusion, and that far from hibernating, village life goes on in all its various subdivisions, at all its branch locales.

There in the Congregational Church basement nineteen nursery school children, among them my son, are busy learning how to make butter, or having snack time, or listening to Nora Thebodo read them a book. In the social room in back Eileen Saunders puts her three-year-olds through their dance lessons, teaching them how to curtsy and bow without bending so low they topple on their faces. Across the road the pickups pull into the general store for sandwiches and coffee, so for the half hour leading up to noon it's a crowded, social rush. Three doors down at Nichol's Hardware, Srimalai Nichols presides over the lunch counter, Thai dishes her specialty, every stool taken, the occupants swiveling around to greet those poor souls coming in merely for nails. Over across the common at the restored, rebuilt school we're all so proud of, Jonathan Freeman, the new principal, a local character already for the extravagance of his neckties, presides over an assembly honoring Martin Luther King, Jr. A mile north of town, in the ice-fishing shacks on the largest of our local ponds, the old-timers let their lines down for pickerel or perch, not catching much, but enjoying the companionship, the way they've re-created a village in miniature there on the ice.

Come summer you could add the community of kids, mothers, and sunbathing teens that gathers on the town beach, the trollers commiserating with each other at the boat landing over the shrewdness of our local trout, the softball players on our local team, "The Rats," or even the little village of Adirondack chairs at the nearest our town has to a resort. These form the outer web of village life, the inner web being made up of all the various organizations, clubs, and civic groups: the Utility Club, the planning board, the local chapter of AA, the volunteer firefighters, Happy Valley Quilters, what's left of the

Grange, the town historians, ad hoc committees to restore this, save that. Of these our town is well endowed, is famous in the region for its high percentage of participants involved in just about any community effort anyone can think of.

These committees and clubs have to cast their net wide to obtain members; after all, we're talking about a population of less than two thousand. As a result, they help overcome what Studs Terkel identifies as the besetting sin of our times, the "Great Divide," wherein people live their lives surrounded by those who think like they do, earn what they do, live like they do, and have little or no contact that isn't hostile with anyone from across the various divisions.

A divide exists in this town, of course—as nice as it is here, the laws of reality are still in effect. Much of it, in the time-honored Yankee way, revolves around how long you've lived in town, something that is talked about quite openly, used as a measuring stick to gauge whether or not we should take someone seriously. Thus, at a recent town meeting the following exchange took place as the latest controversy came up for discussion. Up in front jumps Shine King. "I've lived here for forty-three years," he begins, then launches into his opinion. The moment he finishes, another speaker jumps up, Jack Menge this time. "Well, Shine, I think I top you, since I've been here forty-five years." Fine, he too has his say, speaks with sense, then sits down, only to be replaced by my friend Dan Freihofer, looking sheepish. "I've only lived in town ten years," he begins . . . pregnant pause, everyone staring . . . *"And this is the first time I've gotten up the nerve to open my mouth."*

Hearing these stories, seeing the terse nods that are often all there is by way of greeting, the person I'm showing around town usually gets around to asking, "Uh, how friendly *are* people around here?"

I'll admit this is a real stumper. How friendly are people anywhere? Are Southerners who greet the hell out of you intrinsically more friendly than New Englanders who grunt? Westerners who give you a big "Hi ya boy!" warmer than New Yorkers who use "Fuck you" as their introductory remark?

Certainly there are those in town who, sullen already, like to use the fact they've lived here longer than anyone else as another part of their sullenness, just as there are people who, pompous already, like to use the fact they once went to Yale as another component of their pomposity. But these are more than made up for by those to whom all these artificial distinctions don't matter at all—people who, plunk them down in any environment, any situation, would still have a perspective so warm and large it embraces everyone; people who, in Bertrand Russell's splendid phrase, "remember their humanity and forget all the rest."

My rural bias is strongly at work here. In the country, people who have anything to offer can stand out with more clarity and distinction; there aren't too many of us, so each person still counts. Literary theorists bemoan the fact that "character" no longer matters in the world—that the very notion has been consumed by the faceless indifference of this mechanical, bureaucratic age. And in the greater world this is true—and yet here in these small pockets character is still something explicitly discussed, reputation is everything, and a clumsy move, a petty feud carried on a little too long, a bit of work clumsily done, will not soon be forgiven.

There's a downside to all this—the fact that American small towns are notorious breeders of conformity, viewing suspiciously any deviation from the norm. Our town has escaped most of this, thanks to its position near a college, its traditional New England respect for privacy. Still, compared to the other alternatives the world cooks up—facelessness, loneliness, alienation, indifference—I'd take my chances with conformity, leave it to the strength small places can instill to give our children the courage to break away from it when the time comes.

So in a sense we're back to where we started, the tour nearing its end. Just as all the aesthetic differences between a short story and novel can be traced to the former's smaller size, so too most of the differences between here and anywhere else in the world can be attributed to our lesser, more humane dimension. One thousand nine hundred and ninety-six human beings is just about right—the right number to sensibly govern; the right number to care about; the right number to get to know. It makes us too insignificant for the purveyors of mass this and mass that to bother with (so far), and yet small and responsive enough we're often out ahead of the world on a whole variety of issues.

The last is something I continually marvel at: how a place supposedly off the beaten track as far as history goes, out of the mainstream of contemporary events, often manages to be on vital matters four or five steps ahead. Environmentalism? Recycling got started early in town; there was a handful of people interested, devotedly so, willing to do the hard work to get it started, and in such a small place small groups can perform miracles. So too with our land; this town has more acreage protected in land trusts and conservation easements than anywhere in the state, reflecting a healthy *conserve*-atism that has nothing to do with the current bastardized connotation of that word (this town being a Democratic pocket in an otherwise reactionary state). Equality of the sexes? With it taking eleven to make up a soccer team, kids being at a premium, we've been fielding coed teams for years now, and it works out just fine. World peace? The best church dinner ever given here was for a Russian delegation in a citizen-to-citizen exchange back in 1982 before détente had caught on ... and I remember from that happy laughing night of much good cheer, besides the stuffed grape leaves and tortilla casseroles and warm cherry pies, how patently absurd the whole Cold War business seemed, how old-fashioned and doomed.

Resiliency and stiffness. We have our share of both, just as any small town must in order to survive, the correct balance allowing us to take from the larger world the best it has to offer, while hoarding protectively those virtues the larger world, in contempt or indifference, would take away.

∽

I lied about the tour being over, feel twenty pages on that it's hardly even begun. I haven't had a chance to show off the Connecticut River yet, cleaner than it's been in fifty years, take you down to River Road where the cook boats used to tie up during the log drives at the turn of the century (*"March 7, 1887—John Jewell has a huge force of help on his log job as he has a million feet to put in the river in three weeks; his son Herman, a lad of nine, can handle a pair of horses in the most approved manner"*) explain how the river gives the town its geographical locus, stringing us on the necklace of towns upstream and down. I haven't described the reception we gave Liz McIntyre, the local skier who went off to the Olympics and brought back a silver medal; the parade around the common, the speeches, her own modest thank-yous, and how all the kids in town got to hold her medal (and how one little boy, refusing to be impressed, asked her with a mix of bewilderment and accusation: "How come you didn't win a *gold*?").

And that's just for starters. I could describe the Pumpkin Festival, the kids parading around the common dressed as shopping bags or brontosauruses or whatever cartoon character is currently the rage. I'd like to take you to the general store, let you choose from the bumper stickers placed there by the register: WELCOME TO NEW HAMPSHIRE—NOW GO HOME! LIVE FREEZE OR DIE! NEW HAMPSHIRE—DON'T TAKE US FOR GRANITE! I could do something on the town's sounds: the atonal, far from displeasing effect the town band gives when it's playing Sousa; the hoot and howl of coyotes in winter back of Walter Record's farm; the unearthly shriek on gray March nights of something that may or may not be a cougar; the way the carillon of the little church every night at five-thirty scratches out some static, as if clearing its throat, then launches into its repertoire of hymns in notes that ring out pure across the hills.

And nothing have I said about the farms, the three or four that still operate here, remnants of the old days, but still the town's soul. (*"July 7, 1851—I have been haying two weeks and have finished four acres. This may seem small potatoes to one who mows two or three acres a day, but I feel satisfied as this yielded twelve tons. Corn in No. 4 looks well and grows very fast. Men may sow the field and till with tender care, yet all depends on God's own hand."*) And then the forest that backs them, the streams that still have pockets of native trout, the swampy patches that are best explored during winter on snowshoes or skis, the old covered bridge down on Clay Brook, home to otters . . .

There are times I wish all this were perfect, other times when I accept with relief that it isn't, and I suppose I will go on loving it enough to get occasionally fed up with it until the day the winters finally get to me, or it becomes too crowded to breathe. That morning I took my chance and drove into town to look things over my intuition didn't let me down, for the village I saw out the window, flinty, comprehensible, and solid, is our home now, the home of our children, the place for better or worse—in this age of extinction—we'll make our stand.

January 21:

You could live here a hundred years and not experience all the tricks the weather's capable of dishing out. On Monday, just as the real winter was settling in, a tropical warm front blew in from the south, raising the temperature from below zero to over sixty in what seemed like seconds.

With it came the thickest, most unctuous fog I've ever seen here, which is saying plenty—the kind of fog that eats snow, so when we woke up this morning the ground was absolutely bare, as if trolls had opened up hidden petcocks in the earth to suck away the drifts.

A welcome break? While the January thaw is a well-documented phenomenon up here, we're talking weather more typical of mid-May, temperatures that broke the old records by a full ten degrees. I'd enjoy it more if it didn't seem a suburban plot to soften us up, undermine our foundations. It's turned our dirt road into a real morass, the ruts deep enough to scrape the bottom of the car and everything there attached.

"It's the wildest I've ever seen here," road agent Fred Stearns says when I flag him down. "The frost has let go on most of the back roads and this rain won't help things either."

A true test of character, this false spring. There are those who relish it, the novelty of going around in shorts in the middle of January, others who sourly complain about having to go through an extra mud season on top of the one we'll still have in April. The flies have come alive from the windowsills; the earth smells metallic and salty; when you look up into the sky expecting to have your spirits lifted, they run smack into the low ceiling of clouds, the thermal inversion, so the overall effect is depressing.

There's no skiing of course, no skating. The science museum in Norwich had scheduled demonstrations of sled dogs, and after calling to find out if it was still on, we went down to watch.

Sure enough, the man who owned the team—a friendly, somewhat intimidating man with the crouching strut of a nose guard in football and the fleshy bulk to match—had brought along a sled on wheels instead of runners for just such a contingency, and before harnessing his dogs to it, he called for a volunteer.

Matthew, age four, blond hair draped sheepdog fashion over his forehead, glasses fogged up so he could hardly see, was standing out a little ahead of everyone— far enough that the man took this for volunteering. In a second Matt was tucked horizontally beneath the man's bearish arm, the nylon harness being slipped over his forehead, smoothed down his back, tightened . . . the man hoisting him high in the air so everyone could see, spinning him so they could see both sides, then plopping him down on all fours in the mud to demonstrate how the harness pulled.

Matthew did fine with this—up to a point. I could see him fighting back something that wasn't just shyness. . . . For the first time ever I saw in his expression what I wouldn't have suspected him capable of, not at such an age. Stoicism—the determination to hunker down and get it over with and not move one facial muscle until this was done.

> *The man finishes. . . . Harness comes off again. . . .*
> *Huskies bark in wild envy. . . . Crowd good-naturedly*
> *applauds. . . . Matthew walks back to his dad, sits*
> *between my legs with head in hands, refusing to move for*
> *the next ten minutes, waiting for his dignity to come back*
> *again, pressing his chest as if checking for damage,*
> *embarrassed, unbowed, intact.*

There are those who will insist that I've let my vestigial hankering for place get away from me, making me paint a more flattering portrait than the village really deserves—that its glory days were already over with by the January morning I first pulled into town. I have a poet friend whose opinion I value very much, and he's long since moved north, disgusted at the changes in the landscape he once cherished (*"In recent years my love affair has found itself in trouble. I can no longer take its passion straight; for every moment of the old elation there comes a grimly compensating recognition. All these glories are under attack as never before."*). We have some friendly arguments about this, and while I'm prepared to admit things aren't what they were here, the rest of the country's been losing it at an even faster rate, so, relatively speaking, we still stand out as miraculously pristine.

Of course this involves some sophistry on my part. The town is under assault from a multitude of directions, to the point where only a blind optimist would venture to predict we have any future apart from being sucked into the look-alike mediocrity, this nowhere, the modern world has become.

Externally, the threat is pretty clear; we're not *that* far from the cities, and between people willing or forced to commute suicidal distances, the fact that this new electronic age makes it possible for companies to relocate just about anywhere, and the fact that fewer and fewer people actually make their living *within* this town, suburbanization is a real possibility; all it would take is for the CEO of one medium-sized company to decide he or she wouldn't mind having their work nearer their ski lodge or summer house or alma mater.

Internally, the threats are more complex, and depend on the economic status of who we're talking about. From the rich—and we have our share—the threat is of turning this into a countrified theme park, much as Woodstock has become across the river in Vermont. Our clean air, pure water, and safety have become, in this age, literally priceless, things only the wealthy can afford, and on top of the ridges have gone up some astonishingly ugly versions of what trendy owners think a New England house should be. Yes, they've done a lot to protect the land—but too often in the spirit of locking it up in their own private vault.

The merely affluent—the trust funders, doctors, senior faculty—now send their kids to a nearby private school, not because our own local school isn't first-rate, but because this is what people of their class do—give their kids what they see as a jump-start in the life they all think of as a race. Like their kind around the country, they're abdicating from any kind of commonality, all civic obligations, and the result here is to create in the country the same kind of brain drain from the public school system facing inner-city ghettos.

From those in the middle of the economic scale, many of them exiles from Connecticut or Massachusetts, the danger is in their intrinsically suburban outlook—in the danger of recreating the horrors they supposedly fled here to escape. Often they're more than willing to go along with things their first few years in town—the dirt roads, the lackluster schoolbus service, the dearth of shopping—but then gradually they lose patience, revert to type, want pavement and restaurants and instantaneous gratifications. This is not true of all of them; the litmus test seems to be whether or not they like to hunt, canoe, fish, or hike, care enough about the land to get to know it and, knowing it, grow to care about it even more.

The threat from those on the bottommost rung, the ones who have been here longest, still own great tracts of valuable, subdividable land? Few of them have any idea of the dangers that lurk just down the interstates; never having lived in a place like, say, Long Island, they don't know how monstrous and sterile that world is—and how, tough as things are here, living in that kind of environment would pulverize their proud individuality into dust. As conservationist Mollie Beattie puts it, "It's hard living in a rural area that hasn't changed in two hundred years, and accepting that it could change very fast. There's always an isobar of perhaps fifty or a hundred miles north of where development is that doesn't believe *their* land could ever change." These are the old New Hampshirites who have "Backlash" as their middle name—the ones who, hating any kind of governmental involvement in their lives, any kind of regulation or conservation, become easy marks for big corporations or developers getting involved in their lives in a way that makes the government look like an angel of restraint.

Given these internal contradictions, the demographic pressure we can do little about, it will be a real miracle if this village, any American village, as it exists today will exist twenty years from now. Two things must remain in place: the land and the vestigial hankering for community I talked about earlier. If either one of these goes? Make that ten years—and that's being optimistic. Once there's nothing tactile and visible and distinct left for people to cherish with all their hearts, nothing abstract and moral to long for with all their spirit, they will descend into listlessness, spend all their time indoors, be moved neither by old mountain cemeteries nor the glint of sun on new snow, hardly even know what village it is they live in, this village that once in a forgotten age was theirs.

I think it must have been 1919 when the horse chased my grandfather up the firehouse stairs. The New York City Fire Department switched to motor power in the '20s, so it couldn't have been much after this, and besides that was the year Pop was a rookie, and so fair game for pranks like having a sweet bun snuck into the baggy pocket of his fatigues.

"What was the horse's name?" I would ask, testing him when the story got just so far.

Back it came like a shot. "Ajax. The horse that liked buns. He sniffed it in my pocket, yanked out of his harness, started off after me—boom, right up those stairs, me one step ahead of him all the way. I was crying like a baby. O'Malley and Miller were crying, too, they were laughing so hard. They cried fit to beat the band." He shook his head, moved his hand in an unconscious gesture back around to his rear pocket, as if remembering the hot feel of the horse's breath. "Well, fine. That was how they did things in those days. You took your lumps until you proved yourself at a fire." He closed his eyes, shuddered, made a sound that was like a *brrr* only more bitter, winked to clear away the bad taste, went on. "There was worse than that besides."

I'm not sure when I first heard about the horse that liked buns. It may have been during a canasta game at the family summer house back in the early '60s; we used to play after dinner, and Pop liked telling stories between hands, or sometimes, prodded by my father, even during play. He liked to talk while he shuffled, too, talked even faster while he studied what he'd been dealt, but unless he was prodded this way, his remarks were addressed strictly to his cards.

"Come on. . . . There! . . . Come on. . . . Soup! What a mess you've handed me. What a mess! Soup again! Soup!"

So years later, when I used to go visit him in the upstairs flat he rented in an old part of Queens, I was hearing most of his stories a third or fourth time, though if anything they gained from the repetition, since I knew just what questions to ask to steer him toward my favorites. These visits usually came on Sundays. Downstairs, his landlady, Mrs. Barker, would have a roast in the oven, and the smell would fill the apartment with exactly the right aroma to accompany his stories, just as a tea kettle perking behind us on the stove provided the perfect sound.

"Was that before or after the time you brought back the wrong horses?" I would ask, going over to pour us a refill.

"After. The hook-and-ladder took brown horses and the pumpers took gray and the gray ones were smaller to fit in the harness, only no one bothered telling me that. Fine. Captain Flanagan calls me into his office. 'Wetherell, look sharp now. Here's a requisition for horses and I need two right away, off you go.' The stable was in downtown New York. They all looked pretty much alike to me. I handed in the requisition, the man scratched his head, asked me which color I wanted. I said brown—your grandmother favored brown—thought nothing of it, not until I walked them back. Then there was holy hallelujah to pay. Flanagan roared. He wanted gray! Oh how he roared! How I'd made him the laughingstock of all Brooklyn and there he couldn't have been a dumber rookie in the entire department. For two hours it went on. I put my paper in for a transfer that same afternoon."

Pop was always putting in his paper for a transfer; too many captains turned out to be "bad actors" or "phonies" or, in the most damning of his categories, "punks." He'd shudder remembering how mean some could be, though a few seconds later he would beam all over, shake his head in admiration remembering a Captain O'Donnell who was a "fine man," or a Captain Kennedy who would "give you the shirt off his back," or someone else the men "thought the world of." Pop shuddered a lot when he told his stories, good and bad, as if the past lived so vividly in him all it took to bring it alive was the right little grimace, the vaguest cock of the head, a soft whistling sound, after which 1919 was there in the room with us, centered on the little formica table where we could cup our hands around it, deal it back and forth just like cards.

His most violent shudders he saved for his misadventures with horses. Cleaning up after them, shoving in laxatives, trying to persuade them to go where he wanted them to go. Strictly a city boy, it was a happy day for him when the NYFD switched to trucks.

Or so he thought. Pop had so much energy it was always spilling over into impatience, and this often made him seem clumsier than he really was. Thus, his initial impulse for joining the fire department came after a disastrous one-day career as brakeman on the Brooklyn Bridge trolley—a career that ended when he pulled the brake too hard, causing his trolley to plow into the one just ahead. His unlucky streak continued with fire engines; once on the way to a fire in Bushwick, steering the tiller (the wheel mounted on the back of the long hook-and-ladder engines in order to negotiate sharp city corners), he spun too hard, skidding the back of the engine into the display window of a prominent jeweler. This wasn't the first time such accidents had happened to him either; Pop got into enough hot water that only the intervention of his well-connected Methodist minister kept him from being transferred to whatever firehouse served as the NYFD version of Siberia.

A few years later, the first man up the ladder at a big tenement fire in Flatbush ("Bing bing bing bing! Four alarms—that's us, boys!"), his luck ran out on him again; the ceiling collapsed on his head, and when he woke up hours later in a Catholic hospital, heavily concussed, seeing all the religious paintings, the crosses on the wall—having lived what he quickly remembered was a largely blameless life—he assumed he was waking up in heaven.

Even when I knew him much of this clumsiness lived on. Pop was a great one for dropping iron kettles on his toes, or hammering nails through his thumb, or misplacing his wedding ring in cans of Prince Albert tobacco. This was odd in its way, because if I were choosing adjectives to describe the overall impression his personality cast, it would be ones that had to do with dignity and nobility and even grace.

What kind of dignity? The dignity of a man who spent his life doing what he liked doing, work that was valuable work, work a man could sink his teeth into, work that was valued by society, spiced with danger—work that brought him many fine memories, many firm friends. He wasn't tall, five-nine at the most, and yet he seemed taller, walked, sat, and stood with the posture of someone who fit perfectly into his world, to the point his very muscles and joints knew instinctively just where to go. Behind me on the wall is a picture of his entire company, Engine 227 in Brooklyn, in what must have been 1925 or '26. Pop wears his dress cap lower over his eyes than the other men; he comes across as thinner, sharper, faster looking, and what's more, knows this to be the case, so his expression is cocky—a cockiness that, with age and creases, deepened into the lively dignity I so admired.

There was too much character in his face for it to be described as handsome, not without some explaining attached. His chin managed to be sharp and dimpled at the same time; above it, his nose swelled out like the bow of a clipper ship, blending well into the bulk of his profile, but unmistakably leading the way. His eyes were blue-gray, alert and expressive, setting off the kind of face best described as "memorable"— literally memorable, since right up until the end of his life he was always running into people who recognized him after fifty or sixty years.

I was with him on two of these occasions. Once, walking near the tracks of the Long Island Rail Road, a laborer repairing the rails, a middle-aged man stooped over with care, looked up, spotted us, took off his hat, and said, "Hello, Mr. Wetherell."

Pop squinted over. "Johnny! Long time no see!"

It was one of the boys who used to play around the firehouse in the old days; the firemen would give them quarters to go buy beer for them, and then they would hoist it up the back in buckets, the boys keeping a nickel as their tip. Another time, when Pop came to visit us in the country, he explained to our astonishment that sixty years earlier he used to spend his summer vacations boarding at a nearby farm; later that day, Pop accompanying us to the hardware store to buy some seed, a grizzled clerk with an apron on came up and tapped him on the back. "Well, Walter. What'll it be?"

The grace part? Pop partook of it all right, for all his impatience, those occasional bouts of klutziness. And it's hard to know where it came from, though its manifestations were clear enough. His voice was perfectly wedded to his face—a baritone that had just enough rasp to make it interesting, oddly precise for Brooklyn ("peruse" was one of his favorite words), though with enough *dems* and *does* to let the Flatbush shine through. His handwriting, too. Leaving school in sixth grade, he still managed to learn a beautiful, flowing hand which I marvel at to this day, as if what's stored in those scrapbooks and letters in my parents' attic aren't letters at all, but elegant specimens of embroidery, the secret of which, in our degenerate times, has been irretrievably lost. And he had elegance in his movements, his physical presence; limping along Jamaica Avenue at ninety, holding onto my arm for support, he still kept his head up high, stared with curiosity and interest at everyone we passed—and was stared at with respect in turn.

And yet, for all this, for all the love I bear his memory, it's my fixed belief that the grace in him was not exceptional, but rather the inherited aura of his times, an everyday grace I've seen other men and other woman his age share, so in talking to them, in even meeting their eyes, you're aware that the very conception of man has changed dramatically in the last one hundred years—and not for the better. The spiritual ease that comes with a sense of belonging. The simple, old-fashioned manners that seem so courtly today. The lack of self-consciousness; the lively curiosity that is always and forever looking *out*. Their deep immersion, most of all, in what essayist Wendell Berry identifies as a healthy culture: "a communal order of memory, insight, value, work, conviviality, reverence and aspiration."

These are not just shadings seen in retrospect, a nostalgic overlay, but forces that shaped men and women of my grandfather's generation just as alienation and confusion shape ours, so it's no wonder Pop seemed graceful, resilient, and happy. Born in 1887, dead in 1977, he managed to slip in a life when even a person of modest means and very little education could still look forward to the future with confidence—and perhaps that's epitaph enough for any generation to rest easy under, the bittersweet pronouncement of a grandson who is, at least most of the time, of a completely different species of man.

❦

People nowadays blame everything on their parents—add that to the differences—but Pop lived in an era when character alone was expected to accomplish miracles, and so many times did. Inheriting nothing good from his parents, he refused to blame them for anything bad, and except for one furious gesture I'll mention in a moment, called things even.

His mother was an attractive young woman named Rose—and other than that I know nothing about her at all. When Pop was eight months old she wrapped him up in a warm blanket, put him in a laundry basket, and left him on the steps of his cousin's brownstone, along with a note saying *I can no longer take care of Walter anymore*—a story so pat, so suspiciously like the melodramas that were popular in silent films, that I believe every word.

His father, my great-grandfather, was a different story. He was a small-time Tammany politician, or at least a Tammany errand boy, and whether he had enough guts to be anything more villainous it's hard to judge. What role he played in the abandonment, how he treated his wife—of these I have no evidence, but he must have somehow kept tabs on his son, because one day out of the blue he showed up at Engine 227, introduced himself to his thirty-year-old son, and in the next breath asked to borrow five dollars.

"I counted to ten," Pop said in explaining this, shuddering, his knuckles going white as if he were counting to ten again. "I got all the way to nine, and then it was too much for me. I punched him in the nose."

That was what Pop owed his parents—nothing, at least nothing besides the tough genetic conditioning that made him able to shrug off that kind of neglect. He was much luckier with the rest of his life. He married a lively, sensible woman named Agnes Lang in 1915, having met her at Sunday school, and the story goes that on their honeymoon, spending the night in Albany on their way to Niagara Falls, Pop heard a fire bell go off—and out the hotel he ran to see where the action was, never mind his poor bride. I knew her only slightly, the shy bits and pieces a young boy takes away from an old woman at the end of her life, and yet between these and the stories I've heard it's clear she was exactly the right partner for him, with strength enough to keep his cockiness in bounds, to say nothing of his temper, which without her steadying influence could easily have become a problem. They had three children, in steady and reasonable succession, the oldest being my father, who was born in 1917, and so kept Pop from being drafted when conscription kicked in.

Being in the fire department was considered a good job those years, especially during the Depression, when so many other jobs disappeared. By all accounts Pop took his work seriously, the tradition of physical bravery and no complaints, the raucous teasing and hazing, the real and deep camaraderie (a word as extinct now as the spirit it describes) created between men who knew they were good at what they did, men who at any moment might count on each other for survival. My uncle was walking past Engine 227 once when the alarm went off for a fire a short way down the block. First one out the firehouse was Pop, axe in one hand, pants in the other, him caught between wanting to pull them up to a decent level and wanting to get to the fire first, his bony knees pumping up and down like a fireman version of the Keystone Kops.

Still, after the roof fell on him and he almost died, Pop decided enough was enough, and accepted a transfer to the fire inspector's office—a job that suited him just fine, giving him even more people to make friends with, more material for his stories. Dressed in civilian clothes with a fire cap and badge, he would take the elevated each morning to Atlantic Avenue to inspect the premises of the Jewish, Armenian, and Lebanese wholesalers who made it their base, checking in at the speakeasies to see the goods weren't stored dangerously, then over to Brownsville to inspect apartment fire escapes, handing out shiny uniform buttons to the kids that swarmed around. It was a leisurely job—there was always time to stop in at the local firehouse, catch up on the gossip, drink some strong fireman's coffee, talk baseball scores or shop.

And in this gathering of world-class talkers, it's my hunch Pop more than held his own. He was an extraordinarily good storyteller, one who put real passion into his tales, knew by instinct where to abbreviate and shorten, where to embroider and enlarge—knew where the dramatic heart of his story lay, though he would have blinked at you in incomprehension if you told him any of this was so. He seemed to possess an uncanny instinct for knowing how much patience he could ask of his listeners, and could tell a story in shorthand just as he could tell one at length.

For instance, that picture right behind me, the one of his engine company taken seventy years ago. There're eighteen of them, strong men in uniform, gazes even, unblinking, the only sign of weakness being the awkward, oddly helpless way their hands rest on their laps. If he had to, Pop could describe them all in a minute and a half, tapping them out with his index finger as his voice moved along.

"This one's O'Callaghan, a punk. Miller you know from the time he broke his leg pulling me out of the Bible warehouse. Wagner was brutal, hands of lead. Captain O'Connor, a fine man, cried at his birthday once. Birdwell wanted to be an officer, he was always studying, only it was horses, whiskey, blondes. This one is Finnegan, who taught Sunday school until he went bad. This one is Clancy and the horse chased him up the stairs, too, only him it caught."

Telling longer stories he would settle in like a good novelist, filling in the setting, the atmosphere, and only then bringing on his characters; his voice would change, becoming softer, more suited for the long haul; one long white hand spread apart on the tablecloth, his fingers becoming a map or a chart, to the point where, listening, you would watch them closely, as if they formed a scarred and knobby screen. Even in full gear he would glance over from time to time to check on your involvement, whether you were doing your part as a listener. Storytelling was a collaboration, and he expected a lot from the eyes of whoever was listening.

His longest story I heard him tell only once, late on a rainy Sunday afternoon when I had told him, for a third time, it was time for me to go. Whether it was something in the quality of the grayness that came through his parlor window, some nightmare that had disturbed him during the night, a memory that after long years of incubation was finally demanding its way out, his voice grew softer than I'd ever heard it before; his hand rubbed back and forth across the tablecloth smoothing out the little wrinkles, then smoothing them again until the fabric lay flat.

It was about the big tenement fire at Greenpoint on a brutally cold January night in 1933 when eighteen firemen had died. Five alarms were in, and still the fire spread, until even inspectors like Pop were called in as reinforcements.

"You could feel the flames a mile and a half away, like a wind pushing you back. Jesus, what's this? I wondered. Apparatus was racing past, and back the other way came ambulances, so it was just like war. I spotted Tom Phillips, a decent man I knew from the lodge, his face all coated in oil. The fire had spread to the chemical plant and there had been a big explosion. I borrowed his fire coat and helmet, ripped them right off him before he could yell, kept pressing on until I came to the first stretcher, looked down a moment, kept going . . ."

The flames, the iron tenements burning like matches, the noise of people screaming as they jumped from the roofs—all these he described in that quiet voice, the hand restless, ever moving, the details coming back.

"They were putting water on it but then the pumps failed, and the next thing you know there was a crash you could hear even in the uproar. I jumped over the hoses, skidded on the ice, and what did I see but my old pals from Engine Two

Twenty-seven, or at least their pumper. There was no one manning it, no one I recognized, except this fireman from another company. 'Where are the boys?' I asked him, only I suppose I was shouting it by then. He hesitated, met my eyes, pointed toward where the tenement had collapsed. I grabbed an axe off the back of the truck, fought my way in to what was left standing, embers the size of bowling balls falling all around, so I had to dance to keep away from them, and all the time I was doing that I was shining my flashlight, shouting as loud as I could, 'Twenty-seven! Twenty-seven!'"

He shook his head, looked over at me just long enough that I could see the tears brim up in his eyes, then together we glanced down at his hand—his white, fire-scarred hand that had finally left off its rubbing and gone still.

"Twenty-seven. But no one answered."

∾

It seems a million years ago now—not just my grandfather's memories of Brooklyn and lower Manhattan in a far-off time, but those afternoons I used to sit in an overheated parlor smelling of pot roast in the company of a man whose words could bring it all alive. Pop's was the last great storytelling generation, the last for whom storytelling was one of the common, everyday arts, so it's no wonder I remember it with considerable affection and regret. Again, I think of that phrase by Céline that haunts me: "The time when not being able to sing or tell a story properly was looked upon as stupid, shameful, and sick." Those days are over with now, done away with by TV as surely as if network goons had gone around throttling every good storyteller in sight, in the same way Ford and GM bought all the trolley lines so as to render them extinct. In our age a good storyteller is so rare they've become professionalized, win grants, advertise themselves on posters; even rarer is a good listener, or even a mediocre one, so the ancient collaboration is taking it on the chin from both directions. Ours is an age of chatterers, not listeners; everyone has their mouths open and no one their ears.

But here I am tossing off angry aphorisms while Pop sits there waiting patiently for me to pour more tea, come back to the table so he can start another story, a funny one this time, something that will send me home laughing. But one last conceit before I do this, something else that's vexing me. Those hundreds and thousands of lonely people you see when you visit the city, the ones who mutter constantly to themselves? Sometimes I think they're the shattered hulks of great storytellers cut down in their prime, the words coming to them just as easily as ever, the remembered moments from the past that can be summoned back only with exactly the right order and form, only there's no one out there to listen anymore, no one to care, and so they tell their stories time and time again to themselves, until the words start tasting like gum that has been chewed too long, pasty and bitter, creating a terrible stickiness that will soon glue their mouths forever shut.

And it wasn't just storytelling that was headed for extinction. Those born in the late 1800s were the last generation that routinely sang at family gatherings, played parlor games, dropped in for unannounced visits, sat on front porches of an evening, kept scrapbooks, went calling. Most of all, it was the last that was supported and enhanced by a pervasive sense of belonging, to the point where, hearing my grandfather talk about downtown Manhattan or Bushwick or the other neighborhoods where he lived—that is, of the most crowded sections of the most crowded city on the continent—it was like listening to someone speaking familiarly of a small town, one where he felt perfectly at home, alienation be damned.

Pop's whole world was of neighborhood, club, church, association. In our age, people join groups where the common link is the abuse they've received, or the self-inflicted pain, but in his day you joined groups based on what you hoped for, what you dreamed. For Pop, loving the brotherhood he found in the fire department, it was an organization that took that principle and gave it ceremony and pomp: the Masons, to which he belonged with all his heart and soul. In those days (and perhaps in ours, in forgotten pockets where the past lives on) the Masons had auxiliaries for their children, the DeMolay Boys and the Rainbow Girls, and Pop put much volunteer effort into the latter, becoming a statewide officer and attending conferences and conventions all around.

Community was also reflected in his favorite hobby: the collection of miniature figurines and buildings he bought all year to place around the Christmas tree, a composition which, when we were growing up, was referred to simply as "The Village." There must have been several thousand pieces in this by the time he finished, of all shapes and sizes, materials, and styles (Pop caring nothing for proportion or scale; in the world he had charge of he was a true democrat, an equal-opportunity collector). He would buy these from Jewish wholesalers whose premises he was responsible for inspecting, and at a good price, too, nothing dishonest, but enough of a discount to let the merchants and Pop both feel they were doing business in a sensible, adult way.

Soon after Thanksgiving would begin the long process of lovingly unwrapping these from the tissue and old newspaper they spent most of the year in, placing them around the plywood table on which the tree rested. There was a city side on one half, a country side on the other, the former dusted with snow that resembled mothball flakes, the latter with a grassy carpet that set off sparks whenever you touched it.

What delights there were in that miniature world! Each figure, each building, was set in the exact place it was the year before and the year before that and forever as far as my sister and I were concerned. Cat bands playing tambourines and cymbals and little orange drums. Santas on thin metal skis, so potbellied the merest touch would topple them over. A plastic police station placed way in back because Pop didn't like police stations, shuddered when he put it up. A church that had a dial you could wind to hear it play "Oh Come, All Ye Faithful." Wafer-thin sleds with wafer-thin riders, JAPAN or GERMANY stamped on their bases. Blue plastic men raising their hats to red plastic women as they waited for a double-decker bus. Herds of grazing reindeer, browsing horses, pensive cows. A firehouse with its full complement of apparatus. Shouting boys with newspapers tucked under their arms. A glass skating rink on which penguins turned graceful arabesques.... Each figure, each building, coming with its own story of how and where and when it had been acquired, so the village had its living history of anecdote and epic. This was the Village, the world as my grandfather saw it, a world imbued with as much of his own personality as an autobiographical work of art.

"Beeootiful," he would say, studying it in satisfaction, the Brooklyn coming out. Then, his face darkening, his laugh becoming a troubled frown: "Who moved the street cleaner!" and immediately with an economical and delicate plucking he would move it back to where it belonged, God at creation, the custodian at work.

That in a nutshell was Pop, my grandfather, Walter Davidson Wetherell, who died three days after suffering a stroke in 1977, and seemed to take a whole era with him when that great heart finally stopped. And yet there's still so much more to say, to the point where I feel a great reluctance to sever the connection these words have made, the memory my own stories have rescued from my forgetting. I've said nothing about the way he would watch his favorite wrestling matches, bouncing up and down on the sofa, twisting in empathy, digging his elbows into whoever was sitting next to him. I haven't described, on the funny side, the way he would take his false teeth out when he wanted to amaze my sister and me, nor have I described, on the serious, the loving patience with which he took care of my great Aunt Lyd during her final years.

Still more. The instinctive, stubborn sense of right and wrong that saved him during the fire department scandals of the late '40s, when District Attorney Hogan sent most of his fellow inspectors to the penitentiary. The surprise he gave us at my sister's wedding when he showed up wearing a necktie, him who had worn bow ties for seventy-five years, explaining with that characteristic little shudder of his that he was sick of wearing bow ties, that he needed a change. The appraising stare he would give me when I complained about whatever dead-end job I was currently stuck in—how he'd point up toward the fire department pictures on the wall, tell me I had the look of a good hook-and-ladder man, suggest it still wasn't too late to take the test.

He made people feel good just being around him, Pop did. He could dissolve into laughter, rock back and forth with it, start to cry. Even when I was in my twenties he would slip a dollar bill into my pocket each time I left, tell me with a little laugh, "Go buy yourself a milkshake!" The last time I saw him he was perfectly in character, spilling tea across his lap, yelling "Soup!" at his clumsiness; reaching into his pocket, finding it empty, he called out to me on the steps: "Catch me next time! I'm good for it, you know that!"

Yeah, he was good for it—good for a lot of things. The more time separates us, the more heroic and immaculate he grows, to the point where, twenty years after his death, I can't help thinking of him as a Brooklyn version of Buffalo Bill, one of nature's true ornaments, so, in pronouncing here his epitaph, all I can do is echo e. e. cummings's famous words of celebration and lament: *Jesus he was a handsome man!*

February 2:

First copy of my novel, there in the mail with the seed catalogs and bills. After all the brooding, all the hours alone, the solid heft of it in my hands . . .

To modestly celebrate—and as part of my campaign to show my children institutions that once meant a lot to me but which in a matter of seconds will be gone— I drove them fifteen miles to the lunch counter at Woolworth's, treated everyone to hot dogs, soda, and fries.

A 5&10¢ lunch counter! Talk about your survivors from a different epoch! And I'm happy to report this one seems little changed from the ones I remember sitting at when I was seven. The round Naugahyde stools you could swivel back and forth on, increasing your speed until your mother braked you with a firm hand on the small of your back. The perfectly placed shelf beneath the counter for your hat and mittens—perfect, that is, for forgetting them on. The glossy pictures above the grill showing what's on the menu, everything referred to as a "plate." Try Our Clam Strip Plate! Try Our Hamburger Plate! Try Our Baked Macaroni and Cheese Plate! All still there.

"We'll have the hotdog, uh, plate," I said when the waitress came over. Like the lunch counter, she was the real thing: gum-chewing, laconic, her blouse and apron made of the wispy yellow material once referred to as "chiffon." I half-expected her to say "Hon," felt disappointed when she didn't.

I hardly listened to the kids' chatter while we ate, but sat there studying the current state of things, trying to compare it to those old memories of Grant's and Woolworth's and Greene's. The first change that struck me was in the demographics. Gone were the young businessmen on their lunch breaks, the students reading books, the housewives on their one big excursion of the day, the old black ladies with their shopping bags, their burden of woe. Replacing them were—how can I put it? Loners, misfits, the recently deinstitutionalized, sipping medium-sized Cokes, their hands protectively around the glass as if afraid someone would take it, looking up eagerly as each new person sat down, then, finding no solace in their expressions, no relief from their own isolation, turning back to sip again.

Was McDonald's too much for them, the sterile normalcy? Were they nostalgic lunch-counter freaks who toured the country "collecting" new ones to add to their list, much the same way aficionados collect covered bridges? Or were they sadder versions of what I verged on becoming myself in my worst moments, extinction's chaff?

"Good place to work?" I asked the waitress when she came back. This time I noticed sewn on her blouse the name Barb.

She was startled to be asked something so directly, but not as startled as you might think; in this day of the ubiquitous talk show, everyone goes around ready to answer all kinds of impromptu questions.

"Okay," she mumbled.

"How are tips?"

She looked at me like I must be insane, gestured weakly toward those on the stools.

After she left I tried explaining to the kids how it had been in my day. No fast food, few franchises, what people did was head down to the local drugstore or 5&10 at lunch, find a stool, eat quickly in the noisy hubbub, combine it with some shopping. I also tried explaining how lunch counters had been so central to the American experience thirty years ago that they became the place where the most effective sit-ins had been staged in the early days of the Civil Rights movement, the black students sitting on their stools without flinching while rednecks poured ketchup over their heads, showered them with abuse.

It was good, explaining that. The sun coming through the plateglass window at our backs, the opportunity to watch people going through the nearby checkout counter with their arms full of Band-Aids or light bulbs or string—the novelty of eating off real plates, not cardboard or Styrofoam. Satisfying and good.

By the time we were on our hot chocolates (much as I longed to, I couldn't bring myself to order a vanilla milkshake; there are some madeleines so sacred you should never try to savor them again), the lunch counter had begun to empty out. With that, I began understanding why Barb put up with the lousy tips, the endless spills to clean, the patrons who took half an hour to rummage through their pockets when it came time to pay their bills.

Companionship. There were no assistant managers screaming at her to hurry with those McMuffins, no regimen to follow, no canned spiel she was expected to memorize, the better to push this and that. Along with the other waitresses, the short-order chef, she wandered down toward the far end of the counter, where they could smoke in peace, the five of them chatting—two on stools

in front, two leaning on the counter, one hanging up
cardboard Valentines as the others offered advice. . . .
And I could understand how, for the right kind of person,
this would be worth putting up with any amount of grief:
the us-against-them feeling, the comforting insidership,
that can be found at a lunch counter just as purely as it
can be found at a country club; the opportunity to take
the weight off your feet, be surrounded with people who
didn't demand anything from you at all, if for only ten
minutes at a stretch. These things count, and for some
people they count most.

I left a tip under the edge of my plate, and a good
one. Putting on her coat Erin had trouble finding the
arm, and suddenly there it was being held out straight
for her, Barb smiling for the first time since we came in.

"Here you go, hon," she said. I could have kissed her.

It was fully my intention to bring Pop back for an encore
here, tell the story of his famous, never-to-be-forgotten clam
chowder. Seeing me order it in a restaurant one day (I was
twelve or thirteen), he poked me gently in the ribs. "You like
chowder? Someday I'll make you the old firehouse kind, would
you like that?"

Would I like that? You bet! Pop was a pretty good cook of
the short-order variety, and so we had every reason to believe
any chowder that had his hand in it would be truly exceptional,
a chowder fit for firemen and kings. If anything, our appetite
only increased over the years as time and time again Pop would
say, "How'd you like me to make my chowder?" and yet never
quite found the right occasion to actually do so.

A good story . . . and yet I have to interrupt it for a stop-the-
press kind of bulletin, a last surprise in the story of Pop's life.
Talking with my sister on the phone last week, I mentioned who
I was writing about; she in turn mentioned she'd just gotten a
long family tree from a cousin out West who was devoting himself to genealogy. Sure enough, yesterday's mail brought the
results, and in it, as well as the usual long list of names, births,

and deaths, came two bits of information he had gleaned from his father, Pop's brother—so vivid and telling they all but jumped off the page.

They concerned Pop's mother, the mysterious Rose. The first surprise was that she was six feet tall—a good height for a woman of that era, and further evidence of the tendency to tall-ness in the Wetherells. The second fact was that, in the nomenclature of those years, she was "Hebrew."

The more I've thought about this, the more it seems less a surprise than the key to understanding several mysteries. The first is that it might help explain Pop's abandonment as a baby—that with his father being a good Protestant, there might have been tensions in his marrying a Jew, ones that finally snapped the family apart. The second is that Pop was a great admirer of Jews, spoke of them with the highest respect, and fit in perfectly himself with the noisy, vigorous world of the Lower East Side. Among his most treasured possessions was a black woolen yarmulke, which he had gotten from one of his friends among the Jewish merchants (or inherited from his mother? I wonder now), and which he would bring out on special occasions, place on his head, start jabbering away in what seemed to us pretty good Yiddish . . . all as a joke, and yet with a certain solemnity in it, as if it wasn't quite a joke after all.

Did he know his mother was Jewish? I don't remember him saying anything about her at all, other than the story of his being left in the basket. But it explains a lot, and makes me marvel again at how the past, just when you think it's settled quietly beneath your hands, can come vigorously back to life, suggesting a dozen mysteries for every one it solves.

The clam chowder? Oh, he finally made it all right, about ten years after first mentioning the possibility, by which time we were all but salivating from eagerness to try it. He took all one afternoon to prepare it, and when we arrived (having skipped lunch that day to save room), immediately ladled it out into five big bowls. I took a spoonful, swallowed, looked over at my sister; she took a spoonful, swallowed, looked over at my father; my father took a spoonful, swallowed, looked over at my mother . . . and as if on an invisible signal, we all put our spoons back down on the table. "Uh, *great*," my father finally managed, stifling a gag. Pop, beaming proudly, took his own first spoonful now . . . swallowed, frowned, frowned deeper, put his spoon down, went over to the stove, and without saying a word to any of us poured the entire chowder down the sink.

G ravity, the pull of it, does not at first seem like much of a subject to celebrate, especially if the writer doing the celebrating is as close to his fiftieth birthday as this one is. That subtle and not so subtle tug downward back in toward earth becomes clearer with each aging year, from the heavy way I get out of bed in the morning to the heavy way, sixteen gravity-fighting hours later, I fall exhausted back in. It's there when I'm shaving, too. My head seems to fit entirely in the mirror these days, where always before the top part jutted out; when I have my annual physical, step barefoot on the scales, stand up straight, instead of the seventy-five inches of height I've always prided myself on, the nurse is more apt to put it at seventy-four, that missing inch being the part of a weathered Wetherell that gravity's called home.

And gravity seems all the more burdensome when I watch my children sport around in it, unaware of its very existence, skipping and hopping and jumping so spontaneously, so naturally, so lightly, the only wonder is that gravity is strong enough to prevent their actual flight. It's one of the major differences between young people and old, both in performance and outlook, too easily forgotten in this age when everyone comes mechanized. If in the middle of middle age, in perfect health, in good shape, I still feel as if trolls are yanking down on my shoulders, weighting me with chains—if more and more the horizontal seems to me a much more natural and fitting posture for *anything* to be in than the vertical—it's largely due to the gravitational force becoming explicit, familiar, an everyday presence I've developed an entirely new relationship to from the one I had as a boy.

This isn't all bad, of course, no matter how much I fret at these new limitations. Gravity is the pull of what we live on, our home, and so, even as I long to escape it, I grudgingly concede the rightness of its demands. Though the physics are incomprehensible to me, I understand in each joint, each bone, each muscle, that the planet does indeed exert a force on every object resting on its surface, and to wish yourself permanently free of this force is to ask for a dispensation none can grant. And besides, what are the alternatives? An immature kind of flitty-flightiness? A leap straight out and away? When we were kids we were hardly aware of gravity, sure, but we also spent a lot of time worrying we'd fall right off the planet.

In March, the various tugs by which gravity manifests itself seem particularly explicit, as if the force that's been content to work invisibly most of the year wants to take this opportunity to strut itself out in the open. You can see this most noticeably in the way snowmelt leaves a drift—flowing toward the bottom of the fluted base, cutting a tunnel there, spreading apart on an open patch of ground, narrowing at the patch's lowest point, flowing faster, swelled by other sunny rivulets, sliding now this way, now that, following a declivity so subtle, so imperceptible to the human eye, that only a force with infinite sensitivity could find any declivity at all. And likewise with the other drifts, the other rivulets, the brooks and streams and rivers that, give us a good thaw, roar down our mountain valleys in loud exuberant voice, gravity made aural, the living, rushing evidence of the force residing in contour and contour alone.

And so too with the other signs. Maple sap dripping globularly down into buckets; the dirt roads, crusted up with frost, sagging back down again; the thicker way returning blackbirds and robins carve and shape the sky compared to the chickadees and finches that stay all winter. Gravity is in the air, its light touches and heavy effects both, to the point where a quicker, sharper writer than I am might well be able, with just the right grasp, to clutch its secret in his or her hands.

March can be a funny month in these hills, funny as in ago-nizing—warm one minute, frigid the next. But it's the month when perhaps the greatest variety of outdoor sports is possible, from skiing and biking to hill walking and whitewater canoe-ing. What I like about each of these is the way they harness gravity differently within one overall pattern, so instead of something to labor against, it becomes a force you can coax into being your ally, co-celebrant, and friend.

Take skiing. And by skiing, I don't mean the downhill kind as practiced at Aspen or Stowe, where the whole notion of grav-ity is turned on its ear, chairlifts taking the work out of it, the oomph, so gravity becomes a plaything to be sneered at on the way up and laughed at on the way down. Nope, my kind of skiing is battered old wooden skis, two mismatched poles, a rucksack with an extra sweater, some touring wax, a field guide to animal tracks—and maybe, if I'm feeling especially sybaritic, six squares of shortbread and a thermos of Earl Grey tea. This time of year the snow is pretty well gone from the fields along the river, so, after letting Cider hop up in the back of the station wagon, I drive to the height-of-land, park my car near the old stone dam to Reservoir Pond, smear some klister on the skis, clip my boots into place, harness up the pack, start out.

The old woods road is still heavy with snow; a thousand feet higher here than back on the river, it's a good three weeks behind in the rush toward spring. Still, there are signs. Skunk tracks in a curious back-and-forth pattern in the snow, so you can all but picture the animal sniffing its way along; the distant rat-tat-tat-tatting of a pileated woodpecker working its way around a dead stump; the way the branches of the swamp maples, swollen by sap, are already turned a juicy red. Even the snow seems to be of spring, falling in those big fluffy March flakes that give the landscape not the Brueghel-like spareness it usually wears, but a lusher, more impressionistic feel.

For a change I have the right wax on—and a pair of cor-rectly waxed touring skis is as delightful a means of locomotion as man has ever devised. For every modest expenditure of effort comes a surprisingly long dividend of glide, so here on the level part of the trail I'm hardly aware of gravity at all, but coast along like a boy on a scooter, weight on one leg, weight on the other, whoosh, whoosh, gli . . . i . . . i . . . d e.

Friction, of course, is gravity's near cousin, and yet the klister wax outsmarts it, not only on the level stretches, but when the trail narrows past some birch and starts gradually to climb. Through a neat trick of chemistry, the same substance that rolls the skis along as if on ball bearings now turns out to have gripping properties as well, so for the first hundred yards I hardly have to increase my effort at all.

And yet I'm aware of gravity now—feel it in the extra planting kind of kick necessary so I don't slip back. Gravity's been working on me all along, of course, but now it's become explicit—and then more explicit the steeper the grade becomes. Fifteen minutes of this and the gravitational force becomes internalized, no longer something outside of me hitchhiking on my shoulders, but a resistance in my muscles, chest, and heart, so strong they all beat and strain to it, trying to force the force back out.

There are tricks in the skier's arsenal to keep forging ahead when this happens. One is the herringbone—the duckwalk waddle with ski tips spread that creates a stubborn shape gravity can't get a good downhill grip on—and then, coming to the last steep stretch before the height-of-land, the side step—the slow but efficient ladder climbing that lets you mount gravity's back.

This is hard work . . . sweater off now, sleeves rolled up . . . but it brings the same kind of satisfaction as does a good investment, a CD with a high rate of return, something you've righteously earned, leaving you with the knowledge that, returning later in the day over the same route, you can spend all that stored-up gravity in one exuberant downhill spree.

There's a remote pond where the grade evens off, the source of a river that flows to the southeast. Like many plateaus up high in these New England woods, it has a lost-world kind of feel, especially on a snowy day like this one when no one is about. The trail swings around the southern shore, dips past a beaver flowage, then climbs again on a birch-covered esker that encloses the far side as a decorative rim encloses a bowl.

Easy skiing now—not downhill enough to glide without some pumping, but enough so the effect is matched by gravity's contribution, and in symbiotic harmony I really float along. In my younger days I used to make a practice of skiing down frozen streams, enjoyed feeling that slight but certain downhill inclination the water was responding to in muffled gushes deep below the ice, sidestepping over the open spots where the water was exposed, sliding down the miniature falls on my bottom, skiing flat out on those rare runs where the river straightened.

And so on I glide across the countryside, letting gravity determine my speed, working my way in a northwesterly direction around the pond. Now that the snow has stopped the sky is the color of old pewter—gloomy, if it wasn't for the fact I'm in the mood for it. After what we go through up here it's hard to feel nostalgic for winter, and yet that's exactly what I feel. The giant that held us so tight in its grip is here reduced to a wasted invalid who's slunk off into the woods to expire in solitude, its lower edges harried by southerly breezes, its thickest parts melting away under the humid sky, its flanks reinforced not at all by those huge flakes that come down singly now, the snow, the season, ebbing away flake by lonely flake.

There's enough in the landscape to underline this mood, exaggerate it further. Off to the left of the woods road is a cemetery with only one grave—a story, but I've never found anyone who knows it, and the stone itself is illegible. A little way farther is the foundation hole of an old boardinghouse from the days a hundred years ago when this woods road was a main through route across the hills . . . and past these ruins, the swelling, turkey-like ribs of a dead deer, surrounded by coyote tracks as fresh and unmistakable as those left by my skis. Gloomy stuff on a dark March day, and yet I have no trouble seeing this decay as simply more evidence of earth's irresistible tug, not all that different from the tug that slides me downhill, only slower, more permanent, more sure.

It takes about two hours to circle the pond, allowing time for a lunch break, then a further stop to rewax my skis. Coming out to where the height-of-land tips over toward the valley, I'm ready to cash in on the investment my muscles have earned.

Here we go. A mile ahead of me is the car, downhill all the way, trees on one side, rock wall on the other, a slide of ruts, bumps, bare spots, and ridges—can I do it? I slip my hands out from the pole loops (falling, you want those poles to slip away from you, not have them punch you in the jaw), tie and retie my boots, flex my knees like a ski jumper working up nerve, make sure Cider is well ahead of me so I don't run her down, pronounce the secular version of three Hail Marys (*I think I can I think I can I think I can*), shuffle to the very edge of the lip . . . start down.

Straight into another physics lesson, the strangest, most dramatic, and dangerous one yet. Here all afternoon gravity has been, at worst, a force to labor against; at best, a welcome boost, and now in true presto-chango fashion it becomes totally opposite, a power that speeds me downhill in irresistible and scatterbrained imbecility—not the measured and comprehensible tug it was fifteen minutes ago, but a wild, monstrous yanking that makes it seem the earth is falling away beneath my feet, leaving me no other course but to fall with it, my heart in my mouth.

Even my seeing becomes caught up in this. Things flash past so fast I can no more grab them with my eyes than I could grab them with my mittens. Hemlock, granite boulders, pine, old rock walls blend together as if gravity is smearing them into a greenish-gray paste . . . and then comes Cider, her tongue hanging out, dropping behind as I let out a yell . . . up and over a bump, a moment of wild balancing as my arms shoot out . . . down again . . . down more . . . retaining just enough control to sidestep a bare spot, get my skis back together, bend my knees to absorb the next shock. With no place to turn, a schuss all the way, triumph or tragedy, no middle ground, so all I'm aware of is the gravity inside me that crazily sloshes and swerves, the necessity of keeping all this in equilibrium with the surer, steadier gravity outside—that if I can do this for just two more minutes I will have it made, and that if I don't ... if I brake gravity's force too abruptly, slam into one of those trees, then ...

Then I'm down, the earth swelling up to meet me the way a runway swells up to meet a plane, my skis spreading apart to slow me back from the insane and uncontrollable to the measured and calm.... Cider passing me with a triumphant bark of her own ... and then, exhilarated, gravity's collaborator, partner, and pal, I double-pole myself across the ribbony shreds of winter to my car.

∾

Some years I ski as late as Easter, and there are those who extend the season well past this, heading into the White Mountains to the high glacial cirques where the snow lasts into June. But usually this late March trip up to the height-of-land is it for me; I start thinking about what a broken leg could do to my plans for spring, and even this modest risk seems too chancy.

So it's up onto their pegs in the barn the skis, down from their pegs in the barn the bikes. This time of year the ruts are bad, the pavement still gritty with road salt and dirt, so I'm more apt to borrow my wife's mountain bike than I am to use my own ten-speed. My first trips are usually along the River Road, the long, level section past Tullar's farm where the pavement turns to dirt; high above the Connecticut, it's a good place to spot the mergansers and scaups that are the first ducks back every spring, taking advantage of the sloughs formed in the flooded fields.

A bike's speed is modest compared to a motorcycle's or car's, but especially on those first trips of the year it's breathless enough to make me think of how riding on two wheels must have felt to those pioneer cyclists of the 1890s—to recall what a dramatic advance that represented in man's long struggle over inertia. A bike provides a much more controlled and measured relationship with the earth's tug than does skiing; even coasting downhill, exhilarating as it is, remains within limits thanks to those brakes. It's a more mechanical relationship as well, so rather than the intimate skin-on-skin kind of connection skiing brings, it becomes involved with an intermediary—the gears beneath your feet that transfer your up-and-down pumping into a straight-ahead roll.

But still, the feel of the land's rise and fall, the sense of earning a hill, spending the earnings on the downhill side, remains much the same. Somewhere in Ernest Hemingway's writings is a charming description of biking across the French countryside in the 1920s; in the course of this, he points out that a cyclist gets a much better idea of the terrain than does a walker, with each syncline and anticline becoming engraved on your legs' muscles and lungs in a way that's impossible to erase. And it's true—a road is a totally different experience on a bike than it is walking along or driving upon. The frequent ups and downs, the level stretches that connect them, seem strung on one continuous looping thread, so gravity has a liquid, flowing kind of feel, even on those curves where it becomes centripetal or centrifugal, threatens to spill you.

Our valley is one of the more popular bike-riding spots in New England, thanks to the relatively level terrain by the river, so we get our share of bikers, bikes, fashions, and styles. There are the superserious ones: the young men and women in garish racing jerseys, hunched low over their handlebars, too busy or disdainful to smile or wave, trying to shape their bodies into a curve that will shed gravity off their backs (or gravity's handmaiden, the wind). We get beginners, too, out on their first long trip, wearing those bike shorts that are all the rage, red pennants jutting up from their rear wheels to let cars know they're around; they're apt to maintain a more stately, upright posture on their handlebars than do the pros, their eyes straight ahead of them in concentration and effort. Occasionally we even get bikers who look like they're enjoying the process; they laugh on the level stretches, dig in on the hills, spread their legs out sideways going down and shout in happy delight.

Despite the popularity of bike riding, little has been written on the aesthetics of the sport—little, that is, if you compare it to something like fly fishing or sailing. There's a lot that might be done in that direction. The sound bike riding leaves in your ears, the satisfying white whoosh of it. The way your extended arms act as shock absorbers taking in every little bump or imperfection in the road, transferring it to your palms, then your wrists, then your forearms, the shock easing off the higher up the flesh it travels. How on a late spring day, coasting along, you're apt to feel the gritty, not unpleasant tickle of midges blowing against your face. The way pedaling backward or standing up to pump harder reminds you instantly of being a kid. All the mechanical delights, from the flash of silver spokes to the amazingly light heft of a carbon frame, to say nothing of the fussy satisfactions found in tinkering with a mechanism that is so refreshingly exposed. The familiar challenges of balance—how even to ride an old clunker down a suburban street requires an exact symmetry of forces that, for a few seconds anyway, makes a person seem in sync with nature's most basic harmony. . . . Yep, a lot a good bike writer might do.

But not me. I'm a casual rider, one who likes to bike down to the post office, go out with the kids, and only occasionally is in the mood for anything longer. Those passing cars pass a little bit too close for comfort; the concrete remains a little too concretish. And yet in March, on those first swooping rides along the river, there are moments when I think there could be nothing finer than to ride for hours on end, pumping on the hills, working on the level stretches, resting on those exhilaratingly long glides, the air parting to admit you like the entrance to Aladdin's cave, only over and over, entrance after entrance, cave after cave, an infinity of partings, while you there on the saddle have to do nothing more complicated than lift one foot up and press the other back down, one foot up and the other back down, knowing that if you do this long enough, faithfully enough, gravity will smile on you and roll you right along.

⁓

These New England hills never stand more exposed than they do in late March, and it's not just because there are no leaves yet on the trees. I've already mentioned the runoff—the way every melting snow drift reveals by its furrows the minor declivities of the earth. In much the same way, each patch of land bears a different relationship to the sun, facing it on an inclined plane like a solar reflector, tucked away wallflower-fashion in the shade of a hill, sunk deep into a ravine the sun touches only a few minutes each day . . . and all these exposures can be easily determined by studying where the snow melts first, where it lingers, where it's stubborn to melt at all.

There's probably a half month's difference between snowmelt on a south-facing slope here and a north-facing one, at least in the high country east of town. Tanner's Ledge, our local cliff, is a good example; if I were to hike up the north side today I would need snowshoes, and yet going up the south side yesterday afternoon we hiked in sneakers, found snow only in the soggy depressions behind stone walls.

Celeste was with me, and we brought a lunch. No bugs, no leaves, no mud—a perfect day. The Appalachian Trail winds its way over the ledge, starting out by a huge beaver pond, passing a cellar hole choked with briars, then slanting through open woods at a reasonably steep angle to the cliff's highest point.

Hiking (or *hill walking,* to give it the British term that seems more fitting applied to this kind of terrain) involves a different relationship to gravity than does biking or skiing. It seems more stolid, older somehow; in lifting one boot up, then the other, planting them on ever higher inclinations, we seem to be follow-ing the eternal, trudging footsteps of man through the centuries, never mind our recent hundred-year blip of mechanized speed. *One step at a time*—a worthy slogan, and yet a literal one as well, at least for most of mankind's existence, and it's good for the soul to fall back into this rhythm at frequent, restorative intervals.

It's a quirk of these mountains that each seems to exert its own brand of gravity, and there's a wide variation depending on which one you happen to be climbing. Cardigan, a few ridges east, seems hardly to exert any gravity at all—a quick rush and you're there on the open summit, with half of New Hampshire spread at your feet. Tripyramid, over in the Whites, seems to exert a gravity ten times that of the earth; it's a trudge worthy of Sisyphus, and with few views from the top, there's not much reward for all that effort.

In similar fashion, gravity seems to *shape* itself variously over each mountain, creating a different endomorphy, a different style of force. The rounder and softer the silhouette, the rounder and softer the gravity; conversely, the sharper the profile, the sheerer the gravitational tug, to the point where, on the steepest trails, the force isn't so much *in* toward earth as *out* from it. . . . Sloppy physics, but coming from one who's spent a lot of time walking these hills, the hard pragmatic truth.

It's about an hour's climb to the top of the ledge—not far, but enough for our first time out. At the top, opening on three sides so suddenly, so dramatically, it makes it seem gravity's been cut loose like a helium balloon, is a view that includes mountains from Sunapee to Kearsage to Moosilauke, three remote ponds, and enough wild forest to fill the eye with unbounded delight. Every time I see this I think of Thoreau's grand phrase, "A breadth of view that is equivalent to motion"; staring at it, still panting from the effort of getting there, you experience the same kind of feeling you would get soaring open-mouthed through the air.

Ordinarily, hiking trails are not the best places to find wildlife (animals not so much fearing our presence these days as disdaining it), but the cliffs are a good spot to find nesting peregrine falcons, heroes of a marvelous restoration effort hereabouts. Celeste is the wildlife spotter in our family, and I was just warning her how tough they would be to locate in the pewter expanse of cliff when she pointed her finger and yelled.

There was a falcon all right, a little bit down from the cliff's top, but a safe hundred yards to our north (falcons aren't bothered by anything below them on a cliff, but anything above them drives them crazy). He—or more probably she—was sitting near the dead stump of a birch, with a nesting kind of pensiveness, though there was no sign of a nest yet, not that we could make out. With its white, muscular chest it looked rather like a pigeon on steroids; with its unblinking gaze, its intrinsic nobility, a pigeon with an attitude.

And the falcons weren't the only creatures out enjoying the cliffs either. Across the notch on Elder's Ledge were some miniature *i*'s that gradually revealed themselves to be yellow-helmeted rock climbers, working their way slowly up the steepest bulge, their searching, grasping arms slowly akimbo, so the higher they got the more they came to resemble not *i*'s at all, but stylized forms of Egyptian hieroglyphics.

I did some rock climbing when I was younger, enough to make me feel nostalgic and envious watching them climb. That's one sport where gravity, of course, is a big concern, *the* big concern, and the consequences of not being concerned with it enough are obvious. What I remember is the very detailed, intellectual relationship to gravity being on a cliff brings; finding holds is a complicated and intense form of problem solving, so the whole world narrows to the imperceptible flake just barely within reach, the small fissure just above that, the crack your foot can barely fit in, the rough spot, that if you move quickly, will just take your weight. The first lesson they teach in climbing is to keep your body well out from the rock like a person climbing a ladder, so gravity presses you *down* on the hold, and yet it's a tough lesson to learn, since, feeling gravity so intensely, so intimately, you want to hug the earth—earth which in this case happens to be vertical.

Climbing is a serious subject—and yet its lesson seems to be just what scrappy little odds and ends of geology are needed to support our weight. People that don't climb imagine that all climbers think about is the abyss below, but what they really think about is that small, intense, and very dear world within reach just above.

So, watching the two of them climb up Elder's (a man and woman we saw now; the woman the leader, the better climber), I could feel vicarious tension in my fingers, hands, and feet— and satisfaction, too, when with a wild kicking motion that was in absurd contrast to the delicacy of their previous movements, they sprawled onto the top of the cliff where the earth tilts flat.

Rock climbing? "There is probably no other activity that produces so much pleasure in man as climbing a dangerous Alp," Mark Twain once wrote, watching climbers through a telescope from his hotel balcony in Zermatt. "But, unfortunately, it's a pleasure strictly confined to those who can take pleasure in it."

Time to go. There was a season in our lives when we would have gone down the trail in a third of the time it took us to come up, skidding on the stones, leaves, and pebbles in one long exuberant glissade. The odd thing about age, though, is that it makes it easier to walk uphill than it does to walk down (a phenomenon which has enormous metaphysical implications, natch, but which I'm waiting until I'm fifty to begin figuring out), that collaborative tug on the part of gravity being just a little too enthusiastic for our joints to painlessly absorb. Still, down is indisputably easier on the lungs and heart—all our best hiking conversations come going down—and the grade eventually levels off, bringing us to the meeting place at trail's end where the tug of earth and our own tug find their perfect equipoise, and, like Hansel and Gretel cloaked in Gore-Tex and pile, we walk hand-in-hand through the bright March woods.

∽

And speaking of gravity, I've finished the month off by doing a foolish thing. A warm day, a new canoe, a Connecticut as silvery and slippery-looking as a child's playground slide. But you'll have already recognized these as excuses. Spring was in the air, I'm not yet immune to it, and the way these things happen, I was struck with a notion so startlingly original, so brilliantly conceived, so immediately attainable, it would have been inhuman of me not to give in.

In short, this was my plan. Our extra car, the Olds with 130,000 miles on it, was in the shop getting yet another new muffler. Celeste was working down in Hanover, where I had an appointment for lunch. What better way to get there than to *canoe*, riding back later with Celeste when she drove home.

It sounded good anyway, and in the upshot, it wasn't fatal as so many brilliant ideas turn out to be. The water was higher and faster and browner than it looked from the house, and with the flood gates open at Wilder Dam twelve miles below, the water raced along at a whitewater clip. But, wrapped in my inspiration, lulled by those fleecy clouds, I didn't realize all this until I was launched upon the river, by which time it was too late to turn around.

The worst thing to do in these situations is to waste time berating yourself—I needed a new plan and fast (*A man, a plan, a canal—Panama* ... my daughter's favorite palindrome rushed through my head, and I found it oddly soothing). The safest course would be to hug the Vermont bank so if I capsized I could scramble ashore before hypothermia got me; unfortunately, the high water had brought down some pines, and they stuck out in the water like flippers in pinball, ready to bat me over the moment I came near.

My job—the job my nonextinction depended on—was to keep well out from these and head straight downstream, and when I say straight, I mean *straight.* Any variation, any nervous straying right or left, and the river would roll me over. The longitudinal shape of the canoe had to be kept parallel with the longitudinal shape of the water, which is to say, with the shape gravity was chugging along in, the narrow groove down which spring rolled, and with it, the runoff from the largest watershed in New England.

An hour of this—an hour not without its lighter moments, including a sparrow perching for a moment on the bow, then, judging my prospects, immediately jumping ship—and I glided into the quiet bay below the Ledyard Bridge, safer and drier than I had any right to be. Writing a few hours later, I can still feel the movement in my chest and gut, as if I aligned myself so thoroughly with the river, my very soul has become grooved.

Worth it? Well—perhaps. A battle story to tell over beers, a refresher course in foolishness to help me better understand my kids. But what I remember thinking was how my wild ride seemed to be not just on a river, but along the very back of March itself, spring flowing beneath me in full torrent, carrying me along like I was nothing more substantial or important than a woody chip of bark. That's the tug of earth all right, the full vernal rush of it, and you'd be less than human if once in a while you didn't throw your arms up in surrender and let it do to you what it will.

March 30:
   It's Ivo Andrić I've been reading all winter, the Bosnian-Serb novelist and Nobel laureate who died in

1971, finding confirmation of my belief that even the lesser works of the great novelists will explain more about the world than even the best work of the most astute historian or journalist. The tragic morass in Sarajevo? Here's Andrić writing in 1945:

"*Followers of three different faiths, they hated one another from the day of their birth to their death, deeply and blindly, transmitting this hatred even to those who were no longer alive, and looking upon it as something glorious and sacred, and at the same time a defeat and a shame for their infidel neighbors. They were born, they grew up and died in this hate, this actual physical revulsion toward a neighbor of another faith, and often they spent their entire lives without finding an opportunity to express this hatred in all its intensity and horror; yet whenever due to some great or calamitous event the established order was shaken and laws suspended, this rabble burst down upon the city.*"

And it's another sure measure of a writer's greatness that their work is splendidly portable, universal even in the smaller aspects of life, the everyday texture, to the point where the following, written of Travnik in northern Bosnia, happens to double as the best description of a certain kind of March weather in New Hampshire I've ever read.

"*That indeterminate freak season had gone on for days, for weeks, for days which were as long as weeks which seemed longer than months. Rain, mud and snow, which turned to rain while still in the air and to mud as soon as it fell to the ground. A pale, powerless sun colored the east at dawn with a feeble pink flow behind the clouds, and did not appear in the west until toward the end of the gray day as a bit of yellowish light, before the gray day passed into black night . . . All through the day and during the night, dampness seeped from the earth and from the sky, drizzling, oozing, engulfing the town and permeating all things. Invisible but all powerful, it*

> *changed the color and form of things, the behavior of ani-*
> *mals, the being, thinking and mood of the people . . . The*
> *local residents, accustomed to it all and hardened, put up*
> *with it, with a patience that was always one day longer*
> *than the longest winter."*

So here I am, a celebrant of earth's ancient tug in an age when most Americans go around celebrating the freedom from that tug, its final severance. The ski tourer is run down by snowmobiles, the canoeist by powerboats, the hiker by ATVs. Gravity is dominated, humiliated, bullied, hardly a force at all, but something we thumb our noses at the moment we slip into our machines.

You can see this at its most horribly obvious on any freeway system, where the tug of earth hardly counts at all, not as a living, vital force. Except for whatever malevolent yanking the concrete itself may cast, it's been replaced by individually con-trolled gravitational systems, each one in deadly earnest competition with the ones speeding past it, so what's created during an afternoon rush hour is nothing less than a vicious free-for-all—and to my mind, a much more vivid demonstra-tion of and reason for the violent anarchy of American society than any statistics on murder and crime.

"I hate machines," novelist Thomas Williams once wrote, in what I'm sure wasn't meant to be an overstatement, not in certain bitter moods. "Flighty, dangerous, what they do is remove us from our true lives, speed us loose from what we would be con-tent to be—walking animals upon the slow and beautiful earth."

And isn't that perhaps the cause, at least in an under-ground way, of the rootlessness that so afflicts us—that the bonds of gravity (which don't only weigh us down, but embrace us to earth) have been jettisoned for good? Our vic-tory over gravity has been too sudden, too easy, so it's small wonder it's turned to ashes in our mouths. If the planet no longer tugs us back to itself, no longer grounds us—*bounds us*—in the ancient reality of earth, than anything becomes possible, any evil, any monstrosity, including that bizarre and

ugly swarming of anti-gravitational devices at rush hour—
that mindless soul-rotting blitz that sweeps the meek into the
gutters and for the survivors passes as life.

The cure for all this? Ah, but we're not talking cures here,
not in a book of epitaphs, postscripts, anachronisms, past
tenses, but looking the future square in the eye, spitting at its
ironies with irony of our own . . .

Was he the only reader in the world? There were times those years when he thought so, lying there in his bedroom at the family summer home, or better still, outside on a lawn chair under a vase-like clump of scraggly gray birch. He was thirteen, fourteen, fifteen, smack in the middle of that vital breathing period between childhood and maturity when lifelong passions have their best chance to form. Out the window, above the oval leaves, the sun would be shining with a brilliance so rich it required a dampening effort of self-control not to yell out loud from sheer pleasure, the sky was so blue you could get drunk just looking at it, and yet his eyes stayed fastened on something even more brilliant and deep, a world the center of which he was plunging toward with every ounce of strength he had, even though, to the outside world, he was nothing more than a boy lying down with a book, so motionless and dreamy-looking he was doubtless on the verge of sleep.

Reading, serious reading, can do that to a person, convince you that nothing exists but the book and you. In the other world by the porch his mother would be placing paper plates down on the picnic table for lunch, weighting them with silverware so they wouldn't blow away; off near the garden his father hacked at the tomatoes, his myopia mistaking them for weeds; by the driveway, his older sister talked to whoever her current boyfriend was, a shy one this time, someone who kept reaching down to the gravel to nervously toss some in his hand. All this would be going on, the happy sights and sounds of an endless summer, and yet somewhere between the rectangular object resting on his chest and the deepest, most absorbent matter of his brain, Prince Lyov Nikolayevitch Myshkin was riding the Warsaw train to Petersburg, not "the Idiot" the title had led him to expect, but a fine, sympathetic young man with a well-shaped forehead, heavy, gentle eyes, and an "almost painfully passionate expression" similar to what the boy, in his vainer moments by the mirror, considered to be his own.

He knew he was in for some work with this one, no matter how quickly he had raced through the first ten pages. It was a Modern Library edition, and not only that, but a Modern Library "Giant," which meant five hundred pages at the least. This was daunting—in school, a book's merits were directly proportional to a book's brevity—but not as daunting as it would have been earlier that summer, before a dozen even longer books had turned his imaginative flabbiness into imaginative muscle, taught him something of patience and endurance, especially when it came to the boring parts he knew, even in the greatest books, were inevitable.

Work, in fact, was exactly what obsessed him—understanding what was required of him aside from the simple, unconscious effort of reaching down to turn the page. Forming the letters into words? Well, this was easy enough, he'd been doing it since he was five, ditto with linking words into sentences, understanding the hesitations, emphases, and stops supplied by punctuation. Understanding the words? A bit harder, but nothing he couldn't handle; the authors he was reading now used longer, more complicated ones than the authors he'd read as a youngster—and this is where the work came in, including frequent trips to the dictionary, tearing out meaning from syntax, obsessive re-readings of sentences already read three times before. Following the plot? It was everything to him those years, and so caught up was he in finding out what happened to Prince Myshkin next, he never had to turn to the list of characters, the synopsis, that, as with most Russian novels, was included in the front.

But even these tasks, so straightforward on the surface, so subtle underneath, were only the beginning of what he had to teach himself to do. Blocking out the world he happened to inhabit the better to penetrate the world the author had created for him? Entering the hermitage, the expansive hermitage, of words? This was closer to what the apprenticeship was all about. Here he was spending a week with an author whose name he had never heard pronounced out loud, someone who had been dead for many years, a Russian, and yet, turning those pages, none of that mattered, because what he had to do was give way completely, let the author guide him where he was meant to be guided, and what's more, not do this passively as a passenger riding a coach, but as an active participant, someone whose imagination and understanding, undeveloped as it was, had to help with the pulling . . . and not easy pulling either, but hard, constant, active pulling that left scars in your eyes, a dizzy swarming in your brain, spasms in your midsection, along a twisting mountain path above an enormous and frightening chasm, over which, if the author led wrong or the reader pulled wrong, both would topple, smashed to atoms in that worst of all calamities: a book put down in the middle and never reopened.

Fourteen years old, liver of a life that was sheltered to a fault, spoiled member of a privileged generation, a virgin in every sense of the phrase, yet in those moments under the birch tree he was Fyodor Dostoyevsky's partner, collaborator, and pal, responsible in a way he would have found impossible to articulate for getting Prince Myshkin safely through the adventures and misadventures of all 585 pages—and not just Dostoyevsky's hero, but Steinbeck's Tom Joad and Cather's Ántonia Shimerda, and the hundreds of other characters he stumbled into those summers. And as naive and unformed as this teenager was, one thing was clear: he would have to accomplish this collaboration absolutely and totally alone.

Certain kinds of fourteen-year-olds like to think of themselves as loners anyway, so this wasn't as daunting as it sounds. He was alone by default, at least when it came to books. Nobody he knew liked to read, or read like this—passionately, intently, with everything riding on the next word. His family was tolerant enough to let him devote himself to whatever he felt like devoting himself to—a priceless gift—but they read like most people do, lightly, to kill time, for amusement alone. His teachers didn't love books, not anymore; they had been lecturing about *Spoon River* or *The Canterbury Tales* for too many years, to too many dullards. Literature had become merely a product to them, a subject to grade, and their treason, in Holden Caulfield's words, made him want to puke.

His friends liked to read, at least they used to, but none of them were going at it like this, and he had already learned that Dostoyevsky, Hawthorne, and Conrad were not names you brought up in your average bull session. Loving books in elementary school, they were sick of them by junior high; if English teachers were bored salesmen pushing a product no one had any use for, then they were the sullen consumers, refusing to enjoy what was being forced down their throats.

Family, friends, teachers. No allies there. But there was a further question that perplexed him, one he'd be no closer to solving at forty than he was at fourteen. Did *anyone* read anymore? No one ever mentioned books to him, recommended good ones; nothing was said of them on television; what bookstores were within reach already sold more greeting cards than books. To find his reading he was dependent on a serendipitous network of cross-references and hints (the backs of the Modern Library jackets were a good source for these; they had a list of other books in the series, and he was determined to read every one, from *The Education of Henry Adams* to *Twelve Famous Plays of the Restoration and Eighteenth Century*). When he went to the library, browsed in the shelves, found what he was looking for, or took a chance on something never heard of, he turned to the back of the book to see when it had last been checked out. Five years before, ten years before—even, in some cases, thirty years before, the purple stamp ink looking spidery and ancient, of another era altogether. Here was the temple of literature he was becoming more attached to each day, its power to enthrall, its capacity for solace, and yet as far as he knew no one worshiped at it except him.

A conceit? He was always quick to exaggerate. But isolated as that summer house was in the fold of hills, protected by a

haze of grilling hamburgers, a barrage of flying horseshoes,
softballs, and shuttlecocks, a thick wall of second-growth birch,
it wasn't immune to what was in the cultural air, and this
included, even in the early '60s, a *fin de siècle* burnish strong
enough to make the books glow, even as he held them, with an
autumnal purity that was already bittersweet. Saul Bellow
(whose *Henderson the Rain King* he bought in paperback for
seventy-five cents just because he liked the title) described it
perfectly, what the boy felt then, what the man later discovered.

> Literature, in my early days, was still something you
> lived by; you absorbed it, you took it into your system.
> Not as a connoisseur, an aesthete, a lover of literature.
> No, it was something on which you formed your life,
> which you ingested, so that it became part of your sus-
> tenance, your path to liberation and full freedom. All
> that began to disappear, was already disappearing,
> when I was young.

No one told him that, of course. The disappearing part. The
falling in love with something disappearing part. And even if
they had, his stubbornness might have found it only added to
reading's allure. He had always been a sucker for lost causes.
Indians, Confederates, Davy Crockett at the Alamo, the
Brooklyn Dodgers. So, if he was falling head over heels for
something threatened, sensed this without a word being said, it
only made him give to each book even more of his attention,
even more of his heart.

∽

He often tried picking out the exact moment when the
childhood love for reading, so common, so fragile, kicked in to
something a thousand times more important. He had sharp-
ened his reading skills early; there was a picture of him at five,
holding a newspaper open in front of his face, and not to the
comics either. Like a lot of his friends, the first books he
remembered loving, going out of his way to find, were the
Hardy Boys mysteries—Frank and Joe sleuthing around

Bayport in their yellow roadster. He also liked Clair Bee's Chip Hilton, who lettered in three sports and was always involved in various moral crises, as for instance when the basketball team was caught up in a frenzy for the newfangled jump shot, and Chip had to restore them to shooting old reliable two-handers through his own sterling example.

These were as good as anything to cut his teeth on, even if they were baby teeth, the books themselves the nutritive equivalent of sugar. For getting your neck in shape, your hands, your eyes, teaching you what it meant to spend hours curled up with a book, they did the job. There was another series he liked even better. The Childhood of Famous Americans, wherein Robert E. Lee or Jim Thorpe or Clara Barton would go through all kinds of fictional adventures in the first nine chapters, with a light, edifying touch, only to emerge, *mirabile dictu,* as heroic adults in Chapter Ten.

Seeing his interest in history, his great-aunt Addy bought him a subscription to *American Heritage* magazine—the hard-backed, beautifully illustrated treasure it was in the '50s, coming to the house in its own dignified brown carton. He would read every word of every article—"Burgoyne and America's Destiny," "Perdicaris Alive or Raisuli Dead," "Saint Jane and the Ward Boss," "Seward's Wise Folly," "Blondin, the Hero of Niagara"—so by the time he was twelve, he was a walking, talking encyclopedia of arcane Americana. That same aunt (may the gods protect her!), seeing the affection he had for his cocker spaniel, gave him *All Dogs Go to Heaven,* a novel written from the points of view of dogs lying in a pet cemetery, who tell stories to one another at night about how they came to be there, which was mostly due to their owners' cruel neglect. A book so sentimental and maudlin it made him cry like he had never cried before, to the point where he took out a pen, wrote the following on the flyleaf in vivid blue ink: *This is the saddest book I ever read.*

Animals, sports heroes, detectives, pioneers. He devoured books on all of these, and then when puberty started pumping in its high-test adrenaline, books on exploration, mountaineering, natural disasters, and adventure. *We,* by Charles Lindbergh; *Alone,* by Admiral Byrd; *The Conquest of Everest,* by Sir John Hunt. His favorite books became *A Night to Remember,* by Walter Lord, the story of the *Titanic* disaster. He read each paragraph a dozen times, not wanting it to end—the narrative switching from crew members in the flooded engine room to officers on the bridge to the Astors in the smoking lounge to passengers in steerage; to the deck of the *California* a little way off, its mate staring dreamily over the rail, heedless to the unfolding tragedy; to the iceberg; to the lookout seeing it suddenly loom dead ahead. It was his first big lesson in irony, being in on the world's secret, knowing something the passengers and crew didn't, and it was overwhelming in its way, so this book perhaps more than any other was the vital one, the corner around which he turned from being the kind of reader almost any bright kid is to becoming something entirely different.

A similar process went on when it came to fiction, so there was hardly any interval at all between reading Albert Payson Terhune's novels about collies to reading Dickens and Tolstoy and Dostoyevsky. In those days there was little in the way of "young adult" reading with its phony relevance, its perverse determination to only console and never inspire. When you were finished with kids books you either gave up reading or turned to the real stuff—and the real stuff was what he was reading now, under the shade in the heat of day, up there on the fieldstone porch when the sun got lower, long into the night in the snug, quiet cabin of his room.

He had it down pat now, the actual process. The words taken in quickly and transferred to what they meant; the "business" words, the directional signals, understood and almost skipped; the adjectives subliminally tasted/smelled/heard/felt; the proper names snapping him to attention, signaling him to remember, sort, and file; the rhythm of the sentences causing his head to sway, so he read as much with his ears as he did his eyes. The process alone would have been enough to leave him enchanted, the sheer pleasure to be found in putting all this together, transforming black squiggling lines into roseate sunsets over Normandy or soil-brown rivers in the Congo or the icy-blue summit of Everest. The words disappeared, that was the magic of it. Understood, the words disappeared and you were there.

He read so fast, so thoroughly, so broadly, the subject matter hardly counted, as long as it supplied fodder for that mental alchemy. But he was hungry for information, too—for news of the world, what it was like out there, what he would find when he emerged from this prolonged chrysalis stage and flew forth to life. One of the first real books he discovered was *Jude the Obscure,* and he immediately identified with the stonecutter's hunger for learning—his determination to seize it by force. He went to a good school, had none of Jude's disadvantages of poverty and class, and yet realized from the start that the only kind of education that counted was a self-education, and that he would have to manage this from scratch, his teachers having taught him little that mattered, at least when it came to what he wanted to do in life.

What he wanted to do in life? Any serious physical or moral task demands an unconscious effort of preparation, a blind apprenticeship, that ends up being so thorough and intense it seems, in retrospect, premeditated and deliberate. Henry Aaron spends hours as a kid hitting bottle caps with a stick; Abraham Lincoln lectured to chickens, practicing his elocution; young Dickens is put to work blacking bottles in the darkest of the London slums. Were they deliberately shaping their future or was their future deliberately shaping them? The boy on the lawn chair—who would never be Lincoln or Dickens or Henry Aaron—knew that for who he *would* be he had to read a lot of books, and do it now while he had the time, freedom, and stamina . . . and past that he couldn't see, though it would have comforted him greatly, cleared up many strange and torment-ing things, if he could.

When he was older, looking back, it was clear he'd spent those summers searching for allies, contemporaries, masters, and mentors—in finding out who he would have to read and know and model himself on, and who he wouldn't have to read and know and model himself on. The great thing about reading is that a person finds his contemporaries from a span of two thousand and more years—that the author who means the most to you may turn out to be someone who is actually alive and writing today, or it may just as easily be someone who was alive in the 1500s, who yet manages, thanks to their take on life, their method of expression, their art, to speak to your immediate and very contemporary concerns in a way no one currently writing can ever approach. Melville was more his contemporary than Updike ever was, or even Salinger; Thoreau spoke to him more directly, more youthfully, than any living essayist he could find. Years later he would be puzzled over the uproar regarding "canon," since it had been obvious to him all along that the job of a reader was to find his or her own canon, from a thousand different sources, orthodoxy be damned.

Then, too, when you read with this kind of omnivorous hunger, the books all blend into one enormous and endless whole, so Joyce and Chekhov and James all seem to be chipping away at the same huge block of marble, creating together, the reader becoming the one tool they share, their imaginative chisel—all great books, seen in this light, being installments of something not yet complete—and that this whole, this blend, is what is called literature, and it can best be approached by a young person's huge and indiscriminate gulps.

Years later, reading Orwell's famous list of the reasons why anyone would switch sides in the collaboration, become a writer himself, he was surprised to find missing the only reason that had ever seemed to him compelling: *emulation.* That having experienced the magic power of great prose, the only proper response was to try to create such magic yourself. And the reading he did as a youngster did indeed seem to be leading him toward some enormously extravagant response—he felt this very strongly—though for a long time he assumed the response was to imitate the action of the people *in* the books, to trek to the South Pole or command vast armies, and it took endless hours alone before the great, the disturbing, the overwhelming thought occurred to him that the action he could emulate, the equally heroic action, was the action of the people putting down the words . . . and that this is why, as he poured through book after book, he'd better goddam well understand how they did it.

And so who was he reading? How was that purely individual canon taking shape? Thirty-five years later, it's hard to separate out the chronology, put Tolstoy in his fourteenth summer, when it may well have been his fifteenth or sixteenth that he started reading of them, the earnest, well-meaning Pierre, the vivacious Natasha Rostov, the brave, but nihilistic Denisov, who did them so much dirt. In the same way great books blend into one, a reader's reading seems removed from time entirely, the second and third time through a book blending into the first, so, once started, it's hard to separate the classics you read as a teenager from the classics read as an adult, their circulation being continuous.

Tolstoy was on the list early, as was Turgenev, Dostoyevsky, Pasternak, and Chekhov—the Russians, despite or maybe because they were supposedly our enemy. There was Conrad, too; "Typhoon," "Amy Foster," *The Secret Agency,* and even *Victory*—Heyst alone on his tropic island with Lena, the beautiful, tragic refugee from Zangiacomo's Ladies' Orchestra. Willa Cather's *O Pioneers!* and *My Ántonia,* with their prose so perfectly matched to the plains they describe. Kafka, his stories, his diaries, his endless enigmatic variations (*Somewhere there is happiness and the beaters are driving me there*). Proust, though it took him six tries before he got truly started, only succeeded after an unhappy infatuation enabled him to read the 2,403 pages as a self-help book on jealousy. Hawthorne, the stories more than the novels; Melville, for him, for always, a god. Dickens, of course, in old mildewed volumes that smelled vaguely of bananas. Ring Lardner—not a great, certainly, but he didn't care about that then, laughed at his stories, his crazy plays . . . and then Thurber, who seemed to pick up the story where Lardner left off, especially in *Fables for Our Time,* or "The Night the Bed Fell," wherein eccentric cousin Briggs Beall believes he's likely to cease breathing when he's asleep, and sets off an alarm clock to ring at intervals until morning, and the narrator's grandfather disappears for six or eight days at a stretch, returns "growling and out of temper, with the news that the federal union was run by a passel of blockheads and that the Army of the Potomac didn't have any more chance than a fiddler's bitch."

And there was T. H. White—his Arthurian cycle, which seemed to him far wittier, more profound, than anything he ever found in Tolkien. Kenneth Roberts's novels about colonial days, especially *Rabble in Arms,* which made Benedict Arnold into a hero. Fitzgerald, not only Gatsby (natch!), but *The Beautiful and Damned.* Ralph Ellison's *Invisible Man,* with its Harlem riot so eerily prophetic. The stories of John Cheever, apple-flavored, funny, and sad, the living writer he liked best, at least now that Camus was dead in a car crash. And John Knowles, whose *A Separate Peace,* tragedy circa 1941 at a New Hampshire prep school, moved him like few other books could.

Great and near great, good, indifferent, and downright bad, he read them all, learning which authors he would have to explore further, which ones he could safely drop (good-bye to you, with regrets, William Faulkner; good-bye, with no regrets, the entire world of science fiction). And it wasn't all novels either, but almost equal amounts of history, for instance Francis Parkman, whose books brought the French and Indian Wars so vividly to life it was as if the land of the Iroquois, the *coureurs de bois,* the Jesuit missionaries, began right there in the second-growth forest by his chair.

> The situation of the party was desperate, and nothing saved them from destruction but the prompt action of their surviving officers, only one of whom, Ensign Wyman, had escaped unhurt. It was probably under his direction that the men fell back steadily to the shore of the pond, which was only a few rods distant. Here the water protected their rear, so that they could not be surrounded; and now followed one of the most obstinate and deadly bush-fights in the annals of New England.

He liked Edward Gibbon's *Decline and Fall of the Roman Empire* almost as much, particularly the quirky irony of his stately prose. "The last hope of a people who could no longer depend on their arms, their gods, or their sovereign, was placed in the powerful assistance of the generals of the west, and Stilicho, who had not been permitted to repulse, advanced to chastise the invaders of Greece."

And there was Samuel Eliot Morison, a historian smart and passionate enough to sometimes lose his cool "*Ten thousand curses on the memory of that foulest of assassins, J. Wilkes Booth!*"; Bruce Catton, who wrote so well about the Union side in the Civil War, and Douglas Southall Freeman, who wrote so well about Confederates. He was big on the Civil War, the centennial of which was being celebrated with a flood of new books, but it was nothing compared to the books he devoured on World War II, his parents' war, the one, through their stories, he seemed to have served in himself. Cornelius Ryan, Richard Tregaskis, John Hersey, Bill Maudlin, William Shirer, Winston Churchill, Richard Hillary, the writers on the Holocaust, Anne Frank; if a book had a submarine or a bomber or a stalag fence on its cover, he read it, simple as that.

Nature books? He loved them all—Rachel Carson's books about the sea; Edward Way Teale writing of the seasons; Aldo Leopold, who he discovered early; Hal Borland, whose farm wasn't far away—but his favorites were from authors who lived alone in wild, remote places of extraordinary natural beauty. Gavin Maxwell in Scotland with his otters; Henry Beston alone on the great beach of Cape Cod; John Rowlands's *Cache Lake Country* in the Canadian north; Louise Dickinson Rich, whose books about life in the Maine woods he read over and over. And then the patron saint of all these loners, the author whose name kept coming up in every nature book he read: Henry David Thoreau, whose writings, discovered when he was fifteen, literally changed his life.

Thoreau! There was a time when the name alone could send a shiver down his neck, just as could the words *breast* or *trout*. It wasn't just the vicarious pleasure of living in a cabin by a pond, not just the passionate anger toward the materialism of American life (*"We do not ride upon the railroad; it rides upon us"*), but the absolute and miraculous perfection of his prose, its lyricism ballasted with preciseness, its surprising irony and play of wit, its cadence, and how reading it taught him the rhythm of good prose would always move him more than the rhythm of good poetry, to which, though he read lots of it, he would always remain oddly deaf.

> We had made about fifty miles this day with sail and oars, and now, far in the evening, our boat was grating against the bulrushes of its native port, and its keel recognized the Concord mud, where some semblance of its outline was still preserved in the flattened flags which had scarce yet erected themselves since our departure; and we leaped gladly on shore, drawing it up, and fastening it to the wild apple tree, whose stem still bore the mark which its chain had worn in the chafing of the spring freshets.

In a sense, the list never stops, the names worth mentioning being merely the highest, most conspicuous landmarks on a terrain that was continuous in interest, variety, and beauty. Arthur Conan Doyle's Baker Street blends without discordancy into the Amazonian jungle of H. M. Tomlinson into the rich Mississippi bottom land of Eudora Welty into the Manhattan of J. D. Salinger into the British Columbia trout streams of Roderick L. Haig-Brown into Aleksandr Solzhenitsyn's gulag camps. Stephen Crane, Katherine Anne Porter, Harper Lee, Stendhal, Somerset Maugham, Orwell (another of his gods), Katherine Mansfield, Ambrose Bierce, Edmund Wilson, Emerson, Bertrand Russell (*"Brief and powerless is man's life; on him and all his race the slow, sure doom falls pitiless and dark"*), the memoirs of R. P. Tristram Coffin, Laurie Lee, or Flora Thompson, Sherwood Anderson, Alfred Kazin, C. S. Forester (Captain Horatio Hornblower!), Alain-Fournier, Edna St. Vincent Millay, Apsley Cherry-Garrard of

Scott's last expedition, Theodore Dreiser, Sinclair Lewis, Robert Louis Stevenson, Isak Dinesen ("*I had a farm in Africa, at the foot of the Ngong Hills*"), Vera Brittain, Vilhjalmur Stefansson, Joy Adamson, Joseph Wood Krutch, H. W. Tilman, Robert Frost, Cervantes, Xenophon, Edwin Arlington Robinson, Stephen Vincent Benét, Nordhoff and Hall, Sigurd Olson, Edith Hamilton, Thomas Mann . . . and not just books either, but magazines from *Boys Life* to *Mad,* newspapers (the old *Herald Tribune*!), cereal boxes, dictionaries, and anything else he could get his eyes on, so, when it came to the printed word, he was like a blue whale swimming through an ocean of krill, straining it indiscriminately through his baleen in the certainty that nourishment would take care of itself.

"A regular bookworm!" visitors would say, pointing toward him from the porch as they headed down toward the lake, purple beach towels draped around their necks. Bookworm? Book eagle was more like it (never mind that whale!); from the earliest moments, he never thought of reading as a retreat or refuge, though it was partly those things, but an energetic advance into the world, as vigorous and dangerous an exploration as any he read of in those books. Alone on a lawn chair, in the posture of sleep, a boy seems to doze over an old book propped on the high part of his chest—and yet what he's really doing is closing with a French man-of-war off Honfleur, helping farm animals revolt against their tyrannical master, watching in horror and awe his father shoot a rabid dog on a hot Southern street, or mourning the death of his friend Phineas, dead at seventeen of a broken leg.

∾

Reading, world-class reading, total reading, is never given the credit for being the hard emotional and intellectual work it is. A first-grader becomes a "reader" and that's that; nothing is ever said past elementary school of a person's reading skill, unless they have none at all. But the term is granted too easily; it's as if someone who had the ability to make out a shopping list were called a "writer." In Samuel Johnson's day, the term *reader* wasn't bestowed on a person without good evidence; *a prodigious reader* was about the best thing Johnson could say of a man.

That was the biggest lesson of those summers of discovery: reading is a skill, one that demands talents from the reader to match those it requires from a writer, far beyond the technical how-to. And perhaps the first and broadest of these is a whole-hearted kind of *trust;* the reader must believe, at a minimum, that whatever they are reading is worthy of their time and effort—that translating the squiggles of Tolstoy has commanded be set down on the page will result in an experience far greater, more profound, than the mere jigsaw transformation of squiggles.

Along with this is a quality that is especially important when it comes to reading fiction; the ability, the willingness, to be *transported.* Any great book is a journey—this is one of those clichés everyone recognizes as true—and yet there are many people, slaves to literalness, who can't make that journey, no matter how hard they try. Those that do have to wear the burden of their own surroundings lightly; they need a certain isolation-booth kind of quality, the ability to withdraw from the circumstances of daily life, not go running just because the family golden retriever has rolled in the poison ivy and everyone is shouting. They need to empathize with people far removed from those they know; they need, most of all, the kind of imagination on which another imagination can act—not passively, like a canvas accepts paint, but actively, as if the canvas is creating itself the very moment paint is applied—and this presupposes a certain freedom from the physical, intellectual, and moral circumstances they happen to find themselves caught up in. The reader who is not Russian, not a soldier, not living in the year 1812, must be able to become a frightened soldier standing on the battlefield at Borodino, or a shy girl attending her first ball, or else *War and Peace* means nothing.

And yet this trust, important as it is, can't be granted too easily; the other skill that readers must bring to match it is *discrimination*—they must not let themselves be won over without adequate reason to be won over. The reader can't be too prissy on one side, or too jaded on the other; they must root for the book to succeed, care enough that failure makes them angry or sad. They must have a sense of rhythm to appreciate good style; an ear to hear dialogue; the mental flexibility to accept metaphor, simile, implication, and image; a wide background in having read the best there is in prose so as to form a standard by which everything that aspires to greatness may be judged; a capacity to absorb huge amounts of information, on subjects trivial and profound. A good reader must have patience for tangents—must read for the long haul, be willing to be bored. A good reader must have the ability to believe so intensely that tears can come—be willing, to paraphrase Kafka, to have the stubborn ice inside be melted away by the author's art.

A good reader must have some appreciation for a book as a physical object; must love the compact rectangularity; love the feel of its paper, the perfect compromise achieved between flexibility and stiffness; must have some feeling for the arts of typography and composition—must be the kind who gently peels back the cover before buying a new book to examine the binding underneath.

And readers, the best ones, must "have a life," be actively involved in all its upsets and tragedies, so they can bring to the books that enchant, inform, mystify, and edify them enchantment, information, mystery, and edification of their own; if books teach you about life, then life must teach you about books, so the reading doesn't become merely a refuge, a substitute, a vicarious tower. We hear a lot about the courage it takes to be a writer, take risks; it's time more were said about the matching, risk-taking courage it takes, in this day and age, to be a reader. "We learn *words* by rote," George Eliot once said, "but not their meaning; *that* must be paid for with our life-blood, and printed in the subtle fibres of our nerves."

All these things—and then the rarest gift, the one that almost no one has anymore, the one the lack thereof forms for too many people the excuse not to begin: time, unbounded time, unencumbered time, time in huge chunks, time the boy on the lawn chair was rich in for three priceless summers . . . a space that can be not only filled by words, but illumined by them, so, for those alive to its miracles, the hours spent in reading are among the best and richest in life, books the most precious of man's gifts, time to read them in the second most precious, and the possessor of both, even now, the luckiest person in the world.

April 26:

April is the month we plant trees up here. Pine seedlings from the state extension service, apple trees from mail order in Pennsylvania, a big maple from Elmer Brown's nursery over in Vermont. The instinct to put something in the ground is a powerful one, the kids feel it as strongly as I do, and a seedling six inches in height, when planted tenderly, seems to be a fitting tribute to the earth's new warmth.

We've planted an extra tree this year, one we didn't plan on when we drew up our list this winter. Up on the little rise we call Sunset Hill we put in a crab apple, the biggest, showiest one money can buy, in honor of the children's grandmother who died Easter Sunday after a year-and-a-half battle in which, despite the outcome, it would be more correct to say she defeated leukemia than the other way around.

Our first choice was a plum tree . . . it was Grand-mom's favorite, and was fully in bloom out her bedroom window on Easter, bringing her her last moments of joy . . . but Elmer, smiling up at me from the middle of his perpetual suntan, gently talked me out of it. They can be tricky this far north; the flowering crab does much better with our winters, and is if anything equally showy when it come time to blossom. So be it. A crab apple for Grand-mom. Fine.

We planted it this morning in the teeth of a bright northwest gale. Everything blew away—Matthew's cap, Erin's cap, my cap, the string, the mulch—and yet it was welcome, we needed the vigorous freshness after the events of this month. We dug a hole twice as big as the root ball . . . Dad taking the first hard spade strokes to break the turf, the kids widening it, grabbing at the worms, tossing the rocks away . . . then together we kicked the dirt in and bounced up and down to pack the roots, remembering, before covering it with mulch, to poke some holes in the ground so the tree can breathe.

Finishing, I noticed the kids were reluctant to leave . . . I was reluctant myself . . . and we lingered on talking about Grandmom until it became easier. We talked about trees and flowers and the things she loved. We agreed on how much she would have enjoyed the crab apple if she could see it, and how we had two spots named in that part of the meadow now, Sunset Hill and the Grandmom Tree.

And eventually, sitting under its shade, I hope to tell them something else about their grandmother—how in all the years I knew her I heard her lie only once, and not deliberately either. During her first long stint in the hospital, after all the doctors had decided the chemo had failed, as we kept watch beside her bed waiting for the end, she'd somehow found the strength to write the following down on a yellow pad: I don't have enough courage.

She was wrong on that. She had enough courage to come back to life when all of us had given up hope; enough to have a good year after that, one in which she managed to drive again, enjoy her grandkids, even travel. But courage is not something you can just grab for at the end and expect it to be handy; it has to be something you build a life around, and this my mother did. As a young girl growing up on a farm during the Depression, helping with the chores, walking many miles to school, caring for her mother during a prolonged illness. As an army nurse in England during the war, aiding wounded young boys, dying young boys. In marriage, helping a husband with a severe handicap, never complaining. In daily life—in what Frost referred to as the "trial by

existence." This trial, all these trials, my mother passed
with flying colors, and yet if you told her this she would
have snorted at you in contempt.

And there's one story I'll tell the kids time and time
again, especially when they're discouraged. How, a few
weeks before she died, knowing time was running out for
her, with very little strength left, my mother was bothered
and vexed with one annoying thing—the fact that her
favorite watch didn't work—and insisted over the objec-
tions of everyone on driving through heavy traffic to the
store to get it fixed.

The Grandmom Tree . . . and walking back to the
house, turning to see where Erin has gone, I see her kneel-
ing by the base of it, patting down the soil in exactly the
same emphatic and tender gesture I'd seen so many times
in the woman whose life, in such flashes, she now bore.

There was an article in the paper last night, yet another article, on the problem of illiteracy. Apparently the numbers are
much worse than even the gloomiest surveys previously esti-
mated—that living in what likes to consider itself the best
educated country in the world are close to twenty million
adults who can't read or write at the third-grade level.

The man reading this in the hammock—the boy's succes-
sor—was appalled, as the article intended him to be, but he also
decided the reporter missed an important point. All these
people who can't read obviously suffer from it in jobs and
careers, and yet it's equally apparent that in daily life they function just fine—that in the contemporary world, simple basic
reading is no longer a necessity for many millions of adults.

Appalling—but then I could write some articles of my own.
What about the even higher number of the functionally *aliter-*
ate—those who can read, who have graduated from high school
and college, and yet would never think of picking up a book that
wasn't connected to their job, their studies, or whatever improve-
ment they're attempting to their house, bank account, or body.
Distracted by television, seduced by technology, overwhelmed

by daily life, they lack that essential quality of acceptance real books need in order to be read, what Saul Bellow, with bitter-sweet nostalgia, referred to as *the quiet zone.* They read, but shallowly, celebrity magazines and pabulum, skimming off the words. The well-meaning and earnest long for something better, but—no, the quiet zone will just not come. If Johnny Junior can't read, then Johnny Senior *won't* read, and books are rare items to encounter in most American homes.

Their intellectual counterparts, in the meantime, have signed on as apologists for the visual age, finding all kinds of reasons why *Gilligan's Island* is the aesthetic equivalent of *Hamlet*—why hypertext is the coming thing, printed books passé after a run of a mere four hundred years . . . and what's wrong with that, since books were authoritative and paternalistic to begin with. And let's face facts, the best way to write literature is to imitate sound bites, comic books, or commercials. When it comes to reading, these are the defeatists, turncoats and collaborators—the quislings who do the dirty work for the media barbarians.

Cynics can sometimes be right, of course. Are they this time? Is reading on its way out? There's lots of evidence pro and con. Book sales remain high (if you include romance novels and "true crime"); bookstores flourish (as chains that model themselves on shoe stores); libraries are crowded (especially the video sections); creative writing programs are mobbed (though their students are notorious for not reading books), and computers, rather than seducing people from books, may eventually drive them back in search of news of the soul. Against this is the gut premonition that comes across a lover of reading almost daily—*there's no one doing this anymore but me.*

What's obvious, add all the evidence up, is that a certain kind of reading is truly imperiled—deep reading, serious reading, the kind of omnivorous, passionate reading without which literature cannot survive. There are still millions of readers, of course, but in this last category? The figures couldn't have been very high in the best of cultural circumstances, but now they must number no more than did those early

Christians a few years after the crucifixion, recognizing one another by similar secret signs and indications, at secondhand book sales in church basements, or there in the dark catacombs of the least-visited library shelves. One more sweep by the Roman centurions and they will be gone, their passion extinguished, unless ...

Unless? Driving home from Montpelier last night after a bookstore signing, passing through the working, no-frills city of Barre, home to the marble quarries, I saw something I haven't seen in years. A girl of about fourteen walking down the sidewalk with a book held outstretched before her at eye level, reading as she walked. I couldn't see the book's title, but something in her posture, her intentness, the way she managed to walk and read at the same time (and chew gum, too), gave me the impression she had found it on her own—that it wasn't homework, something assigned, but a book she read because it was delightful and important to read, even more important and precious than the soft April twilight through which she moved.

It's not exaggerating to say that on her slender form, her intentness, the future of reading now rests. Will her absorption, the quiet zone that even on a busy sidewalk so obviously surrounded her, last as far as her front door? Will she be jeered out of it by well-meaning friends? Will she be able to continue that book far into the night, using a flashlight if she has to, or will it be dropped in favor of the gadgets competing for her attention, machines that chatter, chirp, and beep, or taken away from her by the indifference of parents and teachers as surely as if they yanked it from her hands. . . . Or will she be able to take that book to her room, read to her heart's content, one book leading to another, one exploration to another, her bookshelf growing, not only the one she patches together out of cartons in the corner of her room, but the far larger, more portable store of knowledge and wisdom and wonder any good reader carries around with them for life.

I watched her out the side window, taking my eyes too long off the road, then watched her again in the rearview mirror, her shape growing smaller as she walked away—walking, thanks to that book and the effort required to hold it outstretched at precisely the right level, as erect as a princess at a coronation, a pilgrim, the loveliest creature in that April night.

W*e don't have a TV in our house.* Since 99.1 percent of American households cannot make this claim, it may be of some interest to know why. Certainly, our lack of a television has created great curiosity, puzzlement, anger, and awe among those we know, and I suspect even more of these emotions behind our backs. "The Wetherells get by without a TV, why can't we?" "They're into birds, flowers, nature. You know. Tree huggers." "He's a writer, that's why." "It's not fair to their kids, that's what I think." "What are they trying to prove anyway? What are they trying to *prove*?"

We did have a television in the first days of our marriage, a small, black-and-white set Celeste lugged back from Colorado when we moved to these New Hampshire hills. I even remember watching it once—the 1983 World Series, which by sticking the rabbit ears out the window I was just able to make out. I had a concussion at the time—another story altogether—and I remember the dizzy way the images skittered across the screen, as if what I was watching wasn't the Philadelphia Phillies and whoever they were playing, but the confused patterns of my own battered brain. *Nausea made visible*—that's what TV had become, only it took a hard knock on the noggin to understand this was so. A few days later, recovering my senses, we took the set to our local dump, heaved it toward a mound of old paint cans and broken storm windows, shook hands in satisfaction, and have been without one ever since.

Now that my TV-watching days are behind me, I can afford to be nostalgic toward it all. Like other members of my generation,

I was born with the tube, raised on the early days of Milton
Berle and *The Honeymooners,* Pinky Lee and Phil Silvers, Flash
Gordon and Cleo, the talking basset hound. I was there when
Clarabell honked his horn at Howdy Doody; I applauded in
delight when Kukla, Fran, and Ollie danced about their little
stage. I learned to be cool and ironical and flip with Dobie Gillis
and Maynard G. Krebs, fell in love with Yvette Mimieux on
Dr. Kildare, got scared out of my wits by Rod Serling and *The
Twilight Zone,* laughed when Bret Maverick kicked up his heels,
filed into the school auditorium to see John Glenn blast off from
Cape Canaveral, watched in disbelief and horror Jack Ruby fire
his pistol into Lee Oswald's skinny drifter's gut. Walter Cronkite
and *You Are There;* Steve Allen with his mix of intelligence and
craziness, Clint Eastwood in *Rawhide,* David McCallum in *The
Man from U.N.C.L.E.,* Patrick McGoohan in *Secret Agent* and
The Prisoner. I have TV in my bones.

Good nights those. I remember the whole family sitting there
in the living room watching Ed Sullivan, one soft light left on in
the corner, the four of us laughing at the comedians, me going into
my "And now for a really big shooooow" routine the moment the
commercial came on. I harbor no grudge toward those days whatsoever, and yet it seems to me that twenty-some years of watching
television is enough for anyone, and that as innocent as that black-
and-white era now appears, even warmer and more precious in
memory will be these quiet, peaceful years of no TV at all.

Not watching television, of course, is probably the rarest,
most extreme form of dissent left to anyone in our culture.
Reading the paper yesterday, I came across an interview with
John Zerzan, who apparently has become the guru of American
anarchists, what with his call for the "undoing of technology"
and paring life down to "essentials." But the reporter was shrewd
enough to notice that even Mr. Zerzan carries his dissent only
so far. "Asked about his owning a television set, he threw up his
hands in mock embarrassment. 'Like everyone else,' he said, 'I
have to be narcoticized.'"

There are those who would rather not have this happen, feel
no need for narcotics of television's peculiarly invidious

strength. The Wetherells are not smug, self-righteous vegetarians, do not live in a cabin without running water, don't belong to any crank religions or fringe political groups, but in most respects are average, card-carrying members of the consuming culture we inhabit, and have the house, mortgage, and bills to prove it. And yet in this one specific aspect we claim the right to independence, and in anticipation of all the arguments and questions this declaration invariably engenders, I suppose I should get on with my promise to explain. TV, after all, is an integral part of the air we breathe, like it or not, but—and this is what we've proved by our example—not a part everyone has to go along with, its messages, both explicit and subliminal, not ones you necessarily have to swallow, especially if you prefer loving life with all its untidiness to loving the hot, rapid-fire blur of electrons, even if they come neatly boxed.

And while it's not my intention here to engage in random TV bashing, it's only fair to admit I can do my share—quickly, in one fast rush that will allow us to move on to finer things. I hate TV for all the usual reasons. The mindless chatter that gurgles off the screen, the murders offered up for our delectation, the constant violence that you don't need a doctorate to understand breeds violence on the streets, the trivialities that pass as news, the way everything on television is presented with a mocking tone, as if the tube is laughing at us for even watching in the first place, the sneer being TV's inevitable and constant stance toward everything. All these, and then the worst part, the part no one ever bothers talking about, not even the most damning study or article: the commercials, the legalized lying, and how dissatisfied with your life they're intended to make you feel, so rather than just drugging people into insensibility, television makes them bored with their spouses, their children, their friends, their fate, and thus creates the kind of jumpy, nervous materialists this culture turns out by the ton. Bashing? Nope, we're beyond that now, into complete and utter disdain.

It's been fifteen years without TV—enough time for news of this to get around. We find other families are often envious of us in this respect, almost pathetically so, as if they would like to quit watching, too, but are afraid to, don't quite know how. "Well, we don't watch *that* much," they end up saying, glancing automatically toward the corner of the living room, as if staring toward a screen they can't quite believe is not there.

Others ask us for the secret, want tips on quitting—want, I suspect, to find that not having TV is superhumanly *hard*. All I can say to them and to those who might suspect us of a cold and monstrous self-discipline is that not having a television in our house has been accomplished without any undue strain or hardship on our part—that the secret of not having a TV is that it's the easiest, most pleasant thing in the world.

"Ah," people will say, saving their trump for last. "What about the kids?"

Well, what about the kids? Are we sacrificing them to our own selfish doing without? "Television is educational," people will say, often the oldest ones. Educational, and yet all the teachers I know complain constantly about how dumb and passive their pupils have become, the ones who watch many hours of "educational" TV. "They'll be teased by their friends," the sensitive ones add. They would have been twenty years ago, true, but not watching TV is so rare now it's off the mockery scale altogether, so would-be bullies can't even comprehend their going tubeless. "They won't know what's happening in the world," others insist, despite the fact that newspapers and radio answer just fine in this respect. As for mass culture, understanding the current references, things like Barney and Mighty Morphin Power Rangers literally hang in the air, so our kids can talk about them quite well, without having seen them more than once or twice.

It might be instructive in this line to describe what's going on right now in the Wetherell household, at eight o'clock of a beautiful spring evening. Celeste is outside putting in her half of the garden—summer squash, beans, and broccoli this year, keeping it simple. Judging by the wagon full of plants waiting beside her, the pile of mulch, it will be dark by the time she finishes watering them in, leaving her just enough time to read the kids a bedtime story, then read herself before going to sleep.

Erin is downstairs hunting and pecking at her typewriter, putting together an article on the neighborhood dogs for the next issue of our family newspaper, the *Brick Hill Gazette*. Matthew is downstairs in his bedroom listening to a tape-recorded book, the kind that beeps when it's time to turn the page. Downstairs, too, is his grandfather, visiting for the week, listening to tape-recorded books of his own; legally blind, he gets them from the Library of Congress, and the new routine here is for him and Matt to listen together, the two of them with their heads cocked at precisely the same attentive angle.

Me, I'm up here in my study putting in some overtime . . . all of us so busy at what we love doing there's literally no room for television to fit. The two or three hours after dinner is prime time in our house, dearly purchased by the labors of our day, and we're not going to waste them watching "prime time."

But perhaps I'm wrong in saying all this is easy, no sweat at all. Three months after Erin was born, Celeste went back to working twelve-hour shifts on weekends, and I was left alone with the baby from sunrise to bedtime—and with her brother on the same schedule four years later. It's been almost ten years now of this weekend routine, and it's not been easy doing without the kind of instant baby-sitting TV provides. More time spent reading to the kids, more time finding things for them to do, more time just sitting watching them play, more time breaking up the sibling arguments that, when all is said and done, are much healthier than the numbed truce watching the tube provides. Occasionally Erin would ask when we were going to buy a TV, but she hasn't asked that in years, and her brother has never asked for one, to the point where, if by some lunatic whim I brought home a set, they would be the first to demand its riddance.

It's no coincidence that shortly after throwing out that old black-and-white Zenith we purchased our first home—that going without a TV was very much a part of this new, powerful sense of being where we wanted to be. Celeste and I worked a long time, searched hard for many years, to come to this sense, and there was no room in it for what was phony, irrelevant, beside the point. Life was an everyday concern, something that kept us hopping, scalding us from time to time, delighting us at others, but something we were too busy leading to watch other people—flat, boring, gibbering people—lead for us.

∾

Television, of course, is only the most pervasive, obnoxious, and successful assault on our eyes, mind, heart, and hearing that has been going on all century. In the year 1901 the loudest sound a person might hear in the course of a late spring day (at least those who didn't work in factories) was the occasional boom of thunder, or, on special occasions, the pleasant syncopation of a marching brass band; today, many millions of people not only find pleasure in subjecting their hearing to levels of noise that, via electricity and amplifiers, are deliberately designed to hurt, but pay exorbitantly for this privilege. The exponential increase in sound is not the least of the hits humanity has taken in the modern era; if one were asked to choose an adjective to describe the twentieth century—and not allowed to use the word *bloody*—noisy would be the logical and perfect choice.

Writers have been complaining about this for decades, if anyone cared to listen. Open almost any novel of the last hundred years and you'll find evidence they were written with hands pressed over ears to keep out the din. Take John Cowper Powys, for instance, writing of rural England in the early part of the century.

> Wolf began to feel as if he were stranded alone on a high, exposed platform, hooted and shrieked at by thousands of motors and aeroplanes. Beads of sweat stood out on his forehead. It was as if he searched in vain for any escape into the silence of the earth. No escape was possible any more! He was combed out, raked over, drained of all sap! His destiny henceforth must be to groan and creak in the wind of other people's noise.

Or V. S. Naipaul trying to describe life today: "There was always noise, no rest from noise. The impression was of people cooped up and constantly agitated in their small, boxy spaces."

And so on. What a noisy era ours has been! Junk noise that serves no real human purpose (car alarms shorting out in a rainstorm, filling parking lots with their whines), assault noise deliberately designed to offend (the blaring boom box; the mufflerless motorcycle), even well-intentioned noise that ends up contributing to the overall din (those maddeningly shrill beepers installed on trucks and construction vehicles so they don't run anyone over when backing up). Pass any house, even here in the country, and it's wrapped in a throbbing halo of noise—the noise of the television, the noise of the lawn mower, the noise of the radio and stereo, each one roaring to be heard over its competition.

It's perhaps significant that the word *silence* has over the last decade or so become a pejorative term. Silence, once looked upon as something to be longed for after a hard day's work, something celebrated by poets (*"No hammers fell, no ponderous axes rung/Like some tall palm the mystic fabric sprung./Majestic silence!"*) has become in our day a politically suspect condition. Simon and Garfunkel bemoan "the sound of silence," minorities regret the silence of decades, therapists teach us silence is an unnatural and suspect condition, and "silence" has become, in the final dark irony, all but synonymous with sexual abuse. Even writers who you would expect to be the last custodians of silence's virtues are rushing off to writers' conferences, scheming to get on television, issuing CDs, chattering away, so a writers' conference at full blast is one of the noisiest places imaginable—and this in the profession that once spawned Marcel Proust, he of the cork-lined bedroom, he who was smart enough to remember what most contemporary writers have forgotten: "All art is created in silence."

And speaking of centuries—and as anyone who's read this far certainly has guessed—Wetherell is living in the wrong one, by one or two at least. My craving for quiet is undoubtedly the most atavistic, out-of-date longing I possess, the hardest to satisfy, the one that marks me most ruthlessly for imminent extinction. Even in trying to celebrate the virtues of quiet I find myself at a terrible disadvantage; a child of this century, for all my squirming, it's next to impossible for me to recapture what must have been the glorious, unself-conscious quiet this world once enjoyed. Not just the virgin quiet of the American continent before Columbus, or the stillness of these New England woods before the first settlers came up the river, but the quiet my mother's parents must have known on the family farm in upstate New York during the early years of this century, where the soft mechanical click of the threshing machine seemed part of the natural order, just as did the sound of stream water running over a weir, and the rusty creak of a turning windmill clashed not at all with the busy whistlings of the meadowlarks and finches.

Quiet in those days was taken for granted, seldom commented upon, relative to nothing, and yet how serene and harmonious it must have made the men, women, and children caught up under its sway. Read journals and diaries from those days and it's amazing how far sound traveled in that unvexed atmosphere; church bells were discernible from three towns away, a train could still be heard clicking against the rails for thirty minutes after it passed, neighbors could even shout to each other from neighboring farms and carry on a decent conversation. (In our day, the sounds that travel farthest are the ones that carry the worst tidings; a friend of mine, working in his Oklahoma rose garden one morning in spring, heard quite distinctly, like an evil pressure against his ear, the explosion that sabotaged the federal building in Oklahoma City, seventy miles away.) And the fewer the sounds, the better they sounded. Shakespeare could talk about the "concord of sweet sounds" and expect his audience to know what he was talking about; two hundred years later, Wordsworth could still write "The soul of happy sound was spread" and mean it quite literally.

The drumming sound of rain, the billowy slap of wind, the plangent rush of moving water. These must have been the familiar, comforting accompaniments to a good many people's day, at least in rural areas, and even in a city the noises would have been rich, vibrant ones. Cart wheels on cobblestone, the squeak of cordage, steam whistles, peddlers calling, the steady clop-

clop-clopping of horses' hooves. "Too noisy!" a curmudgeon like me might have complained, yelling down the stairs, to describe a decibel level that to our modern ears would pass as silence, sweetly undisturbed.

I've managed to catch the ancient quiet only a few times in my life. Once, walking alone down a beach on Vancouver Island, the fog was so dense it absorbed not only every sound, but even the possibility of sound, so there was nothing loud enough in the world to penetrate it; once, in exactly the opposite experience, I stood on a mountain top in Scotland, heard a cuckoo calling in the distance in air so pure, so perfectly tuned for aural transmission, it seemed there could be no sound anywhere in the world that, wait long enough, wouldn't find its way to my ears.

I catch it, too, when I listen to music. My abilities in this direction, always variable, are not as good now as they were when I was younger, but there are still nights, listening to Schubert or Debussy or Britten, one of those composers who tread better than most the exquisite dividing line between silence and sound, I can sense what it must have been like: the quiet that was so deep and serene and resonant that man couldn't write upon it but in purity and delight. I can sense it in certain voices; Björling, Pinza, Kathleen Ferrier, Janet Baker—those few, precious human voices that by their art and clarity redeem all our chattering.

Pure quiet. Quiet unpolluted and unalloyed. It's hard to catch, and not only because of the background noise of our times, but because I want it so badly it puts a strain in my hearing that's there permanently; even on a trout stream, a beach, or a mountain, I have the sense I'm holding my breath, listening too hard, without that splendidly unconscious acceptance that must once have been quiet's main gift. *Quiet can't be quiet unless you don't know it's there?* Not exactly what I want to say, but near enough to make my point.

"It's so, uh, *quiet* here," visitors will say, making a stretching gesture, like a person waking up after a deep, rich sleep. They're pointing out the obvious, of course—that quiet, like so many other things, is all relative.

Yes, it's quiet up here, at least compared to most places in the world. There are no industries within forty miles, no malls within twenty, and we've been lucky with neighbors who value the peace of our hill as much as we do. Some days I can hear the church bell in the town center three miles away, to say nothing of another church bell less than a half mile across the river. Trains, when they pass along the Connecticut, still leave that lonely rumbling-rambling in their wake (and how many farm boys and girls, hearing that echo in the old days, must have been overcome with longing to follow in its wake). On many nights coyotes nip and paw at the air with that intense, purposeful kind of whining that seems orchestrated by a madman—and always sounds much closer than it really is. Even now, in my pauses in typing, through this open window, I can hear the impossibly elusive, Martian-like beeping of woodcock as they begin their mating ritual, and with it, like a gentle metronome, the satisfying click a trowel make against topsoil as Celeste digs at the weeds.

The sound of tree frogs, peepers, robins. The guttural honk of a heron. The sandy brushing sound the lilac makes against our cedar siding in a fresh breeze. The splendid, scary crack of ice in the winter pond. All these point out the paradox that quiet is not the mere absence of noise, something negative, but a positive, rich kind of melody, to the point where a writer celebrating quiet ends up by celebrating sounds. So many good ones, yet only in this kind of quiet do they have a chance to ring true! Babies cooing to themselves when they first wake up. Kids splashing into icy water, giggling hysterically. The rhythmic singsong as a girl skips rope down a lonely driveway. The soft *tsk tsk* of an old woman listening to a story. The sounds made in love. Given the chance, humanity has its own beautiful voice; quiet is built by these sounds, and quiet deepens them in return.

"But you know," some of our visitors will get around to saying, usually the morning after their first night, "if anything, it's *too* quiet up here."

By which they mean, live in the city or suburbs long enough, the sound of sirens wailing outside the window becomes more familiar and soothing than the sound of crickets. Tonight at midnight, long after every other sound has ebbed away here, my father's tape player will click on downstairs as he tries to fight his sleeplessness with the calm baritone voice on those talking-book tapes—something, anything, to put against the blankness, scrub it away.

"Quiet to a quick bosom is hell," Byron wrote, and there's been enough quickness in my life that I understand him—and my father's insomnia—perfectly. In 1980, having just sold my first book, I used the advance to rent a house beside a quiet salt-water pond on Cape Cod. Too quiet, as it turned out. After years in the suburbs, a bundle of nerves, I grew addicted to the silence too quickly, so any interruption of it became literally unbearable. A teenager who lived up the pond was fond of tearing around in his outboard at all hours of the day and night, to the point where I spent my afternoons plotting how I would swim over to his dock after dark, my face blackened in cork like a commando's, to pour Karo syrup down his fuel tank. Once, at night, driven half crazy by the sound of a dog barking across the pond, I ended up screaming out the window at it, baying, cursing, my violent desire for quiet grown into a tumult (and this behavior W. S. Merwin describes just right: *One dog barks at nothing/Ten thousand pass it on*).

I wrote a short story that summer called "The Next Sound You Hear," wherein a classical-music deejay engages in guerrilla warfare with a hard-rock deejay at the rural radio station where they both work. In the course of it, Silva, the classical man, comes to a terrible admission, one I had no trouble identifying with myself.

"He didn't want listeners. He didn't want to do commercials, take requests, play dedications. It wasn't to anyone's ears he pictured his music traveling when it left the transmitter, but to the deep quiet of the northern night, matching it, reflecting off the stone walls of the abandoned hill farms, the forgotten stands of spruce, the unpeopled hollows to create a harmony so deep and thickly textured that no noise—no hard rock, no blaring commercials, no weirdness—could ever stain its perfection."

Or as Dickens said, with much more pith, giving the words to the immortal Sam Weller: "Anythin' for a quiet life, as the man said wen he took the sitivation at the lighthouse."

∽

The quiet life. Peace and quiet. Serenity. Any discussion of aural quiet expands naturally into a discussion of quiet in this larger sense, though you can hardly pronounce these terms out loud without nostalgia or irony creeping into your tone. If it's impossible in the quiet of our hills to recapture the even more enriching silence that was once theirs, how much harder is it to describe a state of mind and soul that, on good days, quiet days, perfect days, is just palpable enough here to make me long desperately for more. *Tecum habita,* the Bible puts it. Study to be silent, and yet how hard a study that is, a task in life for the misfits, dissenters, the few, rather than a blessing many can share, so we're all striving for something we still have the old names for, but can hardly expect to partake of ourselves.

What would it be like, this quiet in a larger, fuller sense? I think of an environment that still has the capacity to bring to our overburdened, bombarded, assaulted ears—our poor lame drooping ears—tidings of joy. I think of a life where, if we don't immediately see the solution to all our problems, we at least have the quiet to study them out. I think of a time when at least some noises are those of the earth, not of man's domination of the earth; where every mechanical sound is not immediately suspicious and hateful—that the sound of a distant chainsaw could mean a person getting in their winter's supply of wood, and not an old forest's wanton destruction. I think of a time when words like *cascade, echo,* and *chime* were used more often than *throb, beat,* and *pound*—a world not always in forte, not always atonal. I think, not to put too fine a point on it, of a never-never land I'm probably as close to inhabiting at the present moment as I'll ever be, and yet one that still seems unimaginably distant and remote.

You have to go back many years to find a time when this kind of harmony was possible, to someone like Thoreau, to a passage like the following, to understand how when sound and soul were synchronized, a great deal of strong and beautiful music was played.

> Sometimes on Sundays I heard the bells, the Lincoln, Acton, Bedford, and Concord bells, when the wind was favorable, a faint, sweet, and, as it were, natural melody, worth importing into the wilderness. At a sufficient distance over the woods this sound acquires a certain vibratory hum, as if the pine needles in the horizon were the strings of a harp which it swept. All sound heard at the greatest possible distance produces one and the same effect, a vibration of the universal lyre, just as the intervening atmosphere makes a distant ridge of earth interesting to our eyes by the azure tint it imparts. There came to me in this case a melody which the air had strained, and which had conversed with every leaf and needle of the woods, that portion of the sound which the elements had taken up and modulated and echoed from vale to vale. The echo is, to some extent, an original sound, and therein is the magic and charm of it. It is not merely a repetition of what was worth repeating in the bell, but partly the voice of the wood. . . . For the rest of the long afternoon, my meditations are interrupted only by the faint rattle of a carriage or team along the distant highway.

There are times when I know exactly what Thoreau was driving at—spring mornings when the air is so still, so primed with just the right amount of dampness, I can hear bits of conversation a half mile away, Bernard Tullar talking to his son in their field above the river. The words themselves don't come, but their quiet intimacy is transmitted perfectly and is perfectly pitched to the well-tended fields, the Tullar fields, that the words have to cross to reach our meadow and me standing there on its edge. Only a farmer, a countryman, could pitch the tone of his voice so instinctively to the tone of the day; only in these quiet, forgotten pockets can the earth still enhance man's voice. Quiet isn't dead, not here, not on a morning like this. In exile perhaps, but there are still those who take care of it—and while they last, the part of the human spirit that resides in quietude will never be extinct.

But I can't remain in this miraculous refuge of silence, decently silent myself—can't will myself into being a Thoreau, a Burroughs, or a Muir, put myself back in time to an era when junk noise, if it existed, could be avoided by anyone with a little effort, and not by ramming your fists into your ears to block it out. No, I'm going to join with the commentators who drench us with their advice, shove in my own two cents' worth before I'm drowned out by the tidal wave of noise cresting over you in 99.1 percent of American homes—and here it is. Just as aural quiet is one component of the quiet life, so too a quiet life is impossible without a large measure of aural quiet, and the first and most important step toward either begins with—to use an oxymoron which is brutally absurd in every other context—a purifying act of violence: to strangle, to mutilate, to eviscerate, to otherwise destroy, disfigure, and demolish that noisy stranger lurking in our midst to such little good purpose—the television—and then in the silence and space where it had been, see if you can't start patching together that rarest, most threatened of modern phenomena: a life played in harmony; a life that has the quiet in which to ring true.

May 5:

    Some weeks spontaneously group themselves around themes, even what seems to be the theme of a book a writer is currently working on. Thus, it's been dairy week around here, as in good-bye dairy farms and the whole pastoral lifestyle that goes with them.

    On Monday, after fifty years of operation, Brown's Auction Yard in our neighboring town gave what was probably its last livestock auction. There aren't enough farms left in the Upper Valley to support that kind of operation (not too many years ago, five hundred animals would change hands nightly; recently, this was down to

less than half that number), and—since these losses are
seldom caused by just one kind of failure—Mr. Brown
himself, the hoarsest voiced, most exuberant mannered,
and unabashedly avaricious auctioneer in the valley, has
just been convicted of bank fraud in federal court and is
faced with a contemplative spell in the penitentiary.

It's a real blow, losing this. Nowhere was there a
better spot to glimpse the old rural way of life than at one
of Brown's famous Monday night auctions. Anything
might go up for sale, anything a farmer could wedge into
his pickup or coax onto his trailer: heifers, hens, rabbits,
tractor tires, geese, hay, you name it. The cows got the
most critical scrutiny; whenever a good one was led into
the ring the farmers would drift over from the refreshment stand—those farmers who, by their faces and
visages, demonstrated that the words craggy, proud, and
self-reliant were not just stereotypes when applied to
New England farmers. They would come over and lean
elbows-spread on the fence in the timeless posture of
farmers worldwide as Andy Brown rattled off the numbers, cracking jokes, driving up the price on a rushing
fountain of one-syllable grunts, his eyes darting back and
forth so as not to miss a bid, his sons keeping their own
sharp eyes peeled for ones he might miss . . . high, higher
. . . the fountain at its apogee, Andy sensing this a split
second before anyone else . . . then BANG, down comes
the gavel, and the bashful winner, frowning noncommit-
tally, slips a halter over the cow's neck and leads it away.

The last auction was on Monday. On Tuesday came
word that my Uncle Lee is selling off the animals and
equipment from his dairy farm in upstate New York;
battling cancer, his adult children wanting no part of the
long hours and hard work, the farm that's been in our
family all century will be subdivided into housing lots,
and that will be that.

On Thursday, driving home from a hiking trip in the
Franconia Range, I saw something I haven't seen in

years: cows returning through a meadow to be milked at a barn. These days milking cows are kept strictly indoors, fed on specially prepared feed, treated like cloistered nuns, so to see them actually outside is a rare event— rare enough I pulled the car to the side of the road, got out, and watched.

This was a common sight only ten years ago—the common sight in rural America. There were twelve of them, holsteins and jerseys both, their full udders sway- ing in rhythm to the loose skin of their indented flanks as they trudged through the meadow grass . . . looking, so strong was the sun, like cattle marching across an endless Indian plain, with that kind of timelessness, that touch of the divine . . . only then they were into the dappled shad- ows cast by a grove of maple, matching the butterfly pattern of their markings . . . then into the deeper, more absorbent shadows by the first outbuildings . . . until they looked, from that vantage point, like dreams heading nose-first into extinction—going once, going twice, going twelve times, gone.

A married man living in Boston calls his lover living in Cambridge and in quiet tones full of apology tells her that it's over, he's decided to be sensible, there's no use pretending it was anything but a wild, aberrant fling. Putting down the phone, fighting back tears, desperate for distraction, the woman turns on the radio beside her bed—softly, to a classical station—and yet the sound is just loud enough to penetrate the thin wall to the next apartment.

The tenant there, a fussy man of rigid habits, is bothered by the muffled crying sound, the evidence of untidy human life, and so turns up his own radio to a sports call-in program to drown out the sound. A bit hard of hearing from having worked in fac- tories all his life, he turns it up more, to the point where the sound leaves his opened window and crosses the short distance to the three-decker next door. Here a mother of four, trying her best to cope, steal some time for herself, turns the television set louder as the kids, catching the sound of the man's radio, scream they can't hear. The mother yells louder to be heard over the din, the kids scream louder to be heard over her yells, until the sound, a real racket now, grows so large a student living upstairs, calling home to the suburbs, has to shout to be heard long-distance.

His mother, on the phone in their tract house outside Worcester, taking his shouting for real distress, yells, "Are you okay! Are you okay!" which commotion makes her husband so vexed he goes outside and starts the riding mower, spends a half hour cutting the front lawn. His neighbor shouts, "Hello Al!," but can't be heard over the mower's roar, so, shrugging, lonely for something to do, he decides he may as well tidy up the grass himself, and goes into the garage to fire up his new gasoline-powered leaf blower. The man living in back, lying in his hammock trying to relax after a strenuous day selling computers, feels bothered by this aural evidence of industry, becomes guilty enough that he starts up the chain saw to hack away at the fallen pine tree that's been lying across the garden all summer. His daughter, lying on the floor of her bedroom, can't hear her stereo in the angry buzz of it, so she turns up the volume full blast—the beat so rhythmic, so pounding, the teenager three doors down takes out his boom box and turns it to the same station, only these houses are right under the approaches to Logan Airport, the jumbos are coming in one every three minutes, so he has to turn it up even louder in order that the music's pounding finds its way to his chest before the pounding of the lawn mower, leaf blower, chain saw, and jets.

His father has warned him a thousand times about playing his music too loud—too many times, for Dad now snaps, and with a heavy feeling of defeat goes to the garage, climbs into his Corvette, and roars out toward the countryside. Loud as it is, the car's tape deck isn't loud enough to drown out the sound of construction on the highway, the roar of trucks passing him even on the secondary roads, and, an hour later, just short of the New Hampshire line, when a pack of motorcycles passes him like he's standing still—twenty-six of them in line, not a muffler in the bunch—he gives up and heads home.

The motorcycle gang, none of them less than fifty-five years old, heads up toward New Hampshire, since they've heard it's quiet up there, want to be somewhere their engines can be heard to best advantage, an advertisement for their existence none can ignore. Passing a lake, they're heard by a fourteen-year-old boy on a jet ski, a "personal watercraft," that tears across the lake at fifty miles per hour in imitation of the motorcycles, creating such a din that a couple at the far end of the lake who have invested their life savings in a retirement cottage for the peace and quiet end up arguing with each other about whether it was all some huge mistake, yelling at the top of their lungs as the jet ski roars past their dock, an "all-terrain vehicle" tears up the woods behind them, a father teaches his daughter how to shoot an assault rifle . . . the roar, the tearing, the shooting, the yelling making other people in other cottages turn up their televisions to drown out the sounds . . . and so on around the lake and out into the countryside, the noise spreading concentrically across America, then out across the world, then out into the universe—this hoarse, straining voice of an insignificant planet set in quarantine on a silent cosmos's furthest edge.

Meanwhile, in an uninhabited forest mankind by some miracle has missed, a tree falls without making a sound.

John Marshall, at least at first glance, does not seem like the kind of man who would have a brown trout tattooed on his thigh. Of average height and modest demeanor, his mustache tending now toward gray, he comes across as a person who years before and with great difficulty overcame much shyness, so his manner, quiet as it remains, seems dearly purchased and self-contained. Our aggressive in-your-face world being what it is, this might make some people underestimate him and underestimate him badly. But talk to him about fly fishing, watch him in action as he guides clients on a stream, understand the passion and knowledge he brings to the endeavor in all its multifaceted richness, and the only surprise is that the trout isn't engraved right smack over his heart.

The same enlargement takes place when he's behind the oars of the McKenzie River drift boat he uses on his guided trips—the sixteen-foot-long, four-foot-wide fishing machine he imported to Vermont from Oregon, where they're made. His forearms, powering the heavy, rubber-tipped sweeps, seem to swell perceptibly; his eyes, diffident on shore, take on an alertness that is heron-like in comparison. Watching him work, scouting out the river for rising trout, scanning the surface film for the all but invisible insects they're taking, simultaneously guiding the boat past an obstacle course of rocks, provides the kind of delight that comes from watching any living thing perfectly at home in its environment—which in John's case is the blue-ribbon trout water of the Connecticut River round about Lemington, Vermont, and on toward Bloomfield six miles below.

And there's one more clue to John's fishing personality: the care with which he releases those wild trout his clients land. Gently, a manly kind of gentleness in which is gathered all his love for the wild rainbows, browns, and brookies that, even today, inhabit the Connecticut in the kind of numbers more often found in Montana than in Vermont and New Hampshire. Carefully netted, each trout is with even more care detached from the fly, then—John leaning perilously far out from the drift boat's side—swum back and forth in the current until, with a sudden strong turning, it swims off on its own. *This* is the most important moment in fishing to John Marshall. Not the strike, not the battle, but the moment when a wild fish returns unharmed to its lie.

I fished with John this year, floated the upper Connecticut on a day poised right on the challenging border between late spring and high summer. In thirty years of fly fishing, I'd only gone out with a guide once before, preferring to figure out the water and trout on my own. Indeed, this disdain for guides was threatening to turn into a fixed and cranky bias, at least until I met John at a November birthday party of a mutual friend. In the half hour we talked, enough came through to discover we both looked at trout fishing in pretty much the same light, and that he had intriguing clues to a river whose mysteries I was obsessively curious about solving. Before the party was over, we had a date to go out come spring.

Now, there are those who might think that messin' around with boats and trout, getting paid for it, falls into the nice-work-if-you-can-get-it category. And it's true, in the state of Vermont anyone with a dime to call the Fish and Game Department can get listed as a "registered" guide, whereas in Maine and New Hampshire registered guides must pass stringent tests. But in guiding as practiced by John Marshall, a whole variety of skills and talents come into play. Part tour guide, part river pilot, part teacher and chef (John attended the Culinary Institute of America as a younger man, and the lunches he packs for his clients show it), a good fly-fishing guide must also know enough about trout to rank as a semi-professional ichthyologist, enough about the insects they feed on for a minor in entomology, and, in dealing with a variety of clients' egos and demands, have the tact of a diplomat and the patience of a saint.

And all this over the long haul. Marshall guides over thirty trips a season on the upper Connecticut, a dozen more on the lower reaches of the river where he fishes for bass, manages to work in an occasional float on the White River, and finds time for "research and development" trips where he fishes alone. On the day my fishing partner Tom Ciardelli and I went out with him, a typical day for John, he left his home at nine A.M., drove two hours to Lemington, spent a half hour getting his drift boat launched and organized, picked us up, fished with us from noon until midnight, winched his boat back up a precipitous bank I found difficult to climb, served up a midnight snack on the tailgate of his truck, dropped us off at our car, and then drove home—in time to get into bed at three A.M.

All this is a long way from the legendary North Woods kind of guide, who believed the old ways of catching trout were the best ways, allowed that fly fishing was okay as long as you slapped a shiner on the barb, thought the best place for a trout was the middle of a frying pan, and colored his stories with the kind of wild exaggeration sports liked to hear. Instead, the role models for guides like Marshall are more apt to be the guides of Montana and the West—stream-smart workaholics who are right on the cutting edge of new trout-taking tactics and innovative new flies, passionately devoted to the ethos of catch-and-release, believing, as the late great Lee Wulff put it, that "a trout is too valuable to catch only once."

John carries over fifteen hundred flies with him, most tied by himself in the long winters between fishing seasons. He changes them frequently, affixing them to the extra demonstration rods he carries, then handing the rods up to his clients like a gun bearer handing over a freshly loaded rifle. Like most expert fishermen, he worries constantly about getting into a tactical rut, forcing the fish to conform to his way of fishing rather than modifying his methods to fit the trout's mood. He keeps copious notes, compiles a computer data bank to study and learn from off-season, and, on a float trip like ours, is as much student as teacher, trying to understand even more about the river and its fish.

On our day together we had need of all John's expertise and then some. It was unseasonably hot, the water so low and drenched with sun it made the trout as light-shy as vampires. For the first few hours the lack of fish hardly mattered. There was a breeze on the river, more than on land, and it was good to be out there floating at a leisurely pace downstream, with no more sign of man than the occasional rumble of a tractor getting in the hay. The Connecticut around Lemington is, to my mind, one of the loveliest rivers anywhere, with a delightful alternation of slow water and fast, and ever-changing views of the surrounding hills. It's prime trout water all the way, a tailwater fishery kept cool even in summer by the release of Murphy Dam thirty miles upstream. Unlike on most rivers in New England, there's a real possibility of catching something *big,* and it keeps you on your toes, even on a relatively slow afternoon.

Then, too, both Tom and I were fascinated by John's drift boat, curious to know how he'd gone about obtaining it. Seven years ago, tiring of outboards with their noise, stink, and expense, he'd decided to order a drifter from Oregon; it was shipped to Indiana, then John drove out with a trailer and fetched it back to Vermont. Once in possession of a genuine guide boat, John thought it made sense to try guiding, and this—after taking some public-speaking course to overcome his diffidence in dealing with strangers—John proceeded to do.

Since drift boats are a rarity in Vermont, people are always stopping him to ask questions or take pictures, but it makes perfect sense for the kind of float trip the Connecticut provides. It's high, wide, and dry, a perfectly stable and quiet fishing platform, and, with John facing forward as he rows, is highly maneuverable in the rapids, the occasional noisy scrape on the aluminum bottom doing no harm at all. The handiest feature is its anchor, controlled by a winch near the rower's seat, allowing the boat to be stopped instantly when a rising trout comes into range.

I tried rowing myself later in the day to give John a chance to fish. It's heavy, solidly so, and facing forward takes some getting used to. There can't have been more than a handful of such craft ever on the Connecticut, and yet the longer I thought about it, the more I remembered pictures of the rivermen's bateaux that navigated the river back in the heyday of the log drives at the turn of the century—realized how, in their silhouette, they resembled nothing so much as a sleeker version of John's boat.

Around four, as the sun got caught up in the tall silver maples along the banks, we began to encounter rising trout. These were difficult, shy fish, and, with no flies visible on the water, no telltale swallows or swooping kingfishers, there was some puzzlement as to what kind of insects they were taking.

"Emergers," John said at last, after many minutes spent studying the water. "They hatch on the bottom, never quite manage to break the surface film. If the trout don't get them, they're swept downstream. When you put one of these on they'll take it big-time."

Add that to John's qualifications—he's an unfailing optimist whose vocabulary doesn't include the qualifier *if,* but only the more definite *when.*

And so we put on emergers, dry flies with their bottoms sliced off, fished them as John suggested, sunk just below the surface, with slight twitches to imitate their motion. Tom, patient and careful as the scientist he is, a beautiful caster to watch, soon had the knack of it, and began taking good trout, which fought as only wild rainbows can. Me, I fish in a more slapdash manner (*impressionistic,* I prefer to think of it), and it took a little less sunshine for me to begin connecting. But from four to midnight we were casting to rising trout almost continuously, the only intermission being our picnic supper in the shade of the bank.

"Would you like Dijon on your ham?" John asked. Then, a bit later, "I hope you don't mind real whipped cream with your strawberries."

The shade was so deep and cool, the play of light off the river just beyond its rounded, scalloped edge so mesmerizing in its liquid shimmer that we were in no hurry to shove off. The talk turned, as it often does with fly fishers, to whether or not it's possible to tell the difference between wild trout and stocked ones.

Agreement was unanimous—no surprise there. Wild trout are prettier, more delicately shaded, more apt to mirror the environment they live in, harder to catch, spookier, smarter, better fighters, tastier (though we were all a bit tentative in admitting we knew how a wild trout tasted), and, in general, more *alive,* so as far as the debate goes, it's like comparing the aesthetic merits of wildflowers with those of concrete blocks.

I had my say, then sat there nodding as Tom and John continued talking. Listening, I could picture a similar group sitting in a boat thirty years from now, debating in all seriousness whether its possible to tell a wild, natural person from one that has been genetically engineered, the old traditionalists opting for the virtues of the former, while the up-to-date and trendy are saying, yeah, but wait until you see the new mass-produced laboratory model—*that's* a person for you!

There are wild trout and stocked trout both in this section of the Connecticut, and like flatlanders and locals, they are always at odds. Stocked trout—industrial trout—grow up in concrete ghettos, become used to having men about, line up for food, and so act all wrong when they're dumped in a river, running around, as ichthyologist Robert Bachman puts it, "like a motorcycle gang, making trouble wherever they go." They're not responsive to the body signals wild trout send up, don't understand their place in the river, and constantly hassle the stronger wild fish, until the wild fish, with what's easy to believe is a snort of contempt, move to the second- and third-rate lies, where, with less food coming by, more energy needed to fight off the interlopers, they often die, wasted and worn.

And the effects of putting industrial fish in with real fish aren't just temporary. The stocked fish compromise the genetic integrity of wild strains, and can carry the dreaded "whirling disease" that makes trout chase their tails, over and over, until they die from exhaustion.

"I hear the rainbows on the Madison have pretty well been wiped out," Tom said, looking his gloomiest.

"The Gunnison, too," John said, nodding sadly.

"The South Platte," I added. "Upstate New York. It's moving closer."

All three of us turned to look at the river, as if we could see the parasite drifting there in the shallows with the twigs and caddis husks and water spiders, the busy flotsam that floats on a river's surface.

Anytime I run into a game warden or fisheries biologist I make it a point to give them an earful, suggest the state spend more time taking care of its wild trout and less time creating those genetic Frankensteins. They listen politely enough, but always end up trotting out the same dreary company line, which isn't any less dreary for being largely true.

"Most people can't tell the difference," they say, shrugging. "Most people don't care."

Most people don't care. Put that on the tombstone of those of us who like what nature put here, never mind the genetic improvements.

How to explain what's been lost? There's a tributary of the Connecticut called the Waits River, which I fell in love with when I first moved north twenty years ago. It was a delightful place to fish, with plenty of wild trout, browns, brookies, and rainbows. Now, in the seventeen miles of its main branch, in all the connecting miles of its bright, rushing tributaries, it would be hard if not impossible to find a trout actually born in its waters, and no one fishes it until late June when, in the wake of the hatchery trucks, the hordes descend to pull the fish back out of the river as fast as the state pours them in.

And it's not just the wild trout I miss there. When I go back, as I do almost every spring, impelled by nostalgia for its former glories, my optimism which tricks me into thinking the wild trout will have somehow miraculously returned, it's not just the river that seems barren, but its entire valley, since the play of light off its granite boulders, the arcing drape of its bankside willows, the sweet smell of second haying from the fields that roll down to the water mean nothing if there is the fundamental emptiness at its heart. To some of us, the equation is very simple: No WILD

TROUT=NO RIVER ... and it makes me resolve, among the lesser side effects of such despolation, never to write a book about a trout stream again, never risk quite so much of my heart.

This goes along with a *small* article that appeared in all the state's newspapers yesterday, explaining that the Department of Public Health has determined that mercury levels are so high in the state's freshwater fish that young children and women of childbearing age should eat no more than one fish every two months (it says nothing of men in their prime).

"People can and should continue to enjoy angling for and eating freshwater fish," Paul West, spokesman for the Fish and Game Department, said. "They should, however, heed the advice of Department of Health officials and follow the fish consumption guidelines."

That we've poisoned off our freshwater fish doesn't seem to be particularly big news, just as the virtual extinction of New England's offshore fishery hardly made headlines either. This fishery—the one that had flourished for over four hundred years, and been one of the vital forces in world history, to say nothing of the local economy and culture—has this past winter been officially declared kaput, the government having banned nearly all ground fishing off Georges Bank, and begun a program to buy back fishing boats from the fishermen of Gloucester and New Bedford and the other famous New England ports.

What's sad is not only the fish we've lost, but all those fishermen, among the last stubbornly independent men and women in the country, put, literally, on shore. I think too of people like Tom Ciardelli, a scientist doing complex research into immunology, or John Marshall, a person who works when he's not guiding as a janitor at a VA hospital, and how fishing for wild trout, the experience of wildness taken even in small doses, creates a rich and vital life for them apart from the one they find in their daily lives ... and how when wild trout disappear, a fine sort of man and woman will disappear as well.

Moody thoughts—too moody for the kind of afternoon we were having. Maybe those shadows were just a little bit too dark and deep, and it was time to push out again into the sunshine.

"Hey," I said, ready with my answer for everything. "Enough talk already. Let's go out and catch the little bastards."

While they're still here, I was tempted to add. I didn't. I tied on a new fly, bit off the leader ends, ducked as John shoved us out from our tree.

With the evening coolness, a day that had begun a little charily was now full and rich, not just in fish, but in the little incidents and images that being on a river can bring. When I was casting over a particularly heavy rise, a beaver came up and with a tremendous splash whacked the water with its tail, convincing a startled Tom and John, who hadn't see it, that I had hooked the mother of all trout. A bit later, in returning a rainbow to the water, the fish turned belly up, so John lunged again with the net to bring it back and start the resuscitation process over—a lunge that broke one of his spare graphite rods in half. ("Don't write about that," John said, embarrassed, though he shouldn't have been.) As darkness fell, heifers began strolling down to the bank to look us over, wedging each other aside with lowered heads to get a better view. The sun, orange in the dampness, set over the Vermont shore, replaced by a moon just as orange over New Hampshire. And then, on our last break, when I asked about it, John rolled up his pants and displayed for our admiration the serene and dignified brown trout tattooed on his leg.

Midnight now. Both Tom and I were pretty well beat after twelve hours straight of fishing, but John changed flies and tippets just as eagerly as ever, scanning the river with his flashlight to see what insects might be about.

"There's usually another hatch on just after twelve," he said hopefully. It was clear that with the slightest encouragement he was ready to stay out later.

Tom looked at me, I looked at Tom. Our spirits were willing, but our casting arms were shot. It had been as timeless a fishing day as I'd ever enjoyed, and there was nothing more to ask of the Connecticut, not for a while anyway.

John's keen eyes found his takeout place in what to me was just another long expanse of featureless bank, and in a few more

minutes we were landed, the rods taken down, the drift boat
hooked to its trailer and winch, to be reeled in as quickly and
smoothly as any of our trout.

By the light of some spectacular heat lightning we studied a
pocket calendar, made a date right there and then to go out with
John later in the season. He'd done his job and then some, found
us wild trout where we wouldn't have found trout on our own,
and had gone about his work with grace, insight, and patience—
a guide fit for that river, a man who, there in his drift boat, goes
beautifully with the flow.

June 18:

*The big suburban drive-in movie is all but extinct,
and in my opinion it's no big loss. What the car giveth,
the car taketh away, and the gaps left behind the strip-
scape by their passing have already been sutured over by
new fast-food emporiums and boutiques. Yes, aging
boomers will wax nostalgic as they try to describe the
drive-in scene to their kids, but at the same time, heave a
sigh of relief that this ritual courting place is no longer on
the list of their own teenagers' temptations.*

*And yet there was another kind of drive-in that was
much more innocent and endearing. For lack of a better
term, call them* cow field *drive-ins—drive-ins origi-
nated back in the '50s when a farmer or someone with
meadow acreage adjacent to a main road realized how
relatively simple it would be to put in a screen and some
speakers, stick up a marquee, get in on a good thing. With
their pastoral origin, they were apt to remain charmingly
pastoral, even with Tinsel Town's latest up there on the
screen—a reminder of the time when a film coming to a
small New England town was a big event, the viewing of
it a truly communal experience.*

*Miraculously, one of these rural drive-ins still exists
across the river in Vermont. The Dixford Drive-in is a
totally unself-conscious survivor of a bygone era. There are
no frills here, never have been. A screen, a hundred or so*

speakers, a rickety ticket booth, a blockhouse-like refreshment stand, two feature shows on weekends—that's it.

The Dixford Drive-in, of course, does suffer from
that most dreaded of all contemporary qualities: inconvenience. You have to wait until dark to watch the
movie, and it can't be fast-forwarded or replayed. The
rough screen seems small in this day and age; the ground
can be wet and bumpy after a rain; the sight lines from
the sides are tough on the eyes; early in the summer mosquitoes can be a problem, and crickets can sometimes be
more involved in the sound track than purists might
want. Hard by the Connecticut, on damp nights the late
show can seem a bit steamy and damp.

But for many this only adds to its charm. Cars arrive
early for the features, when the heat hasn't quite gone out
of the sky. A minivan disgorges some happy and excited
kids, who, a soccer ball being produced, immediately
start up an impromptu game with the kids in the next
car. Teenagers, aping their city cousin's latest styles, but
somehow innocent in comparison, preen themselves on
the back of their pickups, indulge in all the display posture they want. Fathers, as they stand in line at the
refreshment stand, complain about the Red Sox, shrug
their shoulders and laugh, then, the screen coming to life
behind them, hustle back to their cars, popcorn and
sodas balanced against their chests, their heads bobbing
down to sip some off the top so it won't spill.

It's the kind of place where you remember moments,
not films. I remember one night when the fog was so bad
the screen became invisible and we all were cheerfully
refunded our money. Another night, during an already
scary enough film, a night-flying hawk or owl crossed the
screen, its huge exaggerated silhouette causing someone
in the next car to scream.

And one last quality to add to a drive-in's virtues,
one I didn't realize the force of until I had kids myself.
Was a better, more infallible soporific ever invented? The

coziness of the car, the cool yet comfortable nighttime air,
the distant play of images on a screen no one is forcing
you to watch—the pleasant drone of voices hung there at
your window. It's only the most stubbornly awake who
are proof to these. As the last feature ends, the cars nod
and bump their way back out past the ticket booth
toward Route 5, sleepy themselves, the headlights wink-
ing in the mist as if it's all they can do, a good night
behind them, not to shut.

Our world being what it is, those who write even casually about nature never know whether they're describing the dawn of a bold new age of environmental harmony or delivering the elegy over the natural world's sunset gasps. Is our lyricism merely a prelude to better times? A sad and superfluous postscript? I can see both versions. A realist who hopes for the best, I swing back and forth, knowing full well the deciding vote here will be time's.

In the meanwhile, I'm spending as much time as I can in the here and now on the upper Connecticut River thirty miles from its source, where—if you take your time in small, quiet doses—there are many golden moments to be had yet.

Literally golden. For the night I'm describing, only a few weeks after the trip with Marshall and Tom, was one of those when the river seemed to have gotten into the summer sky, dampening it as ink would a blotter, so it gave off a bluish gray color only a few shades fainter than the water beneath our canoe. One wrong stroke—or so it seemed—and I would glide effortlessly from river to air, find my trout in the upper branches of hemlock and spruce.

A swollen sun was going down on the Vermont side, carrying the high part of the year on its back. Behind me, with perfect timing, rose a yellow full moon. Ten minutes higher, like a vase supporting a flower, its beams fanned out across the water toward the rings of rising trout.

Lots of trout. Trout by the hundreds, strumming the river in a burnished synchronization, delighting and perplexing me all in the same breath. Rainbows, then larger browns. Trout in a river that even in the memory of a youngish man was thought of as little better than a sewer.

Pessimism? Not tonight, not here where all the hard tasks the river has lent its shoulders to over the years have now been reduced to two: to catch and hold the infinitesimal weight of my parachute cahill in the smooth cohesive film of its surface; to flow with gravity the five yards necessary to carry that fly from the light golden shaft of the moonlight to the dark golden dimples of the trout and make the two colors one.

Grasping my rod, moving my fist emphatically upward, I cast my vote toward a future where an untarnished Connecticut runs clear.

My father was never one to com-plain about anything, and so I distinctly remember him coming home from the office that afternoon, angrier than I'd seen him in a very long time. After changing out of his suit and tie, he would sit in the kitchen with my mother, debriefing over coffee, filling her in on his day, then asking about hers. These were calm, easy occasions, at least most of the time. On the after-noon in question, I remember a door being slammed, his voice being raised, my coming to the kitchen in curiosity and appre-hension to see what was up.

"A dollar!" he yelled, obviously not for the first time. He shook his head (a handsome, manly head; at the time everyone compared him to the actor Lee Marvin) in a what-is-this-world-coming-to kind of expression, one I'd grow familiar with, but was new to me then.

"A dollar! For a *sandwich*! Can you believe they have the nerve!"

This must have been 1962, during John Kennedy's brief term; my father was forty-four years old; the place he had lunch with his pals from the office was a typical suburban diner called Cookies; the sandwich that broke the $1.00 barrier—and with it, a little piece of this Depression boy's heart—was his favorite turkey club.

Thirty years later, the same age my father was then, I can understand what he was going through. Sandwiches for $1.00 seem a fantasy from pioneer days; what I have to deal with is seeing those same turkey clubs top out at $7.95, then another 8 percent added when the waiter figures in the tax. Milkshakes I remember enjoying for 35¢ now cost closer to $4.00 (and taste like aerated Kaopectate); books I used to be able to afford at $4.95 in hardbound or 75¢ in paper are now closer to $24.00 and $14.00; opera tickets I could indulge myself in for $5.50 at the City Opera in the heyday of Beverly Sills are now unafford-able luxuries at $60.00; cars that cost $4,000 *new* when I was in my twenties now cost $15,000 *used*; college tuition that was becoming more affordable to more people at $1,500 per year during the sixties is now moving toward an insane $25,000; an apartment I rented for $40.00 a month in a small Vermont town in 1967 is now well over $750 . . . and with each of these changes I yell and gesticulate like my father on that not-so-long-ago July afternoon, feeling another part of the world I once moved in and comprehended coming to an end.

Complaining about rising prices, of course, is one of the surest signs of incipient old-fogyism, but there you are. Anyone in their forties can remember a time when things cost consider-ably less than they do now, and it's almost impossible not to comment on this when the gap is extreme, recalling nostalgi-cally and with a certain retrospective greed (if things *still* cost that, I could go wild!) what more and more seems a halcyon era of general affordability, even though, to our parents, prices were already beginning to climb out of sight.

And yet there are still some things to be said about inflation as a subject, what it does to people, the truth about changing eras it can all too easily hide. It's a word thrown at you whenever you complain ("Inflation," your friends will shrug, the ones who think of themselves as realists) and there are those who have no scruples about blaming it—and thus forgiving it—for everything. There seems to be a logic in place that wants you to counter your natural "It's a lot more expensive" caution with the realization "Yeah, but *everything's* higher," and thereby inflate your notion of what *affordable* and *reasonable* mean, play right into the merchandisers' hands. It puts those with any kind of memory regarding the price of Cheerios or hockey sticks or widgets in the position of having to learn a whole new vocabulary, or rather an agonizing new math.

In short, it's becoming impossible to live with any kind of economic modesty, and this observation has nothing to do with a person's age. One of the clearest pieces of evidence for this is that no one is writing memoirs anymore about how cheap and wonderful life once was—how you could flirt with poverty in the 1970s or '80s and still have a decent and even noble kind of life. To find this note you have to go to the real old-timers, people like Saul Bellow, here reminiscing about life as a young struggling writer in the Chicago of the 1920s:

> No one had any money, but you needed very little to be independent. You could rent a small bedroom for $3.00—a fifty-cent breakfast was served at the soda fountains. The blue plate special at 35¢ was perfectly satisfactory. It cost less than $1,000 a year to be poor—you could make it on $700 or $800. But to be poor in this way also meant to be free.

You can't imagine anyone writing about the 1990s this way seventy years from now, rejoicing in how cheap and affordable everything was—and if you *can* imagine this, God help us all.

〜

My thoughts have been running on economic themes for the last few days, thanks to a question Erin asked when I was driving her to the pond for swimming lessons. We'd gone through the checklist to see she had her lunch and sweatshirt and so on, I'd reminded her what the arrangements were for picking her up, and then, after the kind of silence that used to be called "a pregnant pause," out it popped.

"Daddy," she said, squinting over at me. "Are we rich?"

A real nine-year-old kind of question, and I can recall trying to puzzle this out when I was her age. "Rich as Rockefeller," I sang, remembering the old song, but I could tell by her expression she was serious, so I slowed down and tried giving it the answer it deserved.

Compared to the rest of the world, I explained, compared to all the people who have ever lived on this planet, the poorest person in our town is rich beyond measure, rich beyond most people's wildest dreams. To have a car, a house, warm clothes, food, a good school—these are riches, and we should never become so jaded we forget that fact.

But no—we were not rich, not the way the term happens to mean in our society. Like almost everyone we knew we worked hard to make a living, harder than ever, and her mother and I had to discuss every expenditure carefully to make sure it lay within our resources. This didn't mean we were poor; with a comfortable house in a beautiful setting, two canoes on the lawn, the money to afford a nice vacation every year, we certainly weren't poor.

"Well, what are we then?" Erin asked.

"In the middle," I said, knowing this is exactly what someone her age likes to hear.

But though it seemed to satisfy her, it didn't quite satisfy me, since where precisely the middle ground lies, what compromises, what labors, you have to make to stay there, are becoming increasingly worrisome. So I tried explaining a little bit more, told her that with Mom working as a nurse the paychecks were never very large, it being one of the puzzling things in our society that people who do the most good in their professions often make the least money. With me being a writer, the checks were modest on that side as well, since the other endeavor that wasn't rewarded very well in America was pursuing something you love, particularly if your passion revolved around art.

"We're rich in time," I told her. "Most people don't have much of that. We're rich in experience. In those senses, we're certainly rich."

I tried being as honest as I could with her, but there were other considerations going through my head it wasn't time yet to share. Yes, we're in the famous American middle, and yes, that still means riches beyond the reach of most of mankind. And yet we worry about making ends meet, see our dollars shrinking, resent the fact that we're drowned in paperwork like a small business, find ourselves losing confidence in the future—become increasingly bitter at any conspicuous display of wealth. And certainly, given the insane cost of everything, a person trying to find a sane response is put in a difficult position. He or she can try to keep up, enter the rat race, let money be their goal in life, worship Mammon like so many. He or she can go the opposite route, opt out of the economic race entirely, but this requires courage, and extravagant sacrifice, and is a very difficult option for anyone with kids.

Again, I come back to that "middle" word, since it's the response that lies halfway between the above extremes that we seem to have entered upon ourselves, partly by choice, partly by necessity. Middle with dignity? For someone in this profession, it's uneasy ground. Writers through the years have been great ones for adopting a shabby gentility, wherein they try to rise above straitened economic circumstances by increasingly desperate expedients. The tweed jacket worn far beyond its prime; the borrowing and scraping to send the kids to a prestigious private school; the expensive booze; the Ivy League hauteur. Shabby indeed, and to see what I mean you don't have to look any further than the life of F. Scott Fitzgerald, he of the pathetic worship of the rich, or John Cheever doing Rolex watch commercials just so he could flaunt one on his wrist.

There's another term that's similar, but which, at least to my ears, has a much more positive ring: *genteel poverty.* Literature is full of characters who fall into this category. (*Little Women* comes immediately to mind, the Marches' cheerful mending and making do) and I think the difference lies in the fact that the genteelly poor try to rise above straitened circumstances not by the corrosive expedients of the shabbily genteel, but by moral means—by adopting the belief that materialism is vulgar, conspicuous consumption a sign of bad taste. To the genteelly poor, patches on an overcoat are a kind of badge. To the genteelly poor, a twelve-year-old car is a thing of beauty. To the genteelly poor, using coupons at the checkout to buy economy-sized Cheerios is the mark of an honest and decent soul.

There's another difference. Shabby gentility is now on the rise, genteel poverty on the decline. You can see the former in operation even here in the country, especially when it comes to people's cars. A certain kind of person has to drive a Saab station wagon or risk losing face, another person needs a Mercedes or falls from grace, and there are still more who have to keep up with the neighbors by owning the newest, meanest four-wheel-drive pickup, even if it's way beyond their means. After a while you get so you can detect the peculiar kind of strain car payments put in a payee's face, can guess at the arguments and pleading that goes on behind closed doors, no matter where on the income level these people reside. Emerson spoke of the "surly sweetness possessions bring" and he was a very shrewd man.

Genteel poverty, on the other hand, seems to be becoming rarer—and that's a shame. For all the fact that it's partly a pose adopted by those who have no choice, living modestly, with a certain leanness, brings joys unknown to those for whom money is no object. The delights of making a dying appliance eke out another few months of life; the real and deep satisfactions of mending; the surprise of unexpected windfalls and the luxury of small extravagances; even the pleasures of postponed gratification. Who's left in our culture to sing the praises of these?

It's why so many married couples are nostalgic toward their early days together, when they had to scrape and save and make do, and yet just for that reason knew the kind of happiness inexpensive things can bring. Sleeping bags on the floor, old milk crates for end tables, a couch salvaged from someone's junk, wedding money splurged on a bookcase or painting—and then the take-out Chinese to celebrate special occasions, the treasures found at yard sales, the Gallo burgundy shared with friends. Much later, when life becomes more complicated, more filled with things, these struggling years often stand out as the best, least cluttered ones after all.

Our own stories in this line revolve around the first house we owned, and it requires a bit of explanation. People moving to the country are liable to make one of two classic mistakes. The first is finding a beautiful place that is not only at the end of a winding dirt road, but at the end of a long driveway off that road; deciding, yeah, it will be tough getting in and out come winter, but it's soooo beautiful up here . . . then finding, once winter comes, that they're either cut off from civilization between Christmas and Easter, or spending enormous amounts of money and effort to keep the driveway open.

The other mistake—and the one we walked straight into— is deciding to resurrect an old house. There's a whole mystique built around this, of course, wherein a diamond-in-the-rough is purchased for pennies, plans made to restore it to its mint 1887 condition, work begun, work finished, guests taken around to ooh and ahh at how cleverly modern amenities have been sutured onto the original features—the Jacuzzi built into the outhouse, the exercise room erected in the barn.

What those responsible for perpetuating this mystique don't tell you is that you need either professional do-it-yourself skills and enormous amounts of time to accomplish all these things, or unlimited amounts of money to pay someone else to do them for you . . . and even in these circumstances, you'll always be playing catch-up, one part of the house deteriorating just as another part is restored.

This is what we were faced with when we bought the ram-shackle, circa-1910 gambrel that became our first home, with no carpentry skills between us (putting up shades was about my limit) and, once we paid the deposit, no extra savings at all.

We were the latest in a long line of people without money who had wrestled with that house. (Our theme song of those years was an old blues number: *They say that money talks and that ain't no lie, 'cause every time I get some it tells me good-bye.*) The woman we bought it from had lost her husband in a log-ging accident, and while she had raised four beautiful children there, she'd never had any money to fix anything properly, not even to put in electrical outlets, other than the two or three we finally managed to find downstairs. The old claw-foot bathtub didn't have a shower with it, and was to be the scene of all kinds of makeshift contrivances to serve in its place, none of which worked, their tubes or clamps giving way just when you were soapiest to spray water all over the bathroom—the bathroom that had *two* doors, a front and a back. Built into the hall between the kitchen and living room, when occupied it forced anyone going from one part of the house to the other to put a sweater on and detour outside.

And that was just for starters. The back porch sagged so badly neither Celeste nor I would go out there without warning the other where we were. We put a smoke detector in the unfinished part of the bedroom, but then one day I bumped against it, and it fell deep between the studs and the plaster where we couldn't retrieve it, even with a broom—and so for seven years we listened to a lonely, maddening beeping in our walls as its battery ever so slowly wore down. The kitchen had no counter space at all, *none,* so anyone cooking had to perform marvels of balancing and juggling, my own expedient being to take advantage of my height and do all my mixing and stirring on top of the refrigerator.

The barn door was always falling off its hinges. There were storerooms beneath the barn, where—between the broken glass and cobwebs and the proximity of what passed for our leach field—no one had set foot for forty or fifty years.

The decades can throw a veil over these kinds of experiences, smother all the petty irritants in nostalgia, but I can admit now what I couldn't allow myself to admit then—that there were times I hated that house, even feared it, rued the day we ever convinced ourselves to take it on. It knew too well my weaknesses—my clumsiness with a hammer, my impatience with things mechanical—and seemed to taunt me for these, and taunt me too for not having the disposable income to take care of things right. The house became a constant reproach, so there were mornings, working in the little cramped box of my study, when I wasn't concentrating on my work, but waiting for the furnace to start banging, the water pump to spasm, or one of the other countless groans and squirmings the house would make to tell me another part of itself was now broken.

It was a long struggle fighting back from this notion, working out a rough sort of truce. When Erin was a baby, getting ready to go to sleep, I would carry her around her bedroom having her say good night to the pictures we had hung to cover the bare, broken spots on the walls. "Say good night to the sheep, Erin." "Night-night sheep." "Say good night to the horse, Erin." "Night-night horse."

One night, making the rounds as usual, she suddenly leaned out from my shoulder toward one of the worst spots on the wall. "Night-night hole," she said, blowing it a kiss.

Night-night hole. Take that self-pity. Take that fear and loathing. Take that house.

The good moments were starting to catch up with the bad ones; gradually, between hard physical work on our part and the grudging income I began prying out of my books, we began making some headway. One winter afternoon, just as we had always feared, the back porch collapsed under the weight of snow, and rather than being a calamity, the removal of its roof let a huge amount of sunshine flood into the west side of the house, making it much less gloomy than before. We managed to have a shower installed, and that improved our morale tremendously. By perching recklessly on various old ladders, taking chances I don't like to look back on, I managed to paint the barn. Celeste, in the meantime, cleaned out the old pantry, and we found it a delightful room—cool and fragrant in the summer, taking on the smell of whatever spices we stored there, and giving us a decent counter on which to prepare our meals.

The biggest job, the one I remember most vividly, was tackling the wallpaper. What we'd inherited downstairs was a red-and-mustard-colored paper that was unbelievably hideous; upstairs was somewhat better, at least the color, but the pattern featured cowboys shooting Indians in one bedroom, and the *Niña, Pinta,* and *Santa María* in the other.

I suppose looking up wallpaper patterns in those amazingly thick books they have at the decorator's could be the ultimate in tedium, but Celeste and I enjoyed it and, even more miraculously, agreed very quickly on which paper we would like to have in which room. That decided, I went upstairs with a yardstick to measure the walls and determine how much we needed based on the formula in the book's front. I measured, measured again, wrote the figures down on a piece of paper, did the calculations, then went downstairs with a frown on my face Celeste could read all the way across the room.

"What's the matter?" she asked.

"We can't afford it." I pointed down at my figures. "We need two hundred and twenty-one rolls, just for the hall."

Celeste stared at me—and then burst out laughing. About as competent with figures as I am with a hammer, I'd transposed a couple of numbers, or multiplied where I should have divided, and so was exactly 209 wallpaper rolls out in my calculations—what we needed was twelve.

Time to go to work. As anyone who's ever tried it knows, hanging wallpaper is a painstaking and difficult art, especially when you have a complicated pattern where the edges are impossible to match. Worse yet, we were the fifth or sixth family to occupy that house, and each one had put up their own wallpaper, so, as with an onion, there was an awfully lot to do in the way of peeling. This wasn't without its archeological interest—each new layer gave us clues about the taste and personalities of those who lived there before—but it turned out to be excruciatingly slow, and took up most of my free time for the better part of a year.

We discovered early on that we couldn't use a steamer to speed this up; the layers were too thick, the plaster underneath too delicate. No, we had to do it the hard way, by swabbing down a section of paper with warm water mixed with remover, swabbing it down again, then edging the loose pieces away with a metal scraper, being careful to hold it flat so as not to gouge out any of the plaster.

Wet plaster combined with old wallpaper creates a peculiarly pungent, dismal kind of dust that sickened me after a time; my knuckles, from an hour or two of scraping, would be red, itchy, and scratched. And yet there were satisfactions to be had as well. Getting your scraper under a stubborn little fleck, pulling it back and having a whole foot-long section come off with it was one of these; another was scraping a section clear, and finding beneath it the plaster was smooth and perfect, requiring no filler, so Celeste could go right to hanging. The oldest wallpaper, the last layer before hitting pay dirt, was also the prettiest. Seventy years old, it had a delicate kind of yellow embroidered pattern that seemed perfect for the house; we took a piece and tried matching it at the decorator's, but to no avail.

Sometimes we had reinforcements, and these turned out to be festive, memorable occasions. My parents came to help us paper my study; my mother, an old pro, showing us many time-saving tricks she had picked up over the years; my father, nearsighted but willing, acting as our gofer, taking the wet, discarded strips downstairs in a bucket, coming back with cold lemonade. Before smoothing on the new paper we scrawled our names in pencil across the wall (*The following people hung this wallpaper July 21, 1985*) and if some future owner decides it's time that this lacy blue-brown pattern come down, they'll know, by God, who put it up there in the first place.

Hard work—work that with any sense and a bit more cash we should have farmed out to professionals. And yet I realize now that scraping those walls bare was an important turning point in my attitude toward that difficult, cranky house. Having it under my hands, literally so, shaping it, urging it toward a new conception Celeste and I both shared, if only in wallpaper, made me know it better, sense the history of human effort that had gone into making it a home. People had been born in that house, people had died there—in its space the cycle had been played out. Here people had tried to color and decorate their surroundings in a way that would bring them a small measure of joy, never mind that one day someone else would blot it over. What underlay that pockmarked, battered exterior was an embroidery as beautiful and delicate as that old first layer of paper, a fundamental soundness, an endurance, I was getting at last to know. By the time we finished wallpapering I had begun to forgive the house its weaknesses and foibles, and by a conceit I don't think was totally imagined, began to think that the house was gradually learning to forgive me mine.

∾

There were other lessons to be learned those years that have done well by us ever since. One of these is that we never take anything for granted about our creature comforts—continue to be amazed that we actually have a garage for our cars, and don't have to go outside after snowstorms to dig them clear; amazed that we have two bathrooms, and are spared all the arguments and negotiations that come with having just one. We also learned the joys that come with unexpected windfalls, especially small ones—of how a check for travel expenses, reprint rights for a story, a refund from the insurance company could seem like incredible riches, and allow us to buy the new paint or the new toaster that, so tight was our budget, were extravagant luxuries, their purchase continually postponed.

We learned, too, of the truly miraculous survivability of certain consumer goods, even in this age of planned obsolescence and shoddy disposability. I'm the kind who likes to make things function far beyond their allotted lifespan anyway, so over the years I've been able to make a virtue of necessity, but even without this predisposition, some things really *last*, to the point where sentiment starts to kick in, and you become emotionally tied to things that have served you faithfully through several different epochs of your life.

Clothes top the list here. Having pretty much stayed the same size since my twenties, never having much disposable income to spend, being conservative when it comes to style, I seem to have accumulated a wardrobe of old favorites, things I've been wearing now for nearly forty years. These include a green-and-black-checked Maine Guide shirt purchased from L. L. Bean back in the mid-sixties, which still has the name tag my mother sewed into the collar when I went off to school; old thermal underwear I wore as a Boy Scout, still warm and cozy as ever; various articles of army clothing my father was issued in 1942; a trench coat from high school which I wore not only on my first date, not only to dozens of operas and concerts and recitals back in the days I lived in New York (stuffing it under the seats at Carnegie Hall or the Met, never cleaning it, never having to), but to countries all over the globe, to the point where it now seems a younger, more indestructible version of myself, the coat of Dorian Wetherell, the kind of coat Colline sells in *La Bohème* to buy medicine for the dying Mimi, singing farewell to it in what I always thought is the most moving aria in the entire opera.

"*Vecchia zimarra senti,*" it begins.

Listen, my venerable coat.
I'm staying behind, you'll
go on to greater heights.
I give you my thanks.
You never bowed your worn back
to the rich or powerful.
You held in your pockets
poets and philosophers
As if in tranquil grottoes . . .
Now that those happy times have fled,
I bid you farewell.
Faithful old friend. *Addio.*

My hiking boots are venerable in the same way. They were a Christmas present in 1967, beautiful leather Dunham's that I've hiked many hundreds of miles in, resoled four times, carefully waxing them after every trip, so now—when new leather boots cost upwards of $200—my old ones are as flexible and sturdy as ever.

And clothes aren't the only things that have made it to the survivors' hall of fame. My grandfather's old Hallicrafter shortwave radio, which brings in the BBC clear as a bell. Our old Schwinn bike, a clunker, but indestructible. The dehumidifier in our cellar, a castoff from Celeste's parents, cracked and rusty, but still going strong, having been drying out various basements for a good forty years. My Browning-Silaflex fly rod, purchased with allowance earnings when I was fourteen, and still catching fish, especially when teamed up with my thirty-year-old Pfleuger Medalist reel.

We've found the same kind of immortality resides in some of the kids' things, too, which is exactly where you'd least expect to find it, between the inevitable shoddiness of objects that aren't meant to last more than a few months and the fact so much is outgrown so fast. We bought Erin a bright yellow jogging suit when she was two, and while it was a little big for her, by rolling up the cuffs and sleeves it did just fine. After three or four months we weren't rolling them up anymore—and then in about a year it was beginning to get a little short, but the fabric stret . . . t . . . tched to make up for it, and so on and so on, until she was wearing the top and pants all the way past her fourth birthday, and Celeste and I became convinced the fabric was blessed with magic powers of expansion.

Both Erin and Matthew have also gotten good use out of a Davy Crockett costume my aunt Lyd bought me at the height of the craze in 1957, fringed brown pants and fringed brown jacket, which, stored now in our closet, the survivor of forty-one Halloweens, will undoubtedly one day fit our grandchildren just fine.

⁓

I can't end this without paying tribute to the most heroic survivor of all: the 1976 Oldsmobile Cutlass Supreme my parents gave us just before our wedding in 1983. With over 60,000 miles on it, beginning to show its age, possessing hardly any book value, it had no value to them anymore, whereas we were desperate, the two clunkers we'd been nursing along between us having collapsed in a chaos of leaky valves, dropped mufflers, and scabrous rust.

In most respects, the Olds wasn't our kind of car. Originally a classy beige, it had somehow managed to brighten with the years, so it was now closer to canary yellow; genetically suburban, it didn't like to start in cold weather, and the only way it would stay on slippery back roads was with its trunk weighted down with firewood. It had eight big cylinders, used a refinery's worth of gas. "A getaway car!" one of our friends said when he first got a look at it; our own favorite nickname was Billy the Boat.

It's common in this culture to assume a certain kind of person drives a certain kind of car, and seeing us tool around in this overmuscled powerboat was a source of continuous puzzlement to our neighbors and friends; whatever else Celeste and I were, we *weren't* the kind to drive a Cutlass Supreme. But that didn't bother me; in fact, I began taking a perverse satisfaction in seeing the double takes when I drove up, especially if, as was often the case, my Old Town canoe was mounted on top—for many years, my definition of a mixed metaphor.

Viewed originally as a temporary stopgap until we could afford something better, we ended up driving Billy for another ten years, until the mileage went past the 100,000 mark, and then the 120,000, and then, in a true miracle, up past 146,000. Somewhere along the way the bumper rusted out, and I had to search through four Vermont junkyards before I found one to replace it; the trunk lid went too, and this I special-ordered from a place in North Carolina, paying $75 to have it mailed north; the muffler dropped off I don't know how many times, but the engine never needed a penny's worth of work. The body, too—it seemed impervious to the corrosion that forces so many cars off the road here long before their time.

It's educational, driving an old car. The looks you get, the way the police will stop you out of sheer snobbishness—even the way strangers will come up and casually offer to buy it from you, with the look of someone tossing a beggar a coin. Broke, you listen to every new cough and sputter, hoping it doesn't turn out to be fatal, promising the engine a lube job if it will only get you home, all but praying to it. The Olds took a lot of teasing, some unmistakably angry (How dare you not have the car we expect you to have!), but it had its admirers, too, including our neighbor Henry Marsh, the man who delivered our firewood each summer, who would always go out of his way to run his hands over the chassis in sheer admiration.

We bought a secondhand Honda Civic in 1985, which took some pressure off the Olds, but I continued to drive it, if for no other reason than the air-conditioning, which still worked fine. Its last two winters we took it off the road, put it up on blocks in the driveway, the snow drifts doubling its shape. Each spring when I put the battery back in, primed the carburetor with a splash or two of gas, Billy started up on the first turn of the key, and seemed, as much as anything in our garden, an inspiring symbol of resurrection.

We kept it long enough to be a real curiosity, if not an actual antique—long enough I could understand perfectly why so many people, with the hard sentimentality of the country, like to keep their discarded cars in the back meadow. One summer afternoon, as I was approaching a blind curve, a pickup swerved into my lane, forcing me to take Billy on a wild swing across the adjacent field. No harm was done, at least to me—the seat belt tightened just like it was supposed to, and the car was too tough and solid to be bothered by ditches or rocks. Still, it wiped out the muffler and tailpipe, and after a week of agonized indecision, we decided it was time Billy ended its useful life—that taking care of it further was now a luxury we simply couldn't afford.

As it turned out, I was wrong, at least about its lifespan. I called Henry Marsh next day, and it was quickly agreed we'd trade him the car for four cords of firewood. When I saw Henry this winter, I asked him about the car; with a half-embarrassed grin, he admitted he'd sold it—and for a decent price. This past spring, driving the interstate, I thought I saw it flying along in the opposite direction, a streamlined yellow streak, and for one wistful moment I thought of swerving across the median and giving chase.

I look back on that 1976 Olds Cutlass with affection. A *lot* of affection. Presently I'm driving a 1983 Cutlass, Billy the Boat Number II.

July 14:

I have nothing against the sun—in its place. Shining just right on six inches of snow, slanting obliquely through dark autumn clouds, flooding our summer garden, going down in the west in a soft oranging that gradually widens, flattens to a rusty crimson, slowly ebbs. Seeing what our great and familiar star can do to even the most humdrum of landscapes, the lighting effects it creates, the new life and growth it elicits from a grudging earth, fills me with a joy so exhilarating it's all I can do not to shout out loud, and it's only when it targets

*less hospitable ground, the exposed skin of my forehead,
nose, and cheeks, that the problem, my chronic solar-
phobia, starts making me change my mind.*

*I'm a redhead, with a redhead's vampire-like sensi-
tivity to the sun. Ten minutes on my unprotected face is
enough to cause freckles; twenty minutes, enough to start
a burn; forty minutes, a burn that's trouble. Worse, in a
psychological linkage that has vexed me for years, sun on
my skin makes me irritable, restless, out of sorts well
before the burning starts, as if the command center
responsible is shouting in an excruciatingly nagging
whine* Cover up, dummy! Cover up!

*There are pictures of me taken on Jones Beach when
I was five, scowling so fiercely it's still frightening to look
at, digging grimly away at the sand with a plastic shovel,
my floppy green hat and the war-paint dabs of suntan
lotion across my cheeks doing nothing whatsoever to
soothe my angst. The smell of Noxzema on sunburned
skin; the cool touch as my mother smoothed it on; the
endless series of hats worn in an attempt to ward my
enemy off, each one wider, floppier, more ridiculous
looking than the last; the gallons of sunscreen liberally
applied (industrial strength for me, with an SPF rating of
6,000); the long sleeves worn in summer; the sexual
incorrectness of being pale. All these and more I have
learned with grudging bad humor to endure.*

*And yet, for all the teasing I've suffered over the years
about my solar shyness, it's clear now that currents have
shifted, time is now on my side. Worry about the ozone
hole and what unfiltered radiation can do to our skin; the
premature aging caused by too much sunbathing; the
vaguely out-of-date look a suntan suggests, as if whoever
is sporting one hasn't read the* New England Journal of
Medicine *in a good fifteen years. Even the rage for shade-
loving plants like the hostas. Given these trends, it's my
hunch that paleness, the conspicuous enjoyment of
shade, will be the fashion for the coming century.*

It's important then to remember that shade is more than the mere absence of sun. Shade, particularly the shade of tall trees, can be a positively sensuous pleasure, protective and soothing, nature's sedative, nature's balm. Living in the country, I've become something of a connoisseur, to the point where I often rank trees solely on the basis of the shade they do or do not cast.

Spruces are on the bottom of my list; their shade is too cylindrical, stays too tight in toward the branches, so you really have to hug the tree to gain any benefit. Pines are better, since the branches start spreading higher, allowing you to immerse yourself in a delightfully tart kind of shade—a shade, closing my eyes, I can't help picturing as a dark, almost denim blue. Birch? A bit thin, wispy, four on a scale of ten. Willows are overrated, too; those elegant fronds blow too easily in the wind, so just when you've found a patch on the grass beneath it, the ceiling disappears. Crab apple, pear trees, and apples all throw a decent shade, but there's always the risk, once you doze off, that a piece of fruit, in true Isaac Newton style, will bonk you on the head.

For my money the absolute epitome of what a shade tree should be, a perfect ten, is the sugar maple. Tall, symmetrically branched, its lowest leaves high enough off the ground to create that vital first canopy, round enough that the sun has trouble finding an opening, with very little in the way of seeds or nuts or fruit to clatter on top of you, the maple casts the shade of shades, rich, expansive, fulsome, with just enough sunlight dappling the uppermost branches to add a lively frisson of interest. I planted eight of them last year, and as the July sun begins to lose its intensity, I walk through our meadow in the evening to see how my shade, my shelter, my solace, grows.

Having forecast the demise of so many things, it's time to go out on a limb and predict the imminent resurgence of several features of life that have fallen into disrepute in the course of the past century. This is very much in keeping with all the economic forecasts that have become big business in this country; let's call this "The Wetherell Report," and it's yours for free.

First, it's becoming clearer and clearer, even up here in the country, that servants are again becoming a necessity for the upper middle class. The first hint of this was the tremendous popularity of the *Upstairs, Downstairs* television series twenty years ago, which tapped into a vestigial hankering many people have toward the idea of having people wait on them; another more recent sign was the success of the novel *Remains of the Day,* the main character of which is a butler. The cultural underpinning in place, the return of servants has been introduced subtly—*au pair* became the euphemism of choice (and it's significant that the French has been dropped now, and *au pairs* are being called *nannies*).

But nannies are only the start. I foresee a time not too far in the future when the technological elite must have someone who serves them as butler, though initially they will be called something else (male assistants?). Chauffeurs, of course, are quite common already, and more and more people will employ one, since their time is too valuable to waste it driving. Maids? Well, many of our affluent friends have women who come in and "clean" twice a week; if servants were made redundant by the introduction of labor-saving devices in the home, now there are *too many* labor-saving devices in the home, and extra labor is needed to run them . . . and this at a time when there are more desperate people than ever looking for work.

There will be a literary concomitant to this. I forecast a return to popularity of the comedies of Congreve and Beaumarchais, Figaro-like servants getting the better of their masters, everyone laughing up a storm. Look for P. G. Wodehouse's Jeeves novels to have a resurgence, too.

I also predict the return of hoarding as a widespread middle-class activity—of burying the family savings in a cache out in the yard. Since money is taxed when you earn it, taxed when you save it, taxed when you spend it, more and more people will be burying their earnings out of anyone's sight, and thereby escape means testing and being denied scholarships or Medicare because they've had the temerity to scrape and save. I have a friend who works in a bank and he tells me that already they're overwhelmed with requests for safe-deposit boxes— could rent many hundreds more than their capacity. Yesterday, by way of research, I stopped at our local office-supply store and asked if they still sold those fireproof, waterproof, lockable, airtight metal boxes you can store your valuables in (and bury). Oh yes, the clerk said; not only do we sell them, but by the score.

And my last prediction concerns the return of mending as a common pastime in everyday life. I don't mean knitting as a hobby or crocheting, but *mending*: fixing things yourself so as to extend their useful life. With clothes costing so much, people will find that a few minutes with a needle and thread as the family sits around the living room at night saves them serious money, and doubles as a tremendously soothing antidote to the stress of modern times. Repairs to the house, too—I foresee a return of do-it-yourselfing, which, with decreasing leisure time, has been on a slow decline since its heyday in the '50s and '60s.

Mending—a good metaphor for the coming century. Mending fences, fixing up what the twentieth century has so casually smashed. A century of mending. Yes, I'd like to be able to put that in my forecast as well.

Documentary film buffs will remember Robert Flaherty's black-and-white masterpiece *Man of Aran*. Filmed in the early thirties on the remote and rugged islands off Ireland's west coast, it captures perfectly the old, self-sufficient way of life in the last moments before it was absorbed and erased by the twentieth century.

A classic—and yet one part of the film always bothered me, seemed phony and staged. It involves the boy, the son of the fisherman whose family provides the center of interest. He's about nine or ten—too young yet to go out in the boats for basking sharks or fish, but old enough to spend his days hunting for gannet eggs or trapping eels or letting handlines down the cliffs for cod.

What seemed phony to me is his posture, the stilted way he moves. There he is on the cliff edge, peering over to see whether he's caught anything on his line, back bent parallel to the ground, knees flexed as if he's about to spring off, head extended on what seems a grotesquely elongated neck, his gestures, as he pulls the line up, disturbingly frantic and mechanical, like a windup doll's—and all this within an aura of unbelievably severe intentness. I always thought it was the relatively primitive film quality that made him seem so stagey and artificial, at least until I had a boy of my own, saw him adopt the identical posture in his own version of hunting, the same stork-like movements, realized it's the instinctive, natural posture of the scavenger, the gatherer, the man living by what in this rich and bountiful earth his two quick hands can grab.

Matthew is down on the meadow pond right now, circling the shore with his long-handled net, on the lookout for crayfish, ready to pounce. His mother is there as well, watching from the little rise that cups the pond's upper edge, arms clasped around her suntanned legs, her head resting on the little shelf thus created as she calls out advice. Four years old, Matthew is too young yet to trust alone near water, but that's okay—watching our children forage, trap, pluck, and gather is one of the most enjoyable parts of our life right now, and it's not too far-fetched to say we learn something of mankind while we're at it, which is the nice kind of bonus having kids often brings.

Let's focus on Matthew a little more closely before he disappears through the willows; so intent is he, so watchful, a little return intentness on his back won't even register. He's dressed in black rubber boots, the kind a lobsterman wears; above them, his knees and thighs are bespattered with clay from the pond's bottom, but this only contributes to the camouflage effect of his muddy T-shirt, making him as dark and soggy looking as the pond. He's a blond, at least in summer; he wears his hair in an unruly bang that just licks the top of glasses worn for a lazy (!) eye, glasses that at this stage of his hunting, as he peers toward the brownness of the surface film trying to see past its sun-flecked shimmer, are a millimeter from sliding off his nose.

He sees something, comes to a stop, and crouches, back bent parallel to the water, net tucked underneath his arm the way a vaulter tucks in his pole, his bent knees pressed together so the kneecaps are touching. Alertness, readiness—no rigid setter or pointing shorthair ever suggested more of either. It's a posture designed to peer, to see—the posture of someone whose being has become all eyes, and eyes that are focused *down*.

How long does he hold this? A minute? Two minutes? With a gesture so quick it makes his preceding stillness even more statue-like in comparison, he shoots out the net, rakes it quickly backward, then—with that intensely curious tilt of the head seen in Flaherty's Irish boy—stares into the net to see what fate and skill have won him.

A crayfish, and a good one, its antennae wiggling at the touch of air, its purple-black claws groping at nothing. Matthew rushes over to Celeste to show her, clutching the net closed below the hoop so it becomes a bag.

"A beauty?" he asks, sure of it, but needing confirmation.

"A beauty." Celeste nods. "Your fourth today."

"A beauty!"

Over to the pond he rushes with it. A shake of the net, another shake, and the crayfish drops into the water and scuttles away, by which time Matthew is already on another circuit of the shoreline, going clockwise this time, under the big white pine where the shadows lie deepest and the crayfish grow to trophy size.

A worthy quarry, crayfish are. They lie in mud a few inches from shore, near a rock if they can find one, or under the fringe of grass that overcurls the water. Facing shore, they have good vision, and disappear backward in a milky puff the moment they detect any motion. Matthew had learned to stay well back from the bank to scope out what's there; his stillness is part of this, too, and in the months he's been at this he's adapted his behavior to compensate for the crayfish's caution. Right now, the two forces are perfectly in balance: human intentness and crayfish wariness; human quickness and crayfish speed. About half the time Matthew's net brings in a crayfish; about half the time, nothing but mud.

Last year we didn't find many crayfish bigger than a quarter, but this summer we've gotten into real monsters, some that measure a good six inches from tail ito claw, with shells that are dark and heavy with good health. Herons find them irresistible, and we often see the birds slowly high-stepping their way around the opposite side of the pond, their necks going in and out, in and out, until, with a motion faster than I can write about or even think, they dart, shake, shake a second time, and swallow. Herons eat crayfish, of course, while we put them back alive, but still, to the children, hunting crayfish is a life-and-death game, or at least practice for a life-and-death game, and Celeste and I, when we take a turn with their net, are as slow in respect to the kids as the kids are slow in respect to the heron.

Matthew has worked his way up to crayfish through a careful apprenticeship. Last year, at age three, plain old-fashioned earthworms were still his favorite quarry. With a broad meadow facing south, we're a prime spot for worms—robins find their way back here two weeks before they're seen anywhere else in town. Matthew is good at finding them, uncannily good, and knows just how much turf to turn over in order to find six or seven in a spadeful. But except when we go fishing, he hardly bothers with them now; worms are a bit static to interest him, and he's sharpening his skills on the quicker, livelier game in the pond.

These include the following. Salamanders, spotted ones, turning their graceful underwater arabesques. Brassy minnows sunbathing just below the surface film, drenched in warmth. Yellow perch, most of which we stocked ourselves after fishing trips to fishier ponds, wary, just barely catchable. Frogs, big ones, half submerged in chocolaty mud. Butterflies and grasshoppers living in the jungle of meadow grass and aster that surrounds the water, good reliable prey when the amphibians are skittish. Chipmunks darting in and out of the old stone wall—chipmunks, which one of these days Matthew is going to figure out how to trap. The pond is a paradise to a boy his age, and a paradise for his parents, together on the bank now, a beer between them in a bottle still cold from the fridge—his cheering section, board of advisers, co-conspirators, fellow members of the pack.

Me, I like to take the high anthropological ground sometimes, and part of the delight I take in watching him and his sister at their stalking is knowing that their posture, their alertness, reproduces that of the primitive hunter and gatherer, the man or woman who had as their only weapons—but what potent ones!—their brain and their hands. Whatever else it is, Matthew's posture is *not* that of the man who carries a rifle (that arrogant kind of crouching strut even good hunters unconsciously adopt when in the woods); compared to Matt's kind of hunting and fishing, hunting with a rifle or fishing with a fly rod is artificial and effete. His posture is pre-gunpowder, pre-bow and arrow, pre-sling—the posture of a man whose power does not extend past his reach.

Killing isn't part of this, at least not deliberately. A crayfish is kept a little too long in a bucket, and turns belly-up; a minnow, netted too fiercely, can't stand the shock and folds itself dead. These are the victims of his instinct, the sacrifices that teach him this is far more important and earnest than playing with blocks. Even without a word from Mom or Dad he realizes death is a kind of failure within the rules he's set himself, though an intensely interesting one, offering up a secret he must learn from, try to penetrate. A few weeks ago, when Matt was playing at a friend's, an older boy crushed a frog over the head with a rock, and Matthew was disconsolate, this being one of his first hard lessons in human perfidy. Obviously, his ancestors had no such scruples, and yet anthropology teaches us they too held the dead animal in reverence, regretted having to take its life—that it's always been possible to separate the act of hunting from the act of killing, or at least to feel that this separation is possible; that for man, regardless of the outcome, the hunt, the search, the quest, becomes everything.

There's another lesson in this, too, and it's the reason his mother and I can't help feeling awe tinged with jealousy as we watch him by the pond. Loving nature as we do, living lives that are involved more than most with the cycles of the natural year, we still feel the artificial division that has plagued man for so many centuries, been the cause of so much harm; *nature* versus man, *man* versus nature. For Matthew, for his sister, Erin, this wall hardly exists, not yet at any rate. Frog meadow water net sunshine me *now;* these must all come to Matt in one exuberant unfocused blur whose vocabulary is his swooping net, so it's no wonder he's so happy there, no surprise his instincts are so razor sharp and quick.

❧

Loving the pond as we do, these meadows and woods, there comes a time when we need a change like everyone else, and so this week we've packed our butterfly nets, binoculars, field guides, pails, and shovels and taken our act on the road.

The Maine coast this summer, as it's been for the past seven.
The bright expanse is welcome after the familiar encirclement
of our hills, the way things come weathered and polished by the
one element we don't have at home: the sea, the light the sea
casts. The peninsula we stay on is one of those long fingers that
stretch eastward into the Atlantic; a "drowned coast" geologists
call this, and driving out to its granite tip, passing the yards full
of lobster traps, the modest shops selling driftwood lamps, the
lonely sloops stranded in their cradles amid overgrown meadows . . . passing all these, pointing out to one another familiar
landmarks from visits in the past, we all feel something of this
seaward declination, as if what we're speeding down isn't a road
at all, but a ramp that will launch us with an exhilarating arc
into the surf.

It's a quiet peninsula, unspoiled compared to most of the
coast, with enough rocky coves, pockets, and islands to fill a hundred summers, let alone one. We like it, too, because it has that
rarest of Maine features: an actual, bona fide, honest-to-God
sandy *beach,* lying in a crescent encircled by a necklace of small
islands and glacier-carved rocks, so you can have it both ways, the
yielding sensuousness of sand beneath your back, the craggy
Maine-scape out there for your eyes to sharpen themselves on,
the southwest wind blending things, making them perfect.

And if our own hills are a paradise for gatherers, then the
coast here is paradise squared. So much to take in, or rather *rake*
in—the bounty is everywhere. Ten minutes after we unpack, the
kids are scrambling down to Back Cove to see if the tide has
turned under the little arched bridge. It hasn't turned, not yet
anyway, which gives us time to drive over to Reilly's to buy some
chicken necks, rig them to string with rubber bands, tie on
some rocks for sinkers, then head back down to the cove with
our nets ready to go to work.

The crabs congregate here in unbelievable numbers, feisty-
looking green ones, ganging up in the narrow gut that connects
the deep part of the cove with the inland part, doing their best
to fight the current, clutching and grabbing at the mussel-
covered rocks on the bottom like commuters caught in the

wind from a passing subway. Capturing them is easy, at least once you learn the trick. Lob line, rock, and bait well above the spot the crabs are thickest; let it drift back; then—once a crab takes hold—gently, ever so gently, lift the string up, convincing the crab there is no difference between holding onto a chicken neck underwater and holding onto that same chicken neck in the air.

We're good for an hour of this the first day, then Erin gets restless and wants to move on to the beach. At nine, she feels strongly the tug of the next experience waiting in line, while Matthew isn't aware of limits at all, and would never of his own volition abandon one bright moment for another.

"We'll come back tomorrow," I say. "Here, you guys carry the bucket, I'll take the net. Ready? Hup, one, two, three."

So it's over to the beach and the wonders waiting for us there. Shells, bits of jetsam, driftwood, stranded jellyfish, broken lobster buoys, smashed splinters of traps, huge streamers of kelp. Rocks, too—we've rocks aplenty at home, but they're much shinier here, more desirable, and the larger ones come striated with all kinds of molten, candy-like fillings. Celeste and I make the long trek up the beach with the kids, following the tide line and the sandpipers, laughing when the cold water covers our toes, Erin and Matthew dashing out to chase it, then, as it surges back the other way, running screaming up to where they're safe.

Halfway to the end of the beach they remember what's waiting there, and off they run—Matthew with the wobbly, knee-knocking strides of a four-year-old, Erin with a much more graceful loping as befits her long legs. Tidal pools are what they're running toward—those rocky cups and saucers in the rock the incoming tide floods twice a day, leaving enough water behind that each hollow supports a flourishing marine world.

We've learned the names of the creatures that live in them, thanks to Erin, who insists on knowing. Acorn barnacles, spiky sea urchins, orange starfish, periwinkles, busy hermit crabs, the ubiquitous blue mussel anchoring itself by tufts of filament called byssuses, a name which reminds us all of Dr. Seuss. Erin takes Matthew's hand and starts guiding him about. They're on tiptoe now, their feet tingling on the roughness of the rock, their toes curling downward as they try to gain purchase on the slippery weeds in between; at one point in their progression, Matthew stops and sniffs at the air like a dog, catching that iodine-baked, intoxicating flavor of salt, rock, and weed.

Erin's growing her hair long this summer, and as she stoops to examine each new tidal pool, she has to toss her hair to the side to see, thereby practicing those feminine tosses of the head that so amazed me when I was nine years old myself—how did girls *learn* that? The tidal pools were teaching her, that's how, offering themselves as pellucid mirrors wherein she could examine not only the crusty sea creatures and undulating plants on the bottom, but that increasingly puzzling, absorbing mystery: herself.

"Meditation and water," Melville told us, "are wedded forever," and in such small pools does the linkage start.

On the north side of this peninsula in an otherwise iron-bound coast is a tidal pool the size of a small pond. It happens to be famous—Rachel Carson did research here for her great books about the sea—and since the surf is kicking up tonight, we've come here after dinner (lobsters, natch, washed down by Moxie, that forgotten Maine soft drink that was once so popular its name is in every dictionary as a byword for energy and courage) to watch, listen, and feel it pound.

There's no pool tonight as it turns out; the incoming tide breaks over the rocky depression where it lies and mixes its small contribution of tranquillity into the overall tumult, until there's no hint of it at all. But no matter—nature's cooked up a fine consolation prize. Bouncing and racing toward us comes the surf, an offshore wind blowing back each crest in a horsy gray mane, the combers so solid that, breaking, they cause the rose hips on the bushes behind us to shake, jiggle, and sway. We're country hicks in the face of this—we laugh out loud at the biggest *whoomp*, then, feeling the spray hit us, zip up our sweatshirts and huddle closer to one another on our rock.

As rough as the waves are, the terns aren't having any trouble with them, nor are the gulls or the cormorants or the brant.

I try my best to identify the birds for the kids, but their eyes are drawn to something even more colorful and lively, if somewhat more unexpected. Lobster boats, three of them, darting in and out near the rocky headland just across the water, their owners dressed in yellow slickers, winching up their traps to leeward, but otherwise not bothered by the waves at all.

The harbor we're staying near is still very much a working lobster port, and watching the boats go out in the morning from Shaw's Wharf (coffee fifty cents, donuts a quarter; leave the money in the jar and help yourself to cream) is very much part of our morning routine. Talk about your gatherers! Tending a thousand or more traps, going out in all weathers, knowing the sea bottom better than most people know their backyards, their lives and the well-being of their families dependent on their skill and the vagaries of fate. It's easy to romanticize them, but it's the tough job it's always been, and Matthew, at any rate, saves for them the respectful look of recognition one professional gives to another, with nothing more to be said.

I've talked with the lobstermen here, and they all seem to share the same fierce taciturnity and even fiercer love, though this last is a word they would never use themselves. Part of this comes from the pride any person takes in doing something that's difficult both of mind and of muscle; part, of course, comes from being outdoors in all kinds of weather. But the part I'm interested in, the thread that links them, seems to have to do with the fact that they're among the last people on earth who still manage to live by what their hands can glean from the earth or sea.

This is the love part, the reason they are so fiercely loyal to their environment. They not only know it, they need it, so the symbiotic relationship between nature and man that in most people's lives seems so theoretical is to them an everyday concern, nature being detailed and complex, yet ultimately comprehensible, and comprehensible right smack in their face. The rest of us live on checks, credit cards, abstractions; the lobsterman, quite literally, plucks his dollars off the rocks.

And get shoved around by the waves for their effort. It's obvious the lobstermen are having a tougher time than was at

first apparent, because one boat turns around now, well before
the last green-striped buoy in the line he's pulling, and, with
him being the first to face facts, the other two lose no time in
following him around the headland toward home. A storm is
brewing and a big one—the following morning, all boats will be
confined to harbor, and there are reports of a trawler going
down not twenty miles out to sea—but for the time being the
wind is still offshore, and the waves, fighting it, run out of steam
just short of our rock.

Watching the sea, thinking of the lobstermen, thinking too
of Rachel Carson, her passionate blend of learning, love, and
vision, my train of thoughts begins to travel in a familiar direction—indeed, in those glorious circumstances, the only
direction open.

"Katherine would have liked it here," I say, pointing toward
the granite shelf where the waves chevron apart.

Celeste, catching my mood, nods and stares out toward sea
herself. Matthew, though, looks puzzled. "Who's Katherine?"

That's just what Erin is waiting for. "The one who made
those good chocolate-chip cookies," she says. "John David's
mommy. The one who was so good at catching crabs."

Thinking back, it's not hard to follow the train of associations that brought up Katherine's name. There we were near the
sea's edge, the zone Katherine loved. There were the lobstermen,
which brought to mind crabbing, how good Katherine was at it.
There was the sign honoring Rachel Carson, whose concern for
beauty and the mystery of the world were similar to Katherine's,
and what's more, in a sadder linking, they both died too young
of the same tragic disease. And there were my children, beach-
combers like Katherine, gatherers like Katherine, the two of
them just old enough to remember her, and to have learned
from her, at least a little.

It's not easy to write about Katherine Murray, our friend,
without letting my admiration run away from me in a way that
would have embarrassed her. Born near Baltimore in the year of
Pearl Harbor, she was a star athlete in school, one of those passionate readers who is cut out for serious things, and when she

graduated she spent the next ten years in a convent as a nun, teaching science at various parochial high schools, devoting herself to things spiritual, creating a foundation for all that came later. She never talked much about this phase of her life, except to credit it with giving her "an obscene knowledge" (her own term) of the inner workings of complicated organizations—a knowledge that would come in handy when it came time for her new career in academia, where faculty politics seemed like kid stuff compared to the politics of the Catholic church.

She taught education and anthropology at a small college in Rhode Island. It was there she fell in love with David Thomas, a history professor who was her match in spirit, intelligence, and energy, and by the time I met them they were the devoted parents of a four-year-old son. This was on a saltwater pond along the triceps of Cape Cod, where began a friendship that lasted until her death two years ago of breast cancer and continues still with David and John David and the memories we all share.

The facts, brief as I can put them, and yet they don't begin to capture Katherine's impact. She was of middle height, squarely built, with the kind of physical compactness that suggests great reserves of power; playing Wiffle ball on their lawn after dinner, watching her twirl the bat in her hands, I could never help thinking of Babe Ruth. She wasn't beautiful, not in the conventional sense; but in the unconventional sense, the sense you get when watching a person whose plain features are splendidly humane, she was probably the most beautiful woman I ever knew—ruddy faced, vibrant, with so much warmth in her eyes you felt good just being in their presence. There was a lot of intelligence in those eyes—a *lot* of intelligence; her tongue could be quick as Jesuit's, but the sarcasm always gave way instantly to a brighter, nurturing kind of radiance that supplied the balm for her own sharpness; the effect was that of crossing one part Lauren Bacall to three parts Marjorie Main.

More? She was smart enough to suspect her own intelligence, remain aware of its limits; she was human enough to avoid a foolish and narrow consistency, that hobgoblin of little minds. Once when Erin was little she lectured us at breakfast about how we had to avoid sexist toys that stuck girls in stereotypical roles; later that morning, in a splendid and typical gesture, she rushed Erin out to buy her her first Barbie, and with it all the glitzy glamorous costumes Erin liked best.

There are dozens of people who could say similar things about Katherine, and add much more, but of one aspect of her world I was perhaps a better witness than most. Mornings about eleven, with enough writing finished I could begin to feel easier with myself, I would walk out onto my porch overlooking the pond, drawn by the sound of splashing and the soft, sporadic chatter that goes on between a mother and a small child. There a hundred yards down the pond, a red-shirted Katherine and a naked, nut-colored John David would be following the bright line of the tide as it eased out across the sand, John David with a small net hunting for minnows, Katherine with a large, long-handled net searching the shallows for crabs.

She was good at this, patient, sharp-visioned, and fast, and when she shot out the net, scooped it hard down into the sand, and raked it quickly back, it was hard not to think of the word *ruthless*. For it seemed like every time she did this a crab would be in the net; those times it wasn't, she acted surprised, but unruffled, and would immediately start that same scanning, searching kind of progress through the shallows, missing nothing. Most of the time Whizzer would be right behind her, their yellow Lab; raised there as a puppy, she had imprinted on Katherine early and would comb the flats with the same kind of downward stare, using paws instead of a net, snapping at the water, scratching at the bottom, following Katherine with little yips down the pond.

Vineyard Sound was only a few hundred yards away, reachable under the bridge across the breakwater, and so the pond's salinity was just right for crabs—beautiful blue claws, healthy in their vivid brown and blueness, wet and thriving and dangerous, the big ones with shells measuring six and seven inches across. Hunting for them, Katherine was in touch with the natural world more intimately than any of those summer people sitting on their decks smugly admiring the view. In the world there at her feet, within reach of her net, she found full satisfaction for an inquiring mind—a mind that wasn't so sophisticated it was removed from earthy concerns, or rather, was so truly sophisticated it understood that contact with the springs of life, the ongoing creation, is vital. As I've written before in other circumstances, nature offers the most to persons who ask of it specific questions, wanting something of it, be it a trout, a lobster, or a close-up photo of a nesting bird. And Katherine, this gatherer par excellence, asked of it perhaps the oldest, most fundamental question of all: to give her and her family something to eat.

Katherine netted crabs because she loved eating crabs—it's as simple and healthy as that. Crabs in salad, crabs in cakes, crabs used in stuffings. Katherine was a gourmet cook using even more humdrum ingredients, but with crabs, the produce of their garden, the clams David would tread up from the pond's bottom (luring them in with the deadly quahog whistle he'd obtained from the Mashpee Indians under mysterious circumstances years before), the bluefish John David hooked, she was like a painter blessed with perfect pigments, and there were many masterful dinners on the kerosene-lit Thomas-Murray porch. Meals to Katherine were celebrations of life, of health, of nature's abundance, and because she and David felt it was their responsibility to share this with others, there were often eight or more people crowded around the picnic table, at least some of whom, earlier that day, would have been initiated in the arcane and painstaking art of picking meat out of a freshly boiled crab's orange-red shell.

"Ow! Don't burn yourself like me. Here, use these pickers. Dig! That's it! Tease the flesh out of the cells like—*this.* Did you hear what Reagan said at his news conference? The great communicator, snort, snort. Here, don't forget what's in these claws. We have six more cooking. David! Can you send John David down to check the traps? Shells in the bucket please. Whose motorboat is that, the Hennings'? Our affluent neighbors. All they do is race around. Skimmers—all they do is skim off the cream of life. No shells, please. Absolutely no shells allowed in a

Murray crabcake. Now, let's see. Crabcakes, tomatoes with basil, corn, wine, salad, then we'll get some Portuguese bread down at Costa's. Is that enough? You know any skimmers? Ha!"

And so on for the hour it would take to do the job right, Katherine dispensing politics, philosophy, and good sense from her command center at the head of the table, keeping everyone at it until the silver mixing bowl in the middle of the picnic table was filled with fresh, sweet-smelling white meat.

Toward the middle of those years the family made a trip to Chesapeake Bay, and came back with their pickup loaded with new wire crab pots—familiar stuff in Maryland, but a rare item on Cape Cod. Similar to lobster traps but boxier, anchored on the pond bottom in various choice locales, they proved irre-sistible, and were often hauled in with six or more keepers snapping impotently in the trap's central chamber. Katherine herself, for all her love for the sea's edge, had a long-standing aversion to being in boats, so she farmed out this operation to others, served as the CEO, and when on those rare occasions the traps came up empty, grabbed her old long-handled net and went out to do the job herself.

She was diagnosed with cancer late in the winter of 1992; after the operation, the first rounds of radiation, she was able to have one more good summer on the pond. When we visited in August she came out to greet us wearing a wig, and for the first time ever wore a look of shyness, but it lasted only a moment, we made her take the wig off, and for three days the old times were back in place, though we all knew everything had changed. The doctors were pretty sure they had gotten it in time, and Katherine herself seemed so filled with the life force that it was impossible to believe anything could stop her—as it seems impossible now. When the disease kicked in again after Christmas, she fought it as hard as she had the first time, and for a while it seemed she would be able to spend at least one more summer on the Cape, but this was not to be.

I think of a lot of things when I remember Katherine Mur-ray, have only scratched the surface here in trying to convey her personality. But even remembering the crabbing alone, the way she hunted and gathered in that small, perfect slice of land and water she found herself dwelling upon, it occurs to me that back in the days when *everyone* hunted and gathered for their daily sustenance she would have been one of those natural leaders whose skill, understanding, and insight all would have recognized and looked to for guidance—that back in the days when humanity was thinly, tenuously scattered over the earth, so small in numbers one person alone could make a huge historical difference, she would have been the woman whose influence raised an entire culture a giant step toward civilization, and now in what likes to call itself "civilization" there aren't so many of us that her absence won't be missed.

Once, in the middle years of our friendship, after I'd complained to her in a letter about how poorly my writing career was going, she typed out a poem by her beloved T. S. Eliot, which is now tacked to the wall behind my desk.

> And what there is to conquer
> By strength and submission, has already been discovered
> Once or twice, or several times, by men whom one cannot hope
> To emulate—but there is no competition—
> There is only the fight to recover what has been lost
> And found and lost again and again: and now, under conditions
> That seem unpropitious. But perhaps neither gain nor loss.
> For us, there is only the trying. The rest is not our business.

Some of this is what Celeste and I were remembering, sitting there watching our children play at the ocean's edge, coiling around their arms those wet, pliant strands of seaweed, picking up stones to hurl at the inrushing surf. One comber bigger and greener than the others skips and tosses its way in from the open sea, cresting, breaking on the offshore rocks, growing bigger in the creamy thunder of its own turbulence, until it crashes against the granite shingle with a boom that not only shakes the rose hips at our back, but knocks them from the bushes into the foam.

In the pause that follows the thickest crash, in the brief seconds of silence before the foaming remainders find each other, roll with the smallest stones back out, I gesture toward nowhere in particular, drawing to a point those shreds and scraps of thought that have been ebbing and surging in me since this essay began ... *Gatherer—what a fine, rich word!* ... popping the question I'd been wondering about all night.

"Did she ever get here?" I ask. "Did Katherine ever get to Maine?"

Celeste, not missing a beat, spreads her arms apart toward the surf, the shore, the memories, making a gathering-in motion herself, then, with the smile I love so dearly, delivers the line to end this on, the one that says it all.

"She's here now."

August 18:

It's hard to go on vacation when you already live in vacationland. We drive east to Maine because 1) it's not far away 2) we all get homesick for the sea if we're too long without it 3) we've found a perfect house to rent that sits high on the rocky shoreline overlooking Muscongus Bay 4) midcoast Maine, come high summer, is one of the most beautiful land- and seascapes in the world.

And there have been enough summers now for some family traditions to form. Driving out to old Fort Pemaquid to watch the sun go down. Riding bikes in the morning out toward the Chamberlain post office. Taking a boat to see the sea birds nesting on Egg Rock. Going out for ice cream at the Puffin Shop one night, at Samoset's the next, arguing about which serves the better mint chocolate chip. Going, on rainy days, to the old stone house at Round Pond for penny candy, stopping on the way back to comb through the Carriage House Bookstore and its fine collection of old books.

I've found something of a treasure in the last, at least for me. The nature writer Henry Beston lived most of his adult life just a little way in from the ocean here, a sojourn he wrote about in Northern Farm. *One of my favorites, it was with a great deal of pleasure that, browsing through the dimmest stacks, I found a book for sale that used to be his:* The Voyagers, Being Legends and Histories of Atlantic Discovery *by a Padraic Column. On the flyleaf, in a graceful, old-fashioned hand wielding a light blue ink, is the name* Henry Beston. *At $12, a bargain, and so a part of Beston's library is now a part of mine.*

One of the traditions here is largely Dad's alone. After the sun goes down, with the kids in bed, the fire settled down to a comfortable red glow, the surf reduced to a quiet lapping against the rocks, I go out onto the deck with an old army blanket, settle myself on a deck chair, wait for the darkening night to come alive with light.

Just offshore on the black mat of the ocean is the red bell buoy marking the harbor entrance. Just beyond, much smaller, higher, the distant lighthouse at Port Clyde. In the middle between them, the running lights of fishing boats, lobstermen, the occasional tall ship. These are all lights of motion. The lighthouse spins its 360 degrees of lambent warning; the bell buoy tilts back from one wavelet, then leans with a brassy clang into the next; the fishing boats scatter their reds and greens like embers cast from a fire stirred by an anxious foot. Once, watching all this, trying to focus on the distant halogen of Monhegan light, seven miles out to sea, I saw the horizon come alive with arcs and towers of brightness—fireworks, as the islanders celebrated the 350th year of their discovery by tossing up colors into the night.

What I'm really waiting for, though, is much higher. Andromeda is one of my favorite constellations, but at home, even with our meadow, it's hard to see its true expanse. Here, watching it rise out of the ocean, it seems to stretch across half the sky, from the teapot of Sagittarius in the south to the low cluster of Perseus there in the north—a straight line of four stars, nothing fancy in its asterism, but pleasing precisely because its geometry complements so well the dark straight line of the sea above which it stretches.

Early this morning, hoping to see the sun rise from the sea, I miscalculated and woke too early. In the east, the sky was that burnt amber color that precedes dawn, and yet above it the sky was still dark enough to showcase the last thing I was expecting: Orion, rising from the ocean on its back in a miraculous and awe-inspiring feat of levitation, its expanse, its starry twinkle, magnified by the exaggeration of the atmosphere, so it looked three times larger and brighter than it does even in winter. Beautiful—and yet there was much in the sight that chilled me as well, actually shook me, so when after ten minutes of staring I retreated back to bed I was unable to rest comfortably, and soon gave it up and went out to stir up the fire.

Hard to understand that chill, even now. Partly, it was the effect that comes when discovering the clock you thought was only approaching seven is in actuality approaching midnight; that summer, which I thought so high and full, was already well past its peak. Vacation ending, school starting—these milestones have depressed me for years. And yet it was something else beside that, some involvement of a power that was beyond man entirely, a spiritual dwarfing that even a soul braver than mine could not completely hold off . . . and further than that I can't go with it, other than to say I felt better only when the fire was going, and then, minutes later, when the sun blossomed through its own anticipatory amber into a cloudless morning sky.

Reading back through this chapter, I've discovered that I didn't find room to say anything about berry picking (or fiddlehead picking or mushroom gathering or searching for the increasingly rare New England staple, the butternut). "Berrying" was one of the great social occasions in this village years ago, "berry parties" assembling at a farmhouse, each picker with a bucket, the show-offs with two or three, the best berry finder acting by right as leader, the party on his or her signal starting off through the meadows toward the most promising ledges and canes. These must have been bright and cheerful occasions, as they are in our own modest re-creations. The reconnaissance trip to find out whether the berries were ripe or not, the actual expeditions, the friendly competition to see who finds the first, or picks the fastest, or gathers the plumpest, the eating of them on ice cream or cereal. Enough for a whole chapter all its own.

Driving to Maine, once we were well up the coast, we began seeing Indians selling blueberries along the road. These were back-of-the-truck operations, with an umbrella to keep the sun off and hand-lettered signs. They were doing a land-rush business—no car with New York or New Jersey plates seemed able to resist stopping. Clearly, for these tourists the gathering instinct has been farmed out to others, and the pathetically eager way they stopped, searched through the identical quarts, pulled out their wallets, made you realize what they were missing.

It's no great feat of anthropological divination to say that for most people in our culture the hunting-gathering instinct has been sublimated into all sorts of weird distortions, ranging from the relatively harmless scavenging you see in tag-sale devotees or junkyard scroungers (back in the days where there *were* junkyards, of course) to the more abstract hunt for quarter percent increases in the interest rate that makes capitalist wannabes scan the back page of the *Wall Street Journal* as assiduously as their ancestors once searched for leftover potatoes in a field already gleaned bare.

You can see this vestigial hankering at its most obvious in a modern supermarket, even Reilly's, the modest food store behind the beach where all the summer people shop. These are carnivores well up on the food chain—yachtsmen in after a long day's sailing to stock up on Brie and Dry Sack; leathery summer ladies turning through the corn with a look that combines eagerness (*Ah, real life!*) with disdain (*I won't be fooled!*). Strip off their Sperry Top-Siders and double-knit shirts, cloak them in loincloths, and you'd get a pretty good idea of what they would have acted like back in the days when hunting and gathering was man's diurnal fate.

There are the deliberate ones, those who check the price, the fat content, the competing brands—easy enough to picture them sniffing at the berries and clams, making sure they were fresh before plopping them into their woven-grass baskets. There are the greedy ones, the kind who impatiently reach and grab, pleased to have a full cart, never mind with what. There are the loners, the ones who look at you suspiciously the moment you turn into their aisle, their territorial imperative operating at full intensity. There are the bored, lazy ones, those who expect others to do their work for them, never deigning to take anything off a counter if they have to stoop or bend. The clumsy and diffident who keep putting back everything they take down, or drop spaghetti-sauce jars onto the linoleum— hard not to picture them starving in the wild. The despairing, those who throw their hands up at the prices, complain out loud, and even those mature, confident ones, the pride of the pack, who know what they want from long experience, have smooth, economical motions in plucking . . . and yet aren't so blasé they won't act surprised and delighted at encountering something new, and, on a whim, plopping it into their carts— the kind whose adventuresomeness once upon an ancestral time made for great cultural leaps and Darwinian advances, as for instance when the first Abenaki got up the nerve to try the first lobster.

Easy enough to have fun with all this, though what's operating here is real enough. When I come home from shopping with groceries, I feel . . . well, *manly,* though in this day and age I write that with the requisite blush. Man bringing back the bacon, the forager, the gatherer. How many centuries are we removed from this role, and yet there you are. The sun is bright,

the weather propitious, the game at its most abundant, and—
the clerk having written down my driver's license number on
the lilac-colored facing of the check—the proud and victorious
hunter brings it home.

I n my nightmares I stand in the front of a bus facing forty-four restless tourists of all ages, personalities, expectations, and demands; each carries on their lap a mask representing another aspect of the human personality—over there on the left, a mask of affability; three rows down, a mask of grumpiness; closer to me on the driver's side, a mask of loneliness . . . and so on up and down both aisles. I'm supposed to describe passing scenery to them, supply colorful anecdotes from local history, whet their appetites for lunch, but the windows are all fogged up, and I've forgotten my spiel, other than the words *encompassing three geological epochs.* The bus skids along on its chassis, the wheels having fallen off; a man with a foghorn voice sitting in back shouts out complaints about breakfast; I have marinara sauce on my nose; my driver has lost his way . . . and aside from all these things, of course, I'm standing there stark naked.

Such, twenty years later, is the psychological residue of the three seasons I spent as a tour director for one of America's largest bus-tour companies, leading their Cape Cod and the Islands tour of southeastern New England. Seven days a week, twenty weeks in a row, I worked as a combination nursemaid, lecturer, social director, group psychologist, diplomat, and scout (*shepherd* is the occupation I listed on my tax form each year). It was a demanding job, but not a bad one for an apprentice novelist; a heavy dose of real and not so real life, followed by seven months off in which to recuperate from the mileage and write.

Many of my fellow tour directors—TDs as they were known in company vernacular—depended on cuteness for their style. They were the song leaders, the ones who relied on corny jokes ("Now, folks, you can tell a train just went by, see? It left its—tracks!"). These were the kind who played "Get Acquainted Bingo" with the passengers, celebrated everyone's birthday, ran themselves ragged at night making sure the fussy ones were settled comfortably in their rooms. These were the kind who, not finding anything better to do with their lives, ended up tour directing summer after summer for fifteen years, until the boyishness became seared into their faces, their smiles turned to plastic, then leather, then cement.

My own approach was different. I specialized in being authoritative—a kaiser of tour directors, an affable martinet. I was always warning people we would leave them behind if they were late for a departure time, believed in running a tight ship in general, filled their heads with historical tidbits and local color, but kept them toeing the line. I'm a tall man with a deep voice and I suppose there were tactless moments when I over-did all this. Many times a passenger would approach me at the steps of the bus and ask, all but stuttering, if there was time to use the restroom before we left.

The job was addictive the way travel is addictive. A different town every night, the freedom from humdrum chores, the intoxication of motion—how pleasant it was to be a celebrity, if only in the small cozy world of the bus. "Bus tour" conjures up a shabby image, but the company I worked for believed in doing things first-class, and meals and accommodations—both free for TDs—were luxurious, the most common argument my bus driver, Danny, and I got into every night being whether to follow up our *coquilles St. Jacques* with the lobster or filet mignon.

Then, too, there were the people you encountered in the course of the trip, the ferry captains, hotel owners, dune-buggy drivers, dining-room hostesses, room clerks, et al. A TD accu-mulates many friends of the Willy Loman type, the on-the-road friendships that come in quick hellos, fast jokes, see-you-next-trips. Danny was especially addicted to these; he was always saying "They love us on the Cape, Walt. Absolutely love us!" A wave of recognition from a traffic cop, a waitress who remembered how we liked our coffee. In our essentially lonely life, it was enough to make our day.

The downside to all this? Physical and mental exhaustion. On Mondays, my easiest day, I woke up before six to get everyone ready to catch the boat to Martha's Vineyard, not finishing work until well after midnight when I brought them all back from the summer theater. Day after day, week after week, you wore your public personality like a dirty, unsheddable shirt; day after day, week after week, you explained which Vanderbilt had lived in which Newport mansion, explained why it wasn't possible to drive the bus to Nantucket, counted heads to make sure no one was left behind.

As with any job that deals with people en masse, it was hard not to adopt a protective cynicism, see the passengers as things, treat them accordingly. Stereotypes, too—every time I ran into another TD, we traded stereotypes. Californians were the worst tippers, young people the hardest to please, New Yorkers the biggest complainers, anyone with a string tie spelled trouble . . . and so on ad infinitum.

Looking back, I gave into this far too readily, and it cut me off from getting to know any of my passengers except in the most superficial kind of way. Most of the stories you did end up hearing (at the bar at night, over drinks) were hard-luck ones—we got a lot of widows traveling for the first time without their husbands, lovelorn schoolteachers, people trying to escape this fate or that—so, in the end, I ended up feeling like the eponymous hero of *Miss Lonelyhearts,* with the whole world's problems weighted on my shoulders, wanting to listen, wanting to help, but at the same time feeling a sense of revulsion that made me, once everyone was settled at night, lock the door to my room and refuse to emerge until duty forced me back out the next morning.

Because of this, tour directing was less the education in humanity it might have been, and the lessons I did learn ended up coming from what I would have thought to be the least promising source: the bus drivers I worked with, the ones who—with the two of us out there on the road alone—were my partners, fellow sufferers, allies, and pals. Theoretically the tour director was boss, but you learned right away this was *only* in theory; in fact, the drivers controlled almost everything, since they set the departure times, established the pace of the tour, knew the ins and outs of the road from long experience.

The first driver I worked with treated me pretty roughly in this respect. Sam Curnin was a stocky ex-Marine from Lawrence, Massachusetts, than which there is no tougher place in New England to be a stocky ex-Marine from. In his thirties, he devoted most of his time to a singularly joyless kind of womanizing, disappearing into his room the moment we reached our hotel, emerging an hour later freshly shaved and showered, reeking of cologne, dressed in one of the hand-tailored leisure suits he favored, bedecked with gold bracelets and medallions, off for a night on the town—nights he insisted I be his partner in, since he didn't like to hunt alone.

He had a wife back in Lawrence but this was hardly an impediment. He favored places that had Elvis Presley impersonators singing at the bar (I happened to be with him when he got the news of Elvis's death; I never saw a man look so stricken); putting a twenty-dollar bill down just to let the bartender know he meant business, he would go instantly to work, and an impressive number of times would leave the bar accompanied by a surprisingly beautiful woman ("Car? Nah, I got a bus, wanna see it?"), leaving me to get back to the hotel as best I could.

The second most important thing in Sam's life was driving fast. He was a skilled driver, but pushed that bus to speeds that were criminal and crazy, and many times the frightened passengers would beg me to rein him in. He wanted to give the people only ten minutes at the whaling museum, five minutes in the stores, skip photo stops altogether; the tour, to him, was a kind of madcap sprint through southern New England, and he was always threatening to "slap" me around if I tried to slow him down.

Sam was largely responsible for one of the worst moments in my career. On Wednesdays our itinerary included Provincetown, at the Cape's tip, and heading there on Route 6 (clinging to the rail for dear life as Sam weaved in and out of traffic), I tried to alert people as to what to expect. "Let me put it this way," I would say, after explaining where we would meet the dune buggies, what time to be back. "Provincetown makes Greenwich Village look like West Point."

Which it does—particularly if you happen to stumble into town on July 4th, right in the middle of the annual parade. This was what was in store for us on the afternoon in question. I was used to everything and anything in P'town—enjoyed the ironic juxtaposition between the extravagant locals and the very middle middle-American tourists I dumped unsuspecting in their midst—but nothing prepared me for what was waiting for us up Commercial Street as we tried to cross over to the parking lot near the wharf.

The town, always crowded in summer, was now absolutely mobbed, people everywhere, so navigating the streets was like threading your way through a Moroccan bazaar. For all Sam's speeding, he'd gotten us there a moment too late—the first floats were going by on Commercial, and the police had stopped traffic. Out the window, as my tourists gawked, came a happy blur of red, white, and blue banners, mixed with patriotic rock music and what seemed enormous amounts of lacy chiffon.

Keeping our rendezvous, sticking to schedule—these got so they meant everything to a TD, and so the only thing I could think of was stopping the parade long enough to get the bus across to the wharf and the waiting dune buggies. The door to a bus is controlled by a pneumatic lever that opens it with great force; slamming it forward, I managed to clobber a bicyclist just as he tried to squeeze past, sending him—to my horror—flying across Commercial Street like a man shot out of a cannon.

I hurried over, expecting to find I'd killed him. He was naked, except for a scrap of loincloth, and the first thing I noticed as I helped pull him from the wreckage of his bike was that he covered with black-and-blue marks—that he was *already* covered with black-and-blue marks that couldn't have been caused by his fall.

"Sorry," I mumbled. I pointed toward the bus—my explanation for everything. "Are you all right?"

He nodded groggily, waved his hand by his lips. "Got a light, man? Got a light?"

"A light? Hold on."

I ran back into the bus, found him his match, lit whatever he was smoking, ran over to the nearest policeman intending to ask him to let us through. I had a shock when I reached him. He was crying, really crying, tears streaming down his face. "Oh, you guys make me so *sick*!" he sobbed, waving his arms toward the parade, toward the crowd, toward everything and nothing. "Move along you!" he yelled at the nearest float, trying to blow his whistle, getting nothing but a soggy tweet. "Move along pleeease!"

I ran back to the bus, expecting Sam's adrenaline to be at the bursting point; I wouldn't have put it past him to use the bus as a battering ram, force his way through the parade. Instead, he was grinning enjoyably, reaching back—before I could stop him toward the p.a. system and the mike I'd left on my seat when I rushed out.

"Hey, everybody!" he said in his deep crooner's voice. Forty-four seventy-year-olds from Des Moines looked to where he pointed out the bus's big front window, their mouths dropping open—stared toward the Provincetown Fourth of July parade, the drag queens sitting on their floats coyly kicking their stockinged legs, the transvestites doing the cancan, the cross-dressers blowing kisses, the unabashed panoply of P'town in full display. "See those girls out there? See them, huh? . . . THOSE ARE GUYS!"

～

Sam Curnin, Mr. Subtle. It was unendurable by the time fall came—his constant threats, the way his driving scared all the passengers and so ruined our tips, my covering for him when his wife called the hotel. In a defiant, what-the-hell mood, I called headquarters and told them I wanted another driver, and much to my surprise they complied, though, when I saw who his replacements were, I realized I should have left well enough alone.

For on the next five tours, I had five different partners, each stranger and harder to get along with than the last. There was

Timmy Bonner, also from Lawrence, who was Sam's protégé and modeled himself on Sam's style, from the hand-tailored leisure suits to the fast, reckless driving. Big John Hamola, he of the ever-present comb ever-sweeping through his ever-hand-some white hair, the one who liked to announce at every restaurant, "The only kind of fish *I* like is tuna fish!" Stu Menninger, the intellectual bus driver, moody, aware he was working beneath his capabilities and prickly over this, fiercely proud of the money he'd saved, his favorite reading material being the *Wall Street Journal*. Bobby DiCapia, who'd served time in various New Jersey prisons. Freddy Case, who didn't say a word from one day to the next, then, without any warning, would suddenly grab the mike and start singing songs about chickens. . . . It was quite a crew.

It was partly my fault the chemistry wasn't right. Raised on war movies, Westerns, books about explorers, I had a high con-ception of what male bonding should and could be—wanted, more than anything, to find myself a sidekick in the classic style, someone who would play Pat O'Brady to my Roy Rogers, Georgie Russell to my Davy Crockett, Tenzing to my Sir Edmund Hillary, Pancho to my Cisco Kid. Yes, it occurred to me that the times might not be propitious for this now—that the only two relationships left for men to have were as macho, beer-swigging buddies or serious, no-holds-barred competitors, but there you are . . . my expectations were high. I wanted to some-one who would back me up in tight spots, a good man with wisecracks, a hard worker, someone who was tough enough not to give in to my idiosyncrasies, and yet patient enough to pretty much take me as I came.

One morning as we cruised to Nantucket I was talking about this with the TD who led the other Cape tour. "Who you want to work with is Yocki," he said. "Once you work with Yocki, you won't want to work with anyone else. Yocki is the best bus driver in the world."

❦

I spent the winter alone, holed up in a cabin in the north-western Connecticut woods. After twenty weeks nonstop tour directing, I plunged into solitude the way a burning man would plunge into a pond; I reveled in it, gloried in it, splashed in it, kicked up my heels, the throbbing sensation of too many people chilled into the soothing balm of no people at all. Most days I would manage things so I wouldn't hear another human voice; when I did feel gregarious, a visit to the local store to stock up on supplies acted like a visit to the city, with more than enough human contact to keep me going for another week alone.

Solitude or the mob—it seemed like a pretty clear choice those years, with not much to choose from in between. Still, by the time spring came, having passed the winter as a hermit, I could begin to see some merits in the mob part, especially since my bank account now stood perilously close to empty. When the tour company called to ask if I wanted to come back for another season, I had only one question.

"Is Danny Yockoski driving the Cape this year? If he is, I'd like to team up with him."

He was waiting there on the sidewalk outside the Waldorf-Astoria where our tours began, came right over and introduced himself, pulling off the glove he wore for loading luggage to shake my hand. He was sixty-four years old, short and stocky, with broad shoulders, a heroic chest, and a paunch that would have done credit to Jackie Gleason. He carried it with grace, so you hardly noticed it after a time; what you did notice was his broad, open face, which was alive with the kind of creases, wrinkles, and furrows you'd expect in a man his age, and yet managed to retain an extravagant dose of boyishness, so it was easy to picture what he'd looked like at ten (much later, after much prodding, I found out his nickname at home was Nelson, after Baby Face Nelson, the famous bank robber). The unruly shock of hair; the sparkling eyes; the flashing white teeth set off by a handsome tan—all these were there, too. He had an infectious way of giggling that was partly a giggle at the fact he could still giggle, and combined with those open features, his lightly ironic tone, the bifocals over which he peered with such transparent goodwill, it made for the kind of person everyone liked at first sight.

"Sorry-looking crew if I ever saw one. All full up? Glad to be working with you, Walt, I'm not in a race like your pal Curnin." Wink-giggle-smile. "Look at this! Sisters of Mercy, they don't tip. Nun today and nun tomorrow. . . . Yes, ma'am? No, the eight-day Quebecer is two buses down. Don't forget to tip the driver, okay? . . . Whew! A close one! We're out here for a week, what's the hurry is the way I see it? Whoops, the natives are getting restless; better get them aboard. . . . Not a twenty-dollar bill in the bunch, but what the hell. We don't get paid much, so we'll have some fun. We're number one on the Cape this year, let's not forget that. Legends in our own time. Ten minutes to liftoff, I better get to packing. Think you can handle things?" Wink-wink-smile-double-smile-twinkle. "Or you want a *real* man to take over?"

I hardly had a chance to talk with him the rest of the day, I was so busy getting everyone organized, launching into my spiel ("On your left as we head uptown you'll just get a glimpse of Central Park, created by the landscape architect Frederick Law Olmsted in . . ."). I noticed a couple of things, though, both of them favorable. The first was that I didn't have to cling to the overhead rail to keep my balance—that our accelerations were gentle and even, without sudden surges and swerves. The second was that while the drivers I'd worked with knew a lot of people along the way, Danny seemed to know them *all,* and we didn't pass a tollbooth, didn't stop for gas, didn't meet a waitress, where Danny didn't instantly trot out a name, a memory, a connection.

"They love us out here, you kidding?" he said, the one time I managed to sit next to him on the rail. "I'm getting worried though. Quiet bunch, how come they didn't laugh at your light-housekeeping joke? A little lighthousekeeping? I haven't heard that in, what, three or four years? Shy ones tip lousy. We've got to prime this crew, that's for sure. We get to the hotel tonight, have a drink, then start on the big boy, what d'you say?"

The big boy? "Sure," I nodded, not knowing what he meant. "There's a photo stop up ahead where we cross the Connecticut. Do you think we could stop for five minutes?"

"Nah, let's make it twenty. What's the rush?"

The people could never be things to Danny, never the enemy; he enjoyed talking with them, being in their midst, laughing at their jokes, speculating about their motives, exchanging battle stories about this or that. "Let's mingle," he would say, whenever he sensed my cynicism getting the best of me, and mingle is exactly what we would do, Danny working the passengers like a politician, only without ulterior motives, enjoying, quite literally, the press of flesh.

"They love us out here, Walt. Absolutely love us!"

But even to Danny there came a time when enough was enough. When we reached the hotel our first afternoon there was still a good hour of work for us settling people in, but once we finished the night was ours to do as we pleased, and to Danny this meant a long restorative shower, dressing for dinner in white polyester slacks and a bright Hawaiian shirt, walking up to the restaurant overlooking Vineyard Sound, taking our time over drinks, then the important ceremony of ordering our meal.

"I think I'll start with a King Kong," he told the waitress. "Tell Sugar it's for me."

A King Kong? A Manhattan, straight up, to be sipped and savored as if it were the finest of wines.

"Then after that I think we'll have some squeakers. You got some squeakers today? Tell Joel they're for me and the kid."

Squeakers? Steamers, beautiful little necks, a huge heaping bowlful, Danny picking his out with the appraising squint of a connoisseur, dipping it in broth with a gesture even his thick fingers managed to make exquisitely dainty, dipping it a second time in a little dish of drawn butter, shaking it once as if to dry it out, then . . . with a last squint of appreciation, placing it on the tip of his tongue the way a celebrant accepts the host . . . sucking it back with a slurp that could be heard halfway across the room.

"Nothing like squeakers," he sighed, reaching for another. "You keeping up with me, Walter? We don't want any survivors. Take no prisoners! And save room for the big boy, okay?"

Me, I was still in a daze from being referred to as "the kid." That was it, that was exactly it! Sidekicks! Pancho and the Kid!

Sure, a big boy was fine, whatever that turned out to be. Let's have two while we're at it.

"A double big boy?" Danny looked over at me with new respect. "Okay, if you're up to it. Man against beast, hand-to-hand combat, winner take all."

The words were hardly out of his mouth before the waitress was back bearing two huge platters, one with Danny's two lobsters, one with mine. "Yipes!" Danny giggled, ducking back like he was frightened; he reached for the nutcracker, gave the biggest of his lobsters a rap across the claw just to let it know who was boss, giggled a second time, then went immediately to work, disdaining a bib or even a napkin, pressing his face toward the plate like a scientist on a difficult, painstaking dissection.

"A beauty! We'll start her right about . . . there! Take that! Hah, a stubborn one! A fighter! There you go, fella. What's this? Ow, gotcha! Another claw bites the dust. Two for two and still batting top of the third. How you doing over there, Walt? Got a flopper or a whopper?"

Now crooning, now cursing, referring to it in one breath as a boy, in the next as a girl, using the nutcracker and pickers in tandem with a delicate knitting motion, Danny slowly transferred the lobster from its shell into his mouth. Finishing, he pushed the plate back with its mound of litter, called over to the waitress, "Take this monster away!", patted his stomach, and belched, utterly happy, a man at peace—and only then looked over to where I sat staring at him in complete and absolute wonder.

"Hey, what's the matter?" he said, genuinely alarmed. "You hardly touched yours! You sick or what?"

I hesitated, embarrassed, and it was just long enough for him to reach over and grab my lobsters, dig right in.

"Beauties! We'll start 'em right about . . . there!"

∽

That first dinner in the restaurant overlooking a sparkling, whitecapped Vineyard Sound was the start of a beautiful friendship—a friendship recorded in the stack of blurred, cheaply printed photographs I still have in my file cabinet, the souvenirs of this trip or that, sent to us by passengers who never tired of posing the two of us in front of the bus. We stand there with our arms around each other's shoulder, me tall and angular, Danny short and fat, a perfect Don Quixote and Sancho Panza, the tall one smiling a bit too thinly, too concerned with whatever windmills await him on the horizon, the short one with a smile that seems wider than the bus, his face alive with the joys of the tavern, the marketplace, the road.

"Aw, come on, Walt, lighten up," he would say whenever I got into my worry mode. "You gotta remember one thing. This is not even *close* to being a legitimate occupation."

There were good tours and bad that summer, one in particular being truly disastrous. On our ferry trip to Nantucket we ran into seven-foot-high waves, making everyone seasick. In Newport, the passengers presented me with a petition demanding we change hotels. In Edgartown, the p.a. system broke down, forcing me to search all over town for a megaphone to use instead. ("Oh yes," the salesclerk told me when I finally located one. "This is the model Walter Cronkite uses on his yacht.") In Mystic, my voice gave out, forcing me to use sign language the rest of the trip, imitating a clock with my arms to indicate times. In New London, our right rear tire blew, stranding us for five hours on the hot, dangerous shoulder of I-95.

It was Danny who pulled me through these weeks—grace under pressure was to him no abstract phrase, but the method by which he operated, in big things and small. Flat tire? Peel your jacket off and go right to work, shoving your shoulder into the wheel like a linebacker hitting a blocking sled, shoving and shoving again until the wheel dropped from the axle and the mechanic could slide on a new one. Sick TD? Drive to Hyannis for medicine, see that he takes it. Cranky passengers? Stick cotton in your ears to muffle the complaints, pick out the ringleader, leave their bags behind at the last hotel by way of a gentle hint, and if that doesn't work, leave *them* behind, the hell with the consequences (though in our defense, we did this only twice).

Pretty soon we had our own private lingo, so we hardly needed to do more than mention the right word and a whole train of associations came in its wake. "Martha's" meant the Vineyard and all that went with it—the hassle of the ferry, the snobbery of the inhabitants (it was the only place on the tour where the bus was routinely given the finger), the dangers of driving its twisting roads. "Martha Washington" was the elderly dining-room hostess who always took good care of us when we got to Newport. "Martha Junior" was Nantucket . . . and so on with almost any word that came up in the course of our tour, turning it around until it became what we needed, a shorthand code unintelligible to anyone liable to overhear us talking.

"'Tell them about Squanto," he would say when we got near Plymouth.

"Squanto or Tanto?"

"Nah, neither. I mean Jock Cartier."

"Tonight? With the squeakers?"

"Then bumper cars."

"Not if you scream at me."

"What's wrong with that? You always cut me off."

"Yeah, but in Polish?"

"Stiffs if I ever saw them."

"Lee and Grant?"

"Four rows back."

"Fuck 'em. Triple big boys?"

"Deal."

Always ironic, often obscene, fast, and clipped by its very nature, it was a perfect language for an absurd kind of job. Why bother talking about anything besides what was there out the window, behind us on that bus, ahead of us on the road? Politics? World events? Sports? None of these counted, nothing except the two of us keeping our heads, making things easy for ourselves, not letting the bastards get us down, raking in those tips, chalking up another tour.

We seldom talked about our lives away from the bus. Of Danny's life I knew very little, other than that he had a wife he was crazy about and children who were doing well out on their own. Thus, I remember quite clearly a fall afternoon returning from Martha's, when the two of us sat in deck chairs atop the old

Naushon, knocking back some beers as we watched a purple sun slowly flatten behind the long archipelago of Woods Hole and the Elizabeths.

"What are you going to be doing five years from now?" Danny asked, pointing to nowhere in particular.

"Spieling about pilgrims. Kissing people's asses. Counting heads." I shrugged.

But there was an expression I hadn't seen before on Danny's face—an earnestness that made the boyish features narrow into something much older.

I thought for a minute, tried finding a funny, shorthand way of summing up what I wanted, shrugged at the impossibility, said the nearest I could find. "Living in the country, I suppose. A little cabin somewhere cheap."

"Alone?"

"Of course alone. You picture me married?"

He squinted over at me the way a tailor would sizing up someone for a suit. "Nope." He shook his head—more's the pity, his expression seemed to say.

"How's about yourself?"

This is what he was waiting for. He folded his hands over his belly, smiled like a Buddah on catnip, then leaned his head back so what was left for sunlight took him full on the throat. "We have a place on the Jersey shore, I ever tell you that? No phone, no electricity—heaven. I'll be fixing it up this winter. Retire there. One more year to go. Twenty-one tours, then I'm a free man."

"Yeah? You'll miss it."

He snorted, flapped his hand toward the sky. "This is what I picture. Me getting in one side of the car, Dora on the other. The two of us driving somewhere just for fun. And that's it. No one else in there with us. No one fucking else."

A seagull swooped down over the deck, looking for hand-outs. Behind us a woman in jogging pants aimed a camera toward it while her companion oohed and ahhed.

"So," I said, "one more season?"

"Yeah. With you?"

I could see him looking toward the gull, but it was as if he were staring right smack into my heart.

"Sure. Couldn't leave you out here alone, could I?"

∼

So it was out—we were both dreamers, me of the impossible, Danny of the near-at-hand, but dreamers all the same, sidekicks in this as in so much else. We teamed up for another summer, had a whole new round of disasters and triumphs, made good money, and toward the end of it gave each other, without thinking, little jump starts toward our futures.

Mine came about like this. One of the hotels on the tour was a large family resort on the beach just past Hyannis. The waitresses were college girls earning money for tuition. One of them, a diminutive brunette with a soft, endearing giggle, had waited on us at breakfast for the three seasons I'd been out there, though our conversation never once went beyond "We have omelettes this morning, would you like one?" "Sure." "Coffee?" "Please."

One morning Danny and I were sitting there as usual, sipping our coffees, talking over what lay ahead of us that day, when I noticed the short friendly waitress had graduated into being the hostess—that instead of the drab pilgrim-type uniform the waitresses wore, she was dressed in a stylish skirt and blouse that transformed her entirely.

I pointed over toward where she was standing with an armful of menus, lowered my voice. "Hey, Yocki, know what?"

He glanced up from his coffee. "What?"

"I'm going to ask that hostess out."

He looked back over his shoulder. "Good idea. But you don't have the guts."

"What do you mean I don't have the guts?"

He shrugged. "What are you waiting for then?"

"I'd just like to discuss it a bit first."

"Go ahead and ask her."

"I said I'm thinking about it, I didn't say I was going to actually do it."

His eyebrows shot up into his forehead.

"Okay, I will."

"Sure you will."

"As soon as I finish my coffee."

We could have gone on like this the entire meal, until it was too late to follow through on it, the moment passed, but something was tapping so hard, so unmistakably on my shoulder, there was no resisting. I put my napkin down, dusted the crumbs off my shirt, screwed my courage to the sticking point, walked up to the little dais where the hostess waited for the next guests, her face all but hidden by that huge armful of menus.

"Hello," I said.

She seemed a bit startled, but instantly came the warm smile that attracted me in the first place. "Hello."

"Hey, I was just wondering . . ." I glanced around at where Danny sat smiling benignly, giving me a quick thumbs-up. "If you wanted to go out somewhere for a drink tonight."

The hostess tilted her head to the side, thought for what was probably six seconds, but seemed much longer, smiled even wider. "Sure."

"There's only one problem. I don't have a car."

"I do."

"Great. Meet you outside at seven? We'll be back from P'town by then."

"Okay."

I turned to go back to Danny, stopped. "Oh, I guess I should ask you your name.

"Celeste," the hostess said. Then, smiling beautifully, "What's yours?"

∞

If fate was shouting "Bingo!" at this, moving on to the next life it had to set correctly on track, it still wasn't finished with us—only the next message was a much sadder one, and I want nothing else now except to deliver it as simply and quickly as I can.

Through all our fun together, all those shared meals and drinks, the afternoons when we drove a tennis ball inexpertly around a leaf-strewn court, the times we grabbed the bus and headed for the beach, the nights on the town, I realized that Danny was in some sense living on borrowed time. Paunchy, far too heavy, drinking too much, eating too much, smoking too much, with brothers dead at a young age from heart attacks, Danny was a candidate for trouble, and, like the rest of his friends, it was my fault for not warning him about this more forcefully, lecturing him, nagging him, getting on his ass, until he slowed down. We were sidekicks, but now this was a handicap; the essence of being sidekicks is accepting the other man for what he is, and who was I to talk about diets or quitting the smokes?

He was down to two tours left before retirement—talked about nothing else now—and the trip I'm talking about saw us with a busload of people from Las Vegas, seniors who chatted happily all that first day, despite the fact it was raining buckets. Danny sat over the wheel with what for him was unusual grimness, saying little. When we got to the whaling museum in New Bedford, he didn't even get out of the bus, and I had to go to the local diner and eat our ritual corn muffin all by myself.

That night, getting to the restaurant, settling into our window table overlooking Vineyard Sound, he ordered his usual Manhattan, at ease at last, smiling happily, though he still looked haggard and pale. From the rain, I decided, but then with his first sip he made a chuttering kind of sound, a nodding motion with his head, then slumped from his chair onto the floor.

"Danny?" I said, thinking at first he was fooling. "Danny? Danny!"

In all the confusion of what happened next, the shouting, the people rushing over, the medics, the futile ambulance ride to the hospital, I remember only one moment, the first, as I bent down over him, realized what had happened, wished with all my strength, all my heart, wished as hard as I've ever wished for anything, wished so hard the force of it still tears through me as I write, that he would somehow pull through.

But it wasn't enough, my wishing. He was dead by the time he hit the floor. Sidekicks, legends on the Cape, the two of us against the world. None of this helped at the end. Here I thought what we were embarked upon was a comedy of the absurd, a funny road story played strictly for laughs, and now it fooled me one last time, so it was tragedy after all, and poor Danny Yockoski its helpless puppet.

The people on the bus the next day, as I took the mike to explain I would be leaving to go back with Danny to New Jersey, that another tour director and driver would be flying to the Cape to take our place, expressed their sympathy in the only way they knew how—by tipping me, and not with the crisp tens and twenties we normally got, but with hard silver dollars, Las Vegas dollars, dozens of them, more money than I'd ever made before, literally weighting my pockets so I sagged . . . paying tribute in silver, not to me, not to anything I had done, but to the best bus driver in the world.

September 29:

With the days becoming shorter, I find myself taking up again another of my loves: listening to shortwave radio at night, the room in darkness, the small box of the radio with its yellow dial acting like a magnet pulling in voices from all over the world. Radio Netherland, VOA or the BBC ("This is London!"), Radio Moscow (a pale, weak shadow of its former, Cold War self), the stations in Eastern Europe, Australia, or Radio Beijing. Part of the delight in listening to these is thinking of so much geographic expanse compressed into such a small package; another is imagining how odd it would seem to these broadcasters if they could see me sitting in this small room in the New Hampshire hills, many miles, many time zones, many lives removed from where they themselves sit wondering if anyone is out there listening.

Twenty years ago what I listened for was the music. A string quartet by Bartók, a tone poem by Sibelius, a pianist glorying in Chopin. The distance, the faintness, even the static—all these only added to the music's allure, so I found myself being stirred more deeply by the faint, rough strains than by any live music I've heard. Why? From the effort of hearing—from having to reach for the music with all the force of my attention, rather than passively waiting for it to reach me. That, and the fact that I always imagined it being played live, pictured the trio sitting in a rococo auditorium in some dark northern land playing their hearts out in the middle of the night, and only me in the world to listen and to care.

There's hardly any music on shortwave these days, not even jazz or rock. Hymns, yes—there are a lot of syrupy, badly sung hymns. Religious stations have taken over many of the bands, and the only thing left besides these seem to be stations where the propaganda comes out shrill and nonstop, so, what you get, scanning, is this overwhelming impression of anger and hate. And yes, it's there again tonight; even the right-wing militias have their stations now, and insanity rules the night ("God told me in 1987 to put all my assets in gold, praise be to God!"). I quickly scan on, trying to find that increasingly rare and precious combination: a voice that sounds clear, quiet, and sane.

But tonight by some miracle, on the sixteen-meter band where there's hardly ever anything except silence, I detect strains that are unmistakably those of Bach—and not just any Bach, but the duos for harpsichord and violin I've always loved beyond all his compositions. The rhythmic, crystalline purity of the harpsichord, the more lyric, voice-like violin, the intricate way they weave themselves in and around a melody that seems to rise independently of either. There it is encircled by static, unbelievably remote, seeming to come not from the box of my radio, but from a small tiny transmitter planted deep within the center of the earth, and yet it moves me, reminds me of the old days, and I find myself by the time it's finished very close to tears.

Danny had seen service in the Pacific during the war, and while he wasn't the kind to talk about it much, I gathered by some of his references, the way they framed what for him was unusual silence, that he had seen his share of combat. It wasn't hard picturing him as a GI; he had that hunker-down, take-things-as-they-come kind of attitude you see in a lot of vets his age, a determination to put up with whatever temporary insanity they were involved with until it was time to go home.

And it seems the right moment to pay tribute to his generation—the men and women born in the teens of this century, coming of age in the Depression, fighting the war, then, much to their amazement, enjoying the prosperity that came after. On the historical level there's much that can be said about them good and bad, but it's the personal, everyday level I'm concerned with here—and on the personal, everyday level they were a splendid generation to know. Resilient survivors with surprising steel at their bottom, wisecracking/jitterbugging/full of fun, adaptable from necessity, improvisational, hard workers, upholders of common sense, nostalgic, possessors of a childish hunger for learning, believers in the old verities but not slaves to them, no braver then they had to be but plenty brave when the moment came, good folks to share a foxhole with, skilled in surprising ways, fine and loving parents, they look better with each passing year, to the point where it becomes unbearably sad to think they won't be around much longer, sad to picture those VA cemeteries, their long lines of hearses, the quickly played taps, the folded flags, the disappearance of yet another member of the platoon.

And as I'm a baby boomer, even a reluctant one, it's important to add this about our parents' generation. For fifty years they guarded our flanks for us, took the brunt of the assault, kept us in safety, and the world is a harder place without them, a poorer one, and—for those of us used to their companionship—one that's achingly empty and exposed.

Writing being the business it is, I'm often looking around for alternative livings, at least in my daydreams. Something that is socially useful, intellectually challenging, and reasonably renumerative would fit the bill nicely; anything offering as fringe benefits a certain largess of vision, the opportunity to take chances, court fate would make it, to someone used to the high-stakes gamble of a writing life, even more appealing. And so, in daydreams, I find myself envying meteorologists—and not those smiley-voiced cheerleaders who read "the weather" on the evening news, but the genuine article, the scientists who collect data from all over the world, chart it on their maps, analyze, ponder, probe, and then, with a very human shrug of the shoulders for good luck, tell Mr. and Mrs. America which direction their hair will be blowing as they leave the house for work.

I think of it as a dramatic job, meteorology. Who else in this compartmentalized, overspecialized world deals with matters that are so continental in scope on one hand and so specific in their application on the other? Who in this day and age gets to study the relationship between, say, the ocean currents off Chile and the afternoon sky in downtown Boston? Weather stations send in their reports, satellites beam down their pictures, radar is scanned, computer models generated, records consulted from centuries before, inquiries radioed out to ships at sea. With quick and choppy strokes an isotherm is sketched that bulges from the middle of Oregon out across the Rockies and links their common temperature; a chain of arrows takes in Montana where it's raining; vertical lines resembling a child's drawing of a bridge indicate a funnel cloud over Oklahoma; a broad circle of fair weather extends from Michigan on down to the Gulf states; an arrow warns of high winds over the Carolinas, with a bar and pennant showing its direction and speed; another crosshatch takes in New York and Pennsylvania, and there's still room left on the map for a boomerang-shaped curl over the northward jutting neck of Maine, where, even in September, it's furiously snowing.

All these things meteorologists have at their fingertips, the entire world is combed for its secrets, and not just the ones that will be revealed in the next twenty-four hours, but ones that, as the century nears its end, have implications that approach the eschatological: is man still at the mercy of the elements or are the elements now at the mercy of man?

Drama—and yet I suspect much of this goes on in windowless, air-conditioned rooms that no sunlight penetrates, no wind disturbs, performed by pale men and women of monk-like mien, their shoulders rounded from long hours hunched over those synoptic charts. This is not quite the contradiction it sounds—when a dramatist writes about the human soul, he's not standing in the actual gusts of its dissolution—but only adds somehow to the mystery. Sober and serious are those who divine the fates, Cassandras blessed with the gift of prophecy, but cursed and reviled when they fall short.

My daydream, my fascination with weather's everyday drama, is just vivid enough to make me toy with the idea of taking up meteorology as a serious hobby, invest in a wind sock, a rain gauge, a barometer, and the other low-tech playthings you need to start. The weather is forced to be your hobby in New England anyway, since you'll be left out of 90 percent of the conversations if you can't manage to hold your own when discussing its various permutations and trends. For the changeable weather over these hills is no exaggeration, it being a region that combines wild, extravagant extremes with old-reliable kinds of regularities, so a thoughtful person can draw from it almost any metaphorical conclusion they want. A hard land? Well, there's plenty of evidence, with frosts likely any time after September first, but there are also arguments for softness, clement October afternoons when the temperature crests at seventy-eight, and we all go down to the lake for a last family picnic that never quite manages to be the last, the warmth lingering on for weeks at a time.

The weather, of course, has always been the world's conversational staple, and is usually disparaged as such, as being the trivial and mundane stopgap of folks with little else to say. I've never seen it that way, but find in even the most offhand "Going to rain today?" at least some reflection upon the eternal forces that shape us—considerations that hardly ever come up in conversation at any other time. I happen to be good at such small talk, so this is self-serving of me (I can talk your ear off about the cold front approaching from Canada, or the line storm that snapped off a limb yesterday from our one surviving elm) but I've noticed, with something of a connoisseur's eye, that the ability to do this seems to be on the decline lately, with fewer people able or willing to discuss the weather and its effects at any length.

What they do talk about is the latest weather forecast, which is not the same thing at all; it's the difference between hearing an announcement that a Mozart piano sonata will now be played and actually hearing the music *being* played. Yes, Wayne Smiley Face is predicting rain for this afternoon, but what does that have to do with the beautifully portentous clouds there in the east (for there is always beauty in portent, at least in nature), the actual raindrops on your face? These last, of course, are exactly what so much of modern life is designed to insulate us against, so it's no wonder this fundamental confusion between the thing talked about and the thing itself has become so widespread. Weather's most melodramatic effects can still rivet our attention, but the everyday drama is hardly ever noticed, at least in the city and suburbs, where air-conditioning, central heating, and the automobile have made any real involvement with the weather seem like a relic from another era, something Grandfather may have had to deal with, he who felt the dampness so fiercely in his muscles, limbs, and joints.

Me, I feel the dampness in my joints—and the rain on my neck and the sun on my forehead and the wind in my chest, all of these, via direct and instantaneous transmission, settling deep into the infallible weather gauge of my soul. In short, I'm the kind who's sensitive to the weather, its glories and punishments, its ever-varying bag of climatic tricks. I suspect that if a cross section were ever taken of me it would reveal growth rings as does an oak, with broad ones where the weather was perfect, the wind at my back, and narrow cramped ones from seasons of distress. Weather is the first, most obvious transmission between the world outside and the climate inside, the cards reality has dealt us to play, so it's no wonder I'm susceptible, so quick to let climate color my mood. I'm only surprised to find so many people hardly affected by it at all.

I remember a June morning more than twenty years ago now, walking outside the office on a coffee break with an editor at the third-rate magazine at which we both worked. He was a real Bartleby of a man, pale and cramped from a life behind a desk, with just enough animal instinct left to pay tribute to that kind of day. "Too beautiful to be inside," he said wistfully. The merest commonplace, of course—and yet I remember the words hitting me with the force of philosophic revelation, something so true, so obvious, it had been hiding right under my nose for three long years. *Too beautiful to be inside.* Yes, that was exactly it! I handed in my notice that very afternoon, turned my back on that kind of life forever, started off in pursuit of that intoxicating June breeze because, quite simply, it would have been the death of me not to.

So, for the time being at any rate, I'll not order those weather instruments from Bean's, but will rely instead on the instrument of my own instincts, the weather lore of my remembering, the tactile evidence of what I can see, sense, and feel. Like an old-timer who's lived up here for years, I'll note the fact that the cows are lying down in the meadow and look toward the southwest for clouds; I'll see seagulls in from the ocean and batten down the hatches; notice a ring around the moon and prepare for snow; detect a silver hardening in the pond's surface, look up just in time to take the wind full on my face. I'll sense a lightness in my being when I wake up in the morning, lift the shades to what I've sensed already is a glorious day, with the breeze hard and restorative from the best of all directions here, the cleansing northwest. And while I'm at this, I'll indulge my taste for weather small talk, carrying it further than I get the chance to in casual conversation, taking as my subject the highs and lows of these past six weeks, the bridge from summer over into late fall, which, in a climate that can perform virtuoso tricks at every time of year, still stands out as an absolute masterpiece of rococo variations.

∾

And I'll start with a stark word for a stark condition: *drought*. Not something we ordinarily have to worry about here, but this has been a year of unprecedented dryness, even in the memories of the oldest inhabitants. Little snow during the winter, a spring of brief, useless showers, then five weeks extending into midsummer without any rain at all. One big storm in the middle of July saved the corn, but then we fell back into the doldrums, and went another five weeks without even a thunderstorm to wet down the cinnamon-colored dust that, in this otherwise verdant countryside, seemed like a pestilence imported from abroad.

It's taken its toll, this dryness. The streams in midsummer were so low I couldn't bear looking at them, and the few times I tried fishing I was saddened by the sight of many dead trout. With the headwater streams depleted, wildlife has had to come further down the hills to find water and food; it's been a year of frequent animal sightings, increased road kills, easy targets for the hunters, who find the deer, moose, and bears all but march over to them with their paws raised in surrender, so desperate is their thirst. Like everyone else, we spent all summer waiting for our well to run dry, and I'm still surprised it hasn't.

But if a drought is bad news, nothing to laugh about, at least it's delivered in the sunniest tones imaginable, so only a hydrologist could find it totally depressing. Day after day the weather was perfect, from the first of August right through the first week of October, the sun so high and generous the only adjective to describe it would be Mediterranean, so we all basked in the sensuousness of what has seldom proved so reliable before. Usually, the rain we get around the equinox cools the pond off in a drastic plunging, so my morning swims become a real exercise in masochism, but this year things were different. On October 1 the temperature reached eighty-three and I went swimming; on October 2 it was even warmer and I went back again, and on through my birthday on the 5th, all the way to October 13, two weeks past my last endurance record, and if I was a bit flatter in the torso I might be swimming still, since the sun has warmed the surface layer so much, the top six inches, it's created the effect of a sauna bath suspended over a tub of ice.

Seductive and mellow this autumnal warmth—and yet, lasting so long now, almost to November, it creates an odd sort of unease, as if something deep and basic in the climate is fundamentally out of whack. Is this the Puritan in me at work, the sober outlook of a race that senses clouds in the finest sunshine, chill in the most delightful warmth? Is it from all those articles in the newspapers about global warming, which have turned my head just as poor Don Quixote's was by reading too many books on chivalry, albeit mine in a gloomier direction? Greenhouse gases, noxious emissions, too much carbon dioxide, acid rain. I'm all too aware of these, am prepared to accept that man's hand has become dangerously heavy on the thermostat, and yet I'm also aware of that Puritan doubting, our crisis of confidence, our habitual worry, and how that can affect the way we measure and see, so what I'm left with is that most vexing of riddles—what is screwed up, nature or our way of looking at nature?—and as much as I torment myself over this, I'm no closer to an answer than the most insensitive, unreflective person in the world.

Clearly, things are changing here. The impatiens in our window box look as good now at Halloween as they did in June; mosquitoes bite a month longer than they did five years ago; the asters and Queen Anne's lace are still flourishing out in the meadow; the killing frost that was almost inevitable by the second week of September now holds off until the first week of October; we still had ripe tomatoes in the garden last week; the smallmouth bass bite longer into the fall by a good fortnight; the locusts seem to cling to their delicate leaves forever; we put on our flannel sheets later, take sweaters out of the closet later, burn less wood, and find ourselves, at sunset, still sitting outside jacketless on the porch, listening to crickets, enjoying this extended postlude even as we wonder if a certain type of autumn crispness isn't on its way toward becoming extinct.

∾

It became common this summer to hear farmers and others concerned about the drought say, "What we need is one of those hurricanes. Not the full brunt of it, but just a glancing shot, just a kiss so we get some rain."

Not an unreasonable wish—it's been the busiest hurricane season in decades, with a whole alphabet of storms (including a Hurricane Erin, delighting my daughter, who cut out and tacked on her bulletin board the headline *Erin Sinks Two Ships*)—but as anyone who's ever read a fairy tale knows, you better be careful what you wish for, since it may very well come true.

Hurricanes aren't unknown here, though usually it's the tattered remnants we see, fleeing in haste toward Canada like criminals on the lam, still nasty, still swaggering, but pale shadows of their original brutal selves. When one does hit, the damage can be extraordinary. The famous September hurricane of 1938, after savaging half of Long Island and walloping Connecticut and Massachusetts, still had enough strength left to blow down most of the shade trees in town, then go on to destroy huge stands of forest over in the Whites. You can still see evidence of this if you hike deep in the woods—thick, rotting trunks all toppled in the same direction, so serene in their mossy indolence only a person well versed in meteorological history could understand what had brought them to the forest floor. There was another bad storm in the early '50s, Hurricane Carol, and one of my earliest memories is driving with my parents to the cottage we rented on a north country lake, seeing the trees down, the brown and helpless roots, the sandbags still black from flood water, the broken dams.

This year it took fifteen hurricanes before one named Opal found a path open to it up the Appalachians. This was on October 4, and I'd gone that afternoon to a favorite pond over in the Vermont foothills to watch the geese fly south through the high notch in which the pond lies. They were there all right, along with a gray-black scud of tropical cloud, and by the time the light started to fade, what geese I saw, responding to their own inner barometers, showing admirable good sense, were all flying *north*.

Time to head home now, fill some pots with drinking water, ready the candles, tie down anything liable to blow away. As it turned out, there was rain during the night, enough to help out with the drought if not end it, but hardly any wind. Next day, it having cleared some, I decided to take a hike on my lunch break in the hills east of town. It's higher there, the downdrafts can be tricky, and I wasn't a hundred yards from my car when I began to realize that not only had the wind blown much stronger here during the night, but that it was *still* blowing hard. Hard? Ferocious was more like it, and here I was walking through the forest still anesthetized from the calm back in the valley, so it took a while before the fact that there were fresh trees down across the trail began to register—and even longer for me to realize, with a loud snap that made me jump straight up in the air, that there were trees in the process of falling *now*.

Slow on the uptake, I can still move fast when I have to— and so I hightailed it through the woods toward the ski area that flanks the trail, out in the open where, if the wind could still get at me, the trees couldn't.

There, that was better, at least partially. I stretched out on the meadow grass and let the wind flow on past toward Cider, her ears stretched out straight behind her, her fur flying, her paw coming up to scratch in confusion at the fury in her eyes. A minute of this was enough for her; she headed back toward the woods, heard a tree go down, thought better of it, came running over to nestle against the leeward side of her master, and was rewarded for her prudence by getting the last of his Fig Newtons.

The wind slackened as I sat there watching, the chevroned ripples of meadow grass coming in slower waves, the trees to my right bending, but without those alarming bows. Four or five spruce had already fallen in the line along the ski run's edge, reminding me of those soldiers who, standing too long when the queen reviews her troops, fall straight at attention and are studiously ignored.

Comfortable now, in no danger, I could afford to analyze the wind some, take it apart. Most of the hard blows we get up here come from the northwest, and carry with them not only cold, but the suggestion of unlimited reservoirs of cold, of tundra and arctic expanse. The quality of this wind was entirely different; it was warm, unmistakably tropic, and carried the oddly depressing feel of mistral or chinook. It seemed badly out of place for that reason, Florida imported to New Hampshire, dangerously so, a force the trees and meadow and atmosphere didn't know what to do with, and so hurried to get out of its way. I sat there for a good hour, remembering how John Muir would lash himself to the top of a huge pine simply to feel it shake and sway in the wind, enjoying in a similar way the press and whip of it on my face, the way it billowed my anorak out, then, with a watery little sighing, let it go—probing me, testing me to see if I would budge, going all fluttery when I wouldn't, flowing on toward the trees, its path marked by a whirlpool of twisting red leaves.

By the time I got up again, dusted myself off, started around the fallen trees back toward the car, the wind was barely a breeze. Hurricane Opal, born off Africa, nurtured by the Caribbean, plotted with military preciseness, probed by special airplanes, the subject of watchfulness and fear over a good third of the continent, a notorious destroyer, a proven killer . . . and here it expired in a zephyr just barely powerful enough, Cider turning to follow me, to ruffle the feathery wisps at the tip of an aging retriever's tail.

∽

If the hurricane was something of a bust, the next weather "event" wasn't. October 21, the daylight having faded early from an uneasy purple sky, turned out to be the kind of dark and stormy night you remember for years, with rain that came down in sheets, their mercury-colored fabric illuminated by jagged bolts of continuous lightning. Vampires, monsters, warlocks—a Halloween kind of storm, where supernatural powers seemed to be abroad, and pity those poor mortals caught in their embrace.

As luck would have it, we were an hour and a half from home, we who never go anywhere on Saturday nights, with the necessity of getting back by midnight to reclaim Matthew from the babysitter's. And while a car is one of the most effective insulators from the elements ever invented, in storms like this one its mobility, its hubris, can take you right smack into the center of harm's way.

We made it, of course, but the drive wasn't without incident. Getting in our car, still at the laughing, oh-isn't-this-wild stage, we had to wade through six inches of water, soaking our shoes. The first few miles were on an interstate where even on normal days the signs warn of crosswinds; now, the car's side acting like a spinnaker, it took actual physical effort to hold us on the road—a road slick with the wet, fallen leaves passing tires had smeared into grease. Bad enough, but once on the secondary roads the rain became almost insane in its violence, so the wipers couldn't keep up. Time to pull over, only there was no place to pull over, the shoulders were flooded, and we hadn't passed a light in miles.

"I'm scared," Erin kept saying in the back—not panicking, but merely stating the fact, letting us know it was a kind of shivery cozy fear, but fear nevertheless.

I was cursing myself for having gotten us into this mess, too aware of my own anxiety, edgy with it, pressing. I got out three times to remove limbs from across the road, and the fourth one we hit head on, doing God knows what damage. Ahead of us crawled the red tail lights of another car, one we ended up following on the slow climb over the height-of-land, experiencing that warm, fellow feeling that can come over you in these circumstances. After a few minutes we realized that when their lights started flashing it meant they had encountered a flooded spot on the road, and were proceeding accordingly; one of these flooded spots brought the water up to our doors.

"There's that story by Conrad," I said at one point, ever the litterateur, even under duress. "'Typhoon'? About a captain named MacWhirr who brings his tramp steamer safely through a storm."

"How?" Erin asked.

"How'd he do that? By staying calm. It was loaded with coolies."

"The storm?"

"The steamer."

After two hours of this, singing and talking to keep up our spirits, we came down onto the familiar road that leads toward home. I expected to find trees down over the driveway, the power out, but the only damage we could see was that the rain, blowing horizontally, had come through a window and was lying in puddles on the living-room floor.

"Look at it this way," Celeste said, the eternal optimist. "No more drought, right?"

I started toward the kitchen for towels. "From the frying pan into the fire," I said, too tired to find the proverb I wanted. *It never rains but it pours.*

❧

Drought, hurricanes, storms. We're not immune to these (nor to tornadoes, blizzards, and earthquakes), but when people talk about New England weather as being something out of the ordinary, what they're referring to is the drama evident in the course of even a normal day, especially in autumn, when the equinox, the declining slant of the sun, seems to inject new splendor into the elements, letting them show off their best effects.

Clouds take the lead in this—those dark, adamantine autumn clouds that drift toward us from the Great Lakes, crossing our valley toward the east as the geese follow it to the south. Ordinarily, our clouds are of the middling variety—not as spectacularly awesome and agoraphobic as those you see in Montana or southern Utah, and not as intimate and claustrophobic as what you find elsewhere in northern latitudes, where a sea lies close to the west. The big fluffy ones here are popped apart by our mountains, the low flat ones upraised by our ridges, so the clouds we see coloring the sky, casting shadows, catching the sun, are middle in size, height, and temperament—comprehensible clouds that give you the feeling that if you had just a little more flexibility in the neck, a little more height, you could peek around their circumference to see what lies behind.

That said, there is still room for tremendous variation regarding their shape, texture, and pattern, so, like with a river, you're never staring into the same sky twice. Our clouds expand in October, take on extra air, begin dwarfing our mountains rather than letting themselves be dwarfed. Most of the year their message seems to be that yes, we are a blessed and self-contained island and nowhere else exists, but it's hard to have this illusion this time of year; those spreading cloud layers speak in continental terms, humble us, make us merely another incident beneath the great eastward roll of the sky.

I've tried learning the names of clouds like I have stars, but it's difficult at this latitude; they blend and change so rapidly there is rarely one kind alone. Cumulus is seldom just cumulus, round and cottony, but takes on a lot of stratus as well, so the cotton seems stretched to the sides. Stratocumulus these are called, but with the sun shining through their middles, their edges rolled into doughy logs, stratocumulus undulatus opacus is the more accurate term, so eventually what you're doing is not studying cloud formations, but learning Latin—and a beautiful and suggestive Latin at that. Cumulus humilis, nimbostratus praecipitatio, cirrus castellanus. Meteorologists have the most evocative, lyrical jargon in the world.

There are two types of clouds, more common in autumn than at any other time of year, that deserve special mention. The first of these is the orographic or "lenticular" cloud, created when air rising to get over a mountain reaches its condensation point and forms a cloud over the mountain's summit, often mimicking as it does so the mountain's very shape. On mornings that dawn fair we have a perfect example right out our window, when October, somewhat lenticular in shape already, takes on a dark, cloudy doubling in an otherwise cloudless sky, so it looks twice as high. Other mornings the cloud is white and a little apart from the mountain, like a Santa Claus beard hung around its chin, but in both circumstances it seems a deliberate trick nature has played to get the sky off to a humorous start.

The other cloud is more properly a cloud *effect*. In autumn, with all those stratocumulus about, the sun angled lower in the sky, sunshine often falls toward earth in slanted beams, as if from a filtered searchlight suspended over the earth. Crepuscular sunshine is the wonderful name for this—sunshine that finds an opportunistic hole in the clouds and slants on through, casting a burnished light that speaks so dramatically of the heavens it can hardly be described except in Old Testament terms. Anyone who knows the art of Rockwell Kent, his woodcuts of the Arctic, will recognize the pillar-like pattern of such light; there is nothing the sky offers here that is any finer, and often, driving along the river, I'll catch moments when a half dozen of these searchlights are shining simultaneously, and I'll pull to the side of the road simply to watch.

❧

Anyone writing of a hill-country autumn must include a few words on fog. Moving here from the coast, I thought I knew something about the subject, but if anything the fog can be even more persistent here, and most October mornings we can barely see the meadow from the house. There's a difference in quality, too. Ocean fog is apt to be *foggy* fog, so amorphous it seems spontaneously generated by its own obscurity, whereas valley fog tends to be more shaped and defined, fog in banks, pools, and streamers that fit the terrain over which it collects. The Connecticut River is a short way from the house, and the fog not only seems to raise the river's surface higher, but widens it as well, the fog spilling in slow motion over its banks.

Of all the metaphors we borrow from the elements to help explain the human condition, fog is the one that can be most literally applied. "In a fog" describes a mental state that corresponds exactly to being *in a fog*—the helpless disorientation, the maddening sameness, the cloudy droplets that hide one

moment, distort the next, so you never know where in relation
to reality you stand. And yet if fog has any virtues (aside from
wetting the garden), it lies in this very distortion, how it takes
the familiar and cloaks it in a grayness that lets us see impres-
sionistically, things blending fluidly into other things, their
rigid divisions erased. To the northeast lies a nondescript little
ridge with a ragged fringe of firs along the top; pleasant
enough, but on normal days it can't compete with the view
toward October Mountain or the scene toward the river, so it's
unusual for us to pay it much attention. And yet, give it some
fog, wrap its base in some mystery, and it becomes the most
interesting natural feature visible, the swelling anticline on top
being just high enough to escape the worst of the fog, so it
towers above nothingness, seems miraculously adrift, a brig of
clarity sailing an obscure sea.

So thick is the fog that we never know what the weather is
going to be until ten, when it starts to burn off, turning from an
opaque gray that's seamless to a light blue that's shredded and
torn. Often a wind will come up to stir the tops of the trees,
whisking the last damp streamers away. On a good day the wind
goes on to freshen from the northwest, replacing the haze with
a transparency that seems even more remarkable for the contrast. Talk about your dramatic entrances, the curtain going up!
That's the time to be outdoors here. Using the fog as its scrim,
the sun has climbed high in the southern sky, showing off what
it can still do in the way of warmth; the trees still wear their yel-
lows and reds, so they come instantly ablaze; the wind shakes
them, causes the color to ripple, sends the weakest scattering
out over the meadow in crisp bursts of spray. And many times,
if you follow with your eyes the highest, filmiest remainder still
opaque enough to merit the term *fog,* you'll see a hawk or vul-
ture or osprey or other circling bird, with strong, confident
wings bearing the last of the heaviness away.

∽

Suppressing those lingering doubts, staring out the window
at the here and now, I'd like to go on record as claiming this as the
most extraordinary October I can remember, a once-in-a-hun-

dred-years October, an October of aesthetic significance, setting records in beauty, radiance, and color. Warmth rising from morning coolness in delightful gradations that stop just short of being hot; sunshine so rich and ambient it seems a gift poured into your hands; skies decorated with clouds of every shape, size, and description, none of which could block the sun for very long, and served, come sunset, as the palettes on which a dozen colors were displayed; enough in the way of storms to keep us on our toes, displaying every stroking and streaming effect of which rain is capable; enough frost to put color in the leaves, and breezes light enough to keep them clinging to their branches right through the month. A once-in-a-century kind of fall.

The foliage is talked about with the weather in New England, reported upon and charted on the forecasts, appraised the way a painting is, everyone a connoisseur. There were reports early in September that this would be a dull year for color because of the drought, forecasts that made those in the know snort with contempt, there being—when it comes to chlorophyll, when it will be choked off from the leaves and with what effect—too many variables at work to predict accurately.

As it happened, it turned out to be the best year in the last five or six, the hardwoods turning color exactly the way they do on calendars and postcards. Picture the most vivid crimson you can imagine, the sunniest yellow, give it a papery texture, a crisp earthy scent, then double or triple the intensity, imagine all this spread generously across a hillside slanted to the south, and you *start* to get an idea of what I'm talking about—and then imagine the color prolonged over three or four weeks of perfect weather, and you can sense the exhilaration this brings.

My response to October is always extravagant, even in dull years. Born early in the month, I feel the special affinity anyone has toward the moment in the seasonal cycle they started out upon, so I feel more alive in October than I do at any other time. I write longer in the morning, take the bike out on my lunch hour for exuberantly fast rides, rake leaves just to wade through them with my boots, split wood with gusto, kick a soccer ball around for hours with the kids, break into snippets from opera, go outside simply to inhale. *Here,* nature seems to be telling me—*here, this is the best I'm capable of, make of me what you will.*

This is exhilarating and tormenting both, so there are times on perfect afternoons when I feel an overwhelming urge to somehow grasp the elements that make it so—grasp them, though I can't explain the feeling better than that, me who is reputedly so clever with words, and there were times when I was a younger man when I would feel as much sadness from this as I would exhilaration.

Fall is an odd time to celebrate beginnings, since so much suggests so much coming to an end. The earth's upper hemisphere tilting away from the sun, the birds flying south, the leaves falling, the great abandonment under way. I suppose the older I get the more somber these notes will seem, to the point where someday I will feel an unbearable regret this time of year ... want, with what meager force remains, to have just a month of it again, and if not a month then a week, and if not a week then a moment—autumn condensed in all its bittersweet richness, so *there,* with the last pulse of longing I'm capable of, I squeeze it for comfort in my hand, hoarding it for the afterlife, this precious elixir of fall.

October 2:

A person who values what a culture disdains and disdains what a culture values has two options: silence or crankiness. At a young age, either can be worn with style, even elegance ... the dissenter, the young Turk, the vigorous Cassandra ... but it becomes a weary attitude with the years, and not the least of my arguments with the times is that people like me are being forced willy-nilly into that most comic and pathetic of roles: that of being an old curmudgeon.

We have a friend in town who's adapting to this, and I think she's finally snapped. Seeing the changes in the landscape she loves, remembering how the village she grew up in south of here was spoiled and all but erased by progress, she can't stand to see anymore sub-

urbanization up here, and so last month when yet
another lavish new house was being constructed on her
road, she went to her workshop and fashioned a sign
which she mounted on an easel and placed along the
road so everyone could see.

WHAT'S NEXT? PAVED ROADS? STREET LIGHTS? DON'T
TURN NEW HAMPSHIRE INTO NEW JERSEY!

A week passed, the trucks and bulldozers went
rolling by, up went another sign.

THIS LAND IS WORTH MORE THAN ALL YOUR MONEY!

Another week, another sign, this after someone from
the zoning board came to have a chat with her.

BUSTED! FOR WRITING THIS SIGN!

I can sympathize with her, since there are times I'm
perilously near cracking myself. Earlier this week a thir-
teen-year-old boy, having gotten my number out of the
phone book, called to see if he could come and ask me
some questions about being a writer. Sure enough, yesterday afternoon he showed up right after school, a
fresh-faced, healthy-looking kid, with just enough hint
of shyness to bode well for his future as an artist. His
questions were good ones, but I'm afraid I didn't answer
them properly. Rather than giving him strong advice,
encouraging him with words of optimism and courage,
I launched—through insensible gradations of well-
intentioned realism—into a diatribe against all the ills of
a writing career, the illiterate editors, incompetent pub-
lishers, uncomprehending critics, the lot.

I thought he looked a bit crestfallen when he left, but
there you are—the old curmudgeon was in full gear. This
morning I got a note in the mail that reads as follows.

"Dear Mr. Wetherell. Thanks for taking the time to talk
with me. I really appreciate it and I'm sure it will be an interesting report. I had no idea being an author was so hard."

❧

Two years ago, when we finally got around to enlarging and
refurbishing the small box of our house, needing to adhere to a

strict budget, we allowed ourselves one indulgence: cedar shingles for the siding, white cedar, the kind that weathers over the years, no paint needed, no stain. And while they'll never quite match that burnished silver-gray color they fade to on the coast, they've already been tanned and darkened by the elements depending on which direction they face—the east side grayer than the south, the north side browner than the east, so eventually the entire house will be colored by the years. Someday it may even taken on the patina you see on certain old barns here, where the moss and algae grow right on the weathered boards, and there is no separation between earth and structure at all.

There was a stain we could have used that promised to "weather" the cedar instantly, just as there are jeans you can buy that already come "weathered" out of the box, just as there are tanning salons where people can get a "weathered look" on their face without going outside. The conceit of this, so typical of our era, hardly requires comment, other than to say what a shame it is such a fine, evocative word, *weathered,* should turn out to be for sale like so much else.

The truth is I like a certain weathering in a man or woman, like to see it on their faces. We celebrate youth and a *lack* of weathering so much in this society that it's time more was said in praise of people who aren't ashamed to show what time has done to them, for better and for worse. Was it Orwell or Camus who said that every middle-aged man has the face he deserves? It's a good line, true in my experience, and there's nothing as beautiful as the face of a farmer or fisherman or someone who has worked many hours out in the elements.

People can be weathered by psychological and moral forces, of course—human upset marks the face all too plainly—and yet stare into enough faces and you come to realize there's a difference. Psychological weathering leaves deep wrinkles that tend toward the vertical (all those worry lines, the drooping caused by tears or the tightening of holding back tears), and dark, empty hollows beneath the eyes. Weather weathering tends to wrinkle up the areas around the temples, leather up the forehead, but leaves the eyes young and soft. What I value most in the human countenance is a combination of the two—a face engraved by elements of all kinds, and yet one that hasn't give up to them, so whatever is left seems enhanced and ennobled by a stubborn and quiet sense of pride.

And the older I get, the more I find myself using *weather* in its fine old nautical sense, as a verb meaning "to pass through safely or survive," as for instance, in what surely would be a fine epitaph to rest under, *He weathered his century with aplomb.*

This is an old story, one that's been told many times before, in earlier ages, in other ways, but who knows whether it will be told very often in the future. A young person from the provinces falls in love with a lonely and difficult art, one that dominates each moment of his waking day, and so sets himself what is seen from the first as a heroic, all-but-impossible task—that of mastering it; of finding out whether or not he has what it takes to seize a portion of that art and make it his.

And so a boy living in the drab outlying areas of a major city, of all the things he might possibly fall in love with, becomes desperately enamored with the idea of buffalo hunting, having read every book on the subject he can find, and decides with a sudden, instinctive surge of courage (the impulse of which will never entirely leave him) that *this* is what he wants to do in life, never mind he lives in the suburbs, knows no buffalo hunters, has never seen a buffalo hunter in the flesh. The wild romantic image of the great animal in all its power. The prospect of the glorious country it inhabits. The tradition of bravery, craft, and skill the hunting has always required. The year is 1867, and while the enormous herds that roamed the continent before the white man came have already been sadly wasted and reduced, there are still nearly a million buffalo left on the Great Plains; as crazy as his ambition is, there yet remains an outside chance it might possibly be achieved, never mind that the boy—living among clerks and shopkeepers, petty aspirers, the quietly desperate—possesses not the slightest notion of how to begin.

∾

A good question. Well, there was all that reading I was doing, right from the start. Even as a kid I had the sense I could pretty well reproduce whatever was there on the page before me—that there was a rhythm to words, a certain order, a way of organizing, a tone I could mimic perfectly if anyone ever challenged me to do so. Naturally no one did ... I'm talking ten or eleven years old here . . . but it was an early indication. Then, too, I was searching for something different. I was a serious-looking kid—adults liked telling me I would make a good minister—and felt I was cut out for something hard. I remember finding out there existed a term called *nonconformist,* and, once I apprehended the meaning, deciding yes, that was for me. I was too shy to speak of this to others, so from early days the idea of my future was caught up in secrecy, in stubbornness, in going it alone ... I wrote a poem for the sixth-grade talent contest (this was in the late '50s when NASA was shooting monkeys up in orbit) that started like this: "Maybe someday in June/Perhaps when you look at the moon/You'll see two monkeys instead of a man/One named Harry and the other is Anne." Well, they cheered when I read that, stood on their seats and applauded, and I suppose it turned my head. . . . Wanting to write fiction came later, after working through my teenage share of overwrought verse. I considered journalism and history, but decided the hardest kind of writing, the one demanding the most skill and imagination, the one you could really wrap a life around, was fiction—and so a few days after my nineteenth birthday, entirely unprodded and unprovoked, having dropped out of college for the first time (there would be others), I sat down and wrote a short story on the Ping-Pong table in my parents' basement, in longhand on cheap yellow paper that absorbed the words like a blotter, so the lines seemed to lead like a trail *into* the paper—a faint, barely discernible yellow brick road.

∾

How to begin? There were manuals on buffalo hunting, printed on paper so old it flaked apart beneath his fingers, but such primers seemed too dry and pedestrian to match his

dreams. There were buffalo hunters living in the city, he supposed, retired ones proud with scars, but how did you find
them, approach them, ask them their secrets? His parents knew
nothing of buffalo, other than that those who hunted them
were rough, uncouth men living in poverty. No, the boy would
have to learn buffalo hunting on his own, and so he started the
only way he knew how, with a mock heroic kind of apprenticeship, fasting for days on end to prepare himself for hardship,
going gloveless in cold weather, taking all-day hikes across the
vacant lots that began just west of town, stalking pigeons and
squirrels and rabbits to hone his instincts, trying, as he did so,
to come to terms with the huge and desperate task in front of
him—keeping enough of it in view that it could inspire him
onward; keeping enough of it obscure so reality wouldn't over-
whelm him right at the start.

For many years this apprenticeship to an apprenticeship
went on. His friends had dreams, too, if you could call them
dreams, so common were they, so drab. But he noticed that even
here the dreams often slipped away—that there came a crucial
dividing line, often in the late teens, when the dream had to be
pursued or postponed indefinitely . . . and so, saying nothing to
his parents, gathering what meager supplies he could scavenge
from the pantry, fortified by nothing more definite than the force
of his desire, knowing it was now or never, he walked out of the
house one spring morning and headed for the west, guideless,
following the faint impressions left by wagons in the sod.

❧

The first story was about a hockey player—there may have
been some talking animals in it as well, God forgive me. It went
right in my drawer, as did the second, third, and fourth, which
were even worse. Who would I have shown these to? I remember reading about Hawthorne, how he spent his youth writing
alone in his garret there in Salem, hardly seeing even his sister
from year to year, she who dwelt in the very next room—I
remember reading about him, and feeling he was a backslapping
extrovert, a Kiwanian, compared to me. Years alone in a solitary
room. Was I the last one to go that route? It was a curse and

blessing both, but at least gave me a decently obscure place to fall on my face as I tried figuring out what I had to say and how to go about saying it. . . . Of course. Sure. Any task worth doing requires that initial ordeal. But at least with writing you could embark on the ordeal immediately, this very second, with no grubstake, no scholarship, no begging of favors. Then, too, those years coincided with some severe personal problems, and without writing I would have succumbed to them early, so it literally saved my life—a fact that has kept me eternally grateful in an animal kind of way, even through the sloughs of creative despond. For all the solitude, the menial jobs, all the confusion, writing gave me something to thread a life around. I attended mass in Providence once, and heard the priest repeat an old Portuguese saying: "God writes straight in crooked lines." Exactly! A perfect epitaph for those years. And it took more than eight years of sending my stuff out before an envelope came back containing not the inevitable rejection, but a note that began "Yes!" with a check for thirty-five dollars that actually cleared the bank. But I deserve no credit for stick-to-itiveness, gumption, pluck. Maybe at first, okay, but there was so much discouragement, so many failures still to come, that my dedication became nothing virtuous, nothing to brag about, but a dreary kind of insanity, and you don't credit people with being insane.

∾

Reaching the plains he found them glorious. Their endless roll, the way the sky matched it. The smell of sage crushed in the hand, or juniper wafted out from the sheltered hollows. How the wind came down off the Rockies testing everything in its path, destroying many, but giving those who withstood it an added boost to each step, so he seemed blown willy-nilly toward his future. In his dream he had pictured killing his first buffalo instantly, but he saw now that his apprenticeship was only just beginning. He took menial jobs in the small towns he drifted through, each one sadder and more barren than the last; the people he worked with, decent enough, scoffed whenever he mentioned his dream, told him there weren't enough buffalo left to support a career, were quick to bring up examples of those who had not only failed in their hunting, but died miserably of starvation, friendless and alone. And it was true—there was a conspicuous dearth of buffalo hunters, so even after being out there a year he still hadn't met one. But then one day, having purchased his first rifle, practiced aiming for long hours in the meadow behind the saloon, having saved enough money for a month-long trip into the easternmost strip of the Montana territory, walked there on foot, he came upon his first buffalo—a great brown stillness standing hoof-deep in a rushing stream—and knew in that first intense moment of quiet, of recognition, that the beast was everything he had ever dreamed of, worthy of all his hopes.

∽

Yes. I was always a great one for reading the lives of the famous writers. Two reasons. I had to find my mentors somewhere, and there were no other candidates other than those I could find on the shelves of the public library. And then their lives always turned out to have happy endings; for all the neglect, the suffering, the hardships, the writers ended up being *great,* and that's exactly what a young writer wanted to hear. Melville bumming around the oceans before the mast; Conrad doing the same thing, only as an officer; Proust disguised as a dilettante no one took seriously; Chekhov tearing the serf out of his soul bit by agonized bit; Cather coming to terms with the landscape she had fought so hard to leave behind; Kakfa hiding in the very bosom of the bourgeoisie. The self-taught ones in particular spoke to me, the loners, the great solitaries, though there wasn't a writer I read who didn't seem to offer me one overpowering lesson. Which lesson? That it wasn't just the writing that counted, but a writing life. Dedication, endurance, passion, idealism, daring, strength, dignity, a respect and responsibility toward your gift. These were not relics from a romantic age, but pragmatic qualities a writer still needed, those and a certain way of looking at life, an apartness that managed, when writing, to merge somehow with the whole. . . . That this attitude was old-fashioned there was no one to tell me. And in the meantime, while I tried to fashion my own writing life, I was taking all the usual wrong turns. Each new job I tried to do well; in each of them a moment came when my boss or supervisor called me into the office and asked if I wanted a promotion; each time I responded by immediately giving two weeks' notice, fleeing like Aesop's fox from the dog who had security and comfort and safety, but (the catch!) had to wear a collar around his neck night and day.... Those years saw me burning every bridge I encountered, not only those I crossed, but ones even the hint of whose superstructure rose above the horizon, so after a few more years there was literally no retreat. And I would have retreated. Even now, if a bridge were there handy, there are moments I would retreat. But luckily there are no bridges.

∽

Fast-forward to 1890. Our young hunter, since that first kill, has gone on to slay his share of buffalo, though never losing that initial sense of awe that he should be out there accomplishing his dream. Always when young he had thought of buffalo hunting as a mad and desperate sprint, an art to be seized by force, but now, older, wiser, he began understanding it was a marathon he was embarked upon, one that for all his years on the plains he had just barely started. At the same time, he was beginning to achieve a certain modest reputation, which brought him into contact with other professional hunters whose credentials were much greater than his own. He found them disappointing; too prickly and envious from all that time alone; too wrapped up in their own neuroses, which they had cultivated far too long without anyone calling them on it; too fiercely competitive over a rapidly diminishing supply of success; too quick to adopt the wrong, self-destructive role models, think a proper buffalo hunter had to drink and womanize and carouse; whistling too brightly, too loudly, in the dark foreshadowings of their doom. And yet, talking late at night, once the sham dropped away, there were those among them who could understand him like no one else could.

And it was about this time he realized he was wrong about their number. If anything, there were more buffalo hunters now than ever, at the very moment game was becoming most scarce. There were colleges you could go to in order to major in buffalo hunting; doctorates granted; careers offered in the university where you didn't have to hunt at all, but only talk about hunting; fellowships awarded to those with even the flimsiest claim on ability. He discovered that at Bozeman and Missoula and Fort Benton were held great conferences where buffalo hunters from all over the country gathered to spin their yarns, talk about craft, conduct workshops, and many thousands of would-be buffalo hunters paid large sums for the privilege of attending. . . . That there was a regular bureaucracy of buffalo hunting. . . . That it had its phonies and mediocrities and sophists as in any other profession. . . . That there was no room in any of this established buffalo-hunting order for him, and if he were to continue to hunt successfully, on his own terms, he must avoid it like the plague.

∾

Fighting my way toward a private kind of writing life turned out to be kid stuff compared to finding a public writing life that didn't result in a heavy dose of self-loathing. Anyone will tell you that. Not only the difficulty of making yourself heard through the noise of the fashionable, the trendy, the ruthlessly hip; not only the demands of family and friends, of a social life that expects you to be able to drop the intensity on command and be charming; not only the civic obligations that send us out to lecture, give readings, chat; not only the hack work taken on to make ends meet—no, not only these, but the difficulty of taking something so essentially private and giving it a public face, emerging from the protective sanctuary of the cave, cold and damp as it is, to take our chances in the rough-and-tumble of the marketplace. Each time it's attempted a chastening portion of humiliation is the result. Writers like to whine about this, natch. But aside from the habitual tetchiness, there's something wrong, since bitterness has always been the occupational disease of American writers, as black lung is that of coal miners, and there's nothing that cures it except a decent modicum of success and much old-fashioned toughing it out. For there's another lesson in Melville, other than that things will come right in the end. Do you know *Pierre*? Halfway through it Melville turns his hero into a writer just to get things off his chest:

Now look around in that most miserable room, and at that most miserable of all the pursuits of man. Is there all this work to one book, which shall be read in a very few hours, and, far more frequently, utterly skipped in one second, and which, in the end, must undoubtedly go to the worms? Who shall tell all the thoughts and feelings of Pierre in that desolate and shivering room, when at last the idea obtruded that the wiser and profounder he should grow, the more and more he lessened his chances for bread. . . . Morning comes; again the dropped sash, the icy water, the flesh-brush, the breakfast, the hot bricks, the ink, the pen, the from-eight o'clock-to-half-past-four, and the whole general inclusive hell of the same departed day. . . . Ah! Shivering thus day after day in his wrapper and cloak, is this the warm lad that once sang to the world of tropical summer?

The lesson being—just how far can you afford to let the bitterness go? I mean, shape up or ship out. When the going gets tough the tough get going. Damn the torpedoes, the buck stops here. Hang a slogan over your desk and get on with it, six hours of work today and double that tomorrow. Neglect? Bitterness? Self-pity? All is easy compared to finding those words.

❧

He had two tricks that saved him during the lean times, those seasons when he didn't see a buffalo at all, let alone kill one—seasons when the only sign of buffalo existence were the dusty scuff marks left by their hooves in riverine sandbanks that were themselves crumbling away. The first trick was to remember the fringe benefits that were, for all his complaining, the best of any profession in the world. Being your own boss; having time to do what you wanted, go where you liked; the admiring stares you got from women and children when you rode into town; the self-reliance, freedom, and independence that weren't just pipe dreams, but actual facts of the working day. The other trick, the one that could pull him out of even the deepest funk, was remembering back to the far-off days when he had lived in the suburbs dreaming of someday being what he had in fact become, the satisfaction to be derived from this, seeing things with that young and hungry intensity of want.

Older now, grizzled, arthritis in the shoulder and both knees, with a tendency to stutter and act confused when in company, he turned aside from any hope of making money and pinned all his hopes on hunting one majestic buffalo he had heard rumors of for years—the king of all buffalo, the last one left as huge and fearsome as the bulls of the old days, one the stalking of which would cap his career. In the course of that winter he spent every minute of the waking day plotting out how he would accomplish this, planning his strategy, his tactics, pouring over maps, consulting his journals, making notes, getting ready. Even before the spring thaw he set out, leading his packhorse up into the far northern corner of the buffalo's range, excited as he hadn't been in years, not at all sure he wasn't chasing a phantom, but determined just the same.

It was 1899 now, and out of the four million buffalo that once roamed the Great Plains, there remained a little less than four hundred.

∽

There's this to be said for all the difficulties—they balance what would otherwise be an endeavor so perfect no one could stomach our rapturous celebrations of its perfection. Despite everything the century has tossed at us, it remains one of the true miracles. Out of nothing—a pen, a piece of paper, a notion—*this*. . . . The first dawning of an idea, the way it steals into consciousness by the most subtle of prodding hints, or, changing tactics, flies broadside into your chest like a skater gone out of control, yelling "Catch me! Catch me!" and knocking you over. How all of them come accompanied by little halos of inspiration that make them seem, in that first dawning flash, perfectly splendid, and how, with time, with sober consideration, all but a few of these corrode into ordinariness, leaving the ones that don't all the more crystalline and worthy of pursuit. The incubation period when the idea grows, takes on new and unexpected dimensions, tests itself, survives each more stringent cut. The moment you start, the mix of hopefulness and despair a first line always symbolizes. The satisfaction of knowing a character so thoroughly all the tricks of her being are there beneath your hands; the delight of creating a landscape that matches the world's, yet remains partly imagined; the sheer ventriloquist satisfaction of throwing your voice. The despond, the creative nausea that comes in the middle, endured—as with so much else in the writing process—because and only because it's been endured so many times before. The steadier exhilaration of rewriting, using what experience has taught you, moving away to gauge things from a different, cooler perspective, then narrowing in on the words themselves, the language, hoping to catch a rhythm, pitch everything in key. And then—not always, sometimes, seldom, hardly ever—the idea achieved, or damn near this time, enough for five seconds of satisfaction before the next idea waiting on line forces its way to the surface and the process begins again . . .

∾

. . . for it seemed he had always been chasing this buffalo, springing from the cover of the cottonwoods to gallop madly across the plain, the enormous red beast already running from his scent, so the chase is one-sided right from the start, and yet, through that odd alternating mix of steadiness and fury, the hunter manages to gain ground, the morning air pouring down his throat, the sky embracing rider and horse with its blueness, the smell of the sage dizzying up his head . . . the buffalo closer, closer . . . so that one day, maybe not now, but maybe one day, our hunter will be close enough to lean down and, reaching as far as he's able, pat it briefly on its hump. His only ambition now not to kill it, but to merely draw near, count coup, reassure himself of its existence . . . and then, exhilarated, reining in, watch it lumber off into the sunset, once more to have eluded him, but everything he had ever dreamed.

∾

Rapturous—I warned you. But if someone has to be the last one left to idealize the writing process it may as well be me. The "last" part is something I think about often. It used to occur to me that the reason this may very well be the last generation of writers is that the threat of nuclear war made every practitioner of every profession very likely "the last," from nurses to insurance salesmen to third basemen, and while this is still a real if forgotten danger, far more likely is it that the forces of popular culture will do extinction's dirty work on their own, no bombs needed (the equation being both simple and stark: NO READERS=NO WRITERS). The implications are the same in both scenarios: if we are the last ones, we better get it right.... And so a writing life still counts, because we need all the human forces we can muster to sustain our passion during these times, when it's impossible to talk about the gift of technical skill, a facility with language, a lively and inventive imagination, without talking about the guts and stamina and dignity to back them up.

When I started this I was pretty certain the buffalo in my analogy represented readers, our fast disappearing collaborators, who have been harassed and chivvied to the point of extinction. Now, I'm not so sure it doesn't represent more than this, so atop the bisons' shaggy heads I see gathered the larger, fainter impression of great books, of great aspirations, of goals so important and unobtainable it hardly bears mentioning them out loud. Not just writing and reading, but the part of the human soul that is hungrier than ever for understanding and form, wisdom and insight, drama, comedy, and verve. Certainly, those who view writing as the hardest, more important art form, the best means ever devised for entering the mind, heart, and soul of another being, may be in for a prolonged Dark Age, so the eternal question that has vexed young writers at the start of their careers. *Do I have the talent it takes?*, has shifted to the harder, more gut-wrenching question, *If I have the talent, will anyone notice, will anyone care?*

The good news is that there are fifty thousand buffalo in the country now, not four hundred. The bad news? There isn't a single professional buffalo hunter left in the world.

But remember this young writer when despair gets you down. I've been to Yellowstone many times now, have stared in fascination and wonder at the buffalo herds grazing in the luxurious meadows of Hayden Valley or along the Lamar, seemingly unchanged from the days when the white man last came face to face with something commensurate with his capacity for wonder. I remember in particular the way they looked during the great fires of 1988, when the smoke settled thickly around their shoulders and they pawed in puzzlement at the black burning embers that littered their trails. Dim, stolid, forgotten in the excitement, the chaos, they grazed on, being the only thing they knew how to be but being that beautifully, buffalo—waiting for someone to pay them attention, and yet perfectly ready to wait there forever if that's what it takes.

November 30:

It's six P.M., do you know where your children are? Yep, coming through the mudroom door, their hair still white with the first snow of winter, Celeste bringing up the rear, whiter still, having given in to an irresistible impulse to make angels in the drifts. All three talk at once. Reports on how deep it is, Matthew's arm going way above his head; inquiries about dinner, Erin grinning from ear to ear; a quick shedding of coats, sweaters, and scarves, and then into the kitchen by the woodstove for what is undoubtedly their father's most legitimate claim to fame: the best home-cooked spaghetti and meatballs between Boston and Montreal.

Family dinner. It's getting to be harder to choreograph already, what with activities and meetings and work, but most nights we somehow manage it—the four of us sitting around the kitchen table, talking, eating, sharing our day. And while we don't say prayers or ask a blessing, we do believe in starting it off with a little ceremony: holding hands for a moment, going around the table to say out loud our favorite things about the day.

Easy for Matthew. "The snow!"

Erin thinks a bit longer. "The whole day."

Celeste still has snow in her hair. "The way it slanted down through the spotlight."

I'm reaching over toward the meatballs. "Starting a new story," I say, though the snow ranks right up there. "Did anyone remember to feed Cider?"

Whoops. There, Erin takes care of her, Celeste pops up to put another log in the stove, Matthew reaches over for what's already his second helping of garlic bread, and I pour out two glasses of a modest Italian red wine. While we take being together seriously, preparing real food (which I define as food that takes longer than thirty minutes to cook), we're pretty informal about everything else, and I suspect, to an outsider, the Wetherell family house at dinner time might seem relatively chaotic.

Often the kids will have a friend over, and they sometimes seem ill at ease, not sure how to behave. After some gentle prodding it usually comes out that their family never eats together—everyone eats at different times and usually alone. Their evidence is backed up by what you learn in conversation with their parents. Family dinner? You mean the whole family sitting around at the same time eating dinner? You mean like on Thanksgiving and Christmas? You mean like in the old days? No, we mean like on every day of the year.

For this is the tie that binds. Sitting here together for a half hour at the tail of day. This—as simple and difficult as this.

And while I could wax on at length about the spiritual benefits eating together brings, it would perhaps be another way of coming at these by celebrating the pragmatic ones instead. Tough day at school? Problems at work? There, the evidence is right there in their demeanors, the way they pick at their food, hardly respond to any questions—something that will have to be looked into more closely once the dishes are cleared. Plans needing agreement upon for the weekend? As good a time as any, the four of us sitting there in the family parliament, one man, one vote, the debate is opened. Anything interesting in the newspaper? Yes, a new planet

discovered near a star in the Big Dipper, with the possi-
bility of water and hence life.

"Humans?" asks Erin.

"Well, not quite," I answer.

"Martians?" Matthew chimes in.

"Something in between."

Part council of war, part therapy session, part semi-
nar, debating society, and long-running play, our dinners
together accomplish more family business than we often
manage the rest of the day combined.

Even the kids are reluctant to break this tie. Erin has
a habit of asking to be excused, then, her freedom estab-
lished in principle, lingering on in her chair to listen to us
talk. Matthew, for his part, likes to play Tall-Short, a
game he and I invented that consists primarily of him
doing deep-knee bends on the edge of my chair while I
support his back (giving me the chance to notice his hair
is flaked not with snow now, but Parmesan cheese). Ten
minutes of this, and they're off to homework or flute prac-
tice or play, while Celeste and I sit there over a slow cup
of tea, the lord chancellors off duty, tired ones at that, but
the fatigue only pulls us that much closer together, so our
voices soften, glances become all it takes, and, for once in
the day, there is no blessed hurry at all.

Now that the end draws near, I've just finished reading back
through this book before drawing in my breath for the final
chapter. Several things surprise me when I compared my first
intentions to what's actually here. The first concerns how many
more celebrations I could include had I the space—celebrations,
that is, of aspects of life that are worthy of extravagant praise, and
yet aren't likely to last very far into the new millennium.

One of the chapters I *won't* write would have been called
"The Kindness of Strangers." In it, I would have written about
those occasions in life when I was troubled, suffering true
despair, sometimes in actual physical danger, and perfect
strangers appeared to save the day—those times, and the more

commonplace encounters that come in the course of everyday living (a quick conversation with someone sitting in a diner at the next stool; a hiker encountered along a mountain trail; a fellow passenger in a plane), bringing with them a flash of insight, understanding, and empathy, no less important for being so brief. And I would have had to talk a little about how this quality seems to be disappearing like so many others—that common civility, mocked by cynics, but one of life's real pleasures, seems to be on a precipitous decline, so it's more than most people can do these days to exchange the curtest, quickest of nods.

But some things are too sad to write about. No, even if there were the time and space, I would find this hard. Another chapter would have been on birds, for we live in something of an aviarian paradise here. With the meadows, broad bands of trees, the pond, a major river, a big farm, all within the area of a single square mile, we have the kind of edge many species favor, from waxwings to snow geese, turkeys to kestrels, and watching them on their busy rounds has given my family many hours of delight. But here's where extinction plays its wretched trump. When I start to read about them to learn more, the very first fact I come upon is that almost every species of songbird is threatened by loss of habitat, and this disheartens me from studying further, since my baggage of lost enthusiasms is already heavy enough.

And this brings me to the second thing I've noticed in these pages. Despite never forgetting the irony of the above, I've managed to put more of bitterness behind than I expected I would, thanks to the balm the celebration has engendered. Or rather, I've become aware that there seems to be an eternal quality common to everything I praise, and yet existing independently of any—a complicated thought, but perhaps one I can come at again in a final chapter. And while I've never thought of writing as being as therapeutic as some claim, there's no denying it can be an effective way of getting at what eats you, so there's been this in operation as well. I think what's helped even more is that writing is a form of conversation, any book a refuge, so I've constructed what is in essence my own national park (one of the less-visited ones), where things like hills and books and ponds can flourish unharmed by the ravages of time. Whether this is a good thing or bad one is beside my immediate point, which is to try to understand how I've managed to hold bitterness off as long as I have.

I hadn't expected there would be as much specific human loss to recount as there's been; like the sorcerer's apprentice, I thought I could contain the note of elegy to aspects and qualities of life, not have to include actual relations and friends. It's become more of a memoir than I anticipated, and a peculiar sort at that, since what I'm writing of, with a memoir-like sheen, is for the most part the present, though the press of the future makes it already read as though it's a pastoral from a long-vanished world. I suppose this note becomes predominant in anyone's middle age, when the realization comes that everyone and everything dear to us is held by necessity only briefly, these being the terms, the bargain, by which life operates. In previous eras we could take a great deal of consolation from the fact that what we love in life could be cherished by our children and grandchildren, but now I worry this consolation may no longer exist.

God knows we need it—the habit of taking our pleasure from the ages, not minutes. *Optima dies prima fugit,* Virgil put it—the best days are the first to go—and yet what's sad about our era is how unnecessarily soon we throttle what's best, how passively we bear our losses, this needless civil war.

As for me, as I near the book's end, what I'm aware of most is how much in the world still lies waiting for celebration . . .

Here at the end I have to record two deaths that bring no sadness with them, but only wonder, that a being as frail as man is, victim to so many upsets, can yet in some circumstances achieve over a century of life.

The first is that of George Seldes, age 104, who died this past summer in the old Vermont farmhouse that had been his home ever since his pal Sinclair Lewis convinced him to move north sixty years before. A legendary journalist, a thorn in the side of the establishment, one of ignorance's dedicated foes, his career began in Pittsburgh at the turn of the century, when as a young reporter he watched men pluck horse turds off the cobblestones to hurl at marching suffragettes. During World War I he served in France, and went on in the twenties to cover Europe as foreign correspondent for the *Chicago Tribune;* later, after his reporting became too honest for any paper to risk, he began his own independent weekly, and, on the side, wrote best-selling books almost until his death. He's in *Bartlett's* for his famous put-down of Mussolini (whom he knew well as a fellow journalist), "Sawdust Caesar"; a short list of people he knew and interviewed would include Lenin, Hitler, Freud, Pershing, Jung, Dorothy Thompson, Hemingway, and both Roosevelts. While he wasn't the last man alive to know some of these people, he was probably the last man alive to know them all, and for this if for no other reason he was a true miracle, the survivor of survivors, the eyes that, by the time they closed this summer, had perhaps seen more of world history than anyone else's.

I met him twice, through some close mutual friends. The first and longest of these occasions was at a fishing club high in the hills, where my friends brought him for a barbecue and drinks. Thanks to his friendship with the radical John Reed, he had just made an appearance in the movie *Reds,* and was full of stories about the filming, including how they had made him talk all morning without giving him breakfast. Finding out that Calvin Coolidge had once been a member of the fishing club, he was full of Coolidge stories, too, and described an occasion when, hearing he had just gotten back from a long trip to Russia, Coolidge invited him to the White House and pumped him for information on what Lenin was up to: Silent Cal, at least according to George, was nowhere near as dumb as people claimed.

I was fascinated by these stories, of course, but even more so with George himself. He was short, gnome-like, pale except on the nose, dressed impeccably in jacket and tie, with the faintest trace of a moustache. Watching him, I was aware not so much of the twinkle that any person his age manages to cast, but an aura beyond that, a freshness, a youthfulness, that seemed of the 1920s, though I never quite managed to pin down what visual evidence I was responding to. He wasn't a fisherman, had never been to a fishing club before, but it was just one more exotic locale to add to all the others he had been to in his day, and sitting on the porch, drink in hand, surrounded by receptive listeners, he was right at home.

I spoke with him once more, a year or two later in our local college town where he'd been ferried by a friend to run some errands. He was over one hundred then, and yet if someone had challenged you to pick out the most vigorous, remarkable man on the street, your eyes would have gone immediately to him. He kept up that fine, unflinching crankiness right until the end. Once, just before he died, someone asked his opinion of one of the current radio call-in hosts. "He's a fascist," George snarled. "Leave me alone." The kind they don't make anymore, and, at least where George Seldes is concerned, that ain't no cliché.

The other passing was of someone whose life was quite different; Pearl Dimick, age 102, our town clerk of many years, a woman who except for one brief spell working in the city never left the small circle of hills in which she was born. A farm girl, someone who not only survived the old rural life of self-sufficiency and isolation, but flourished there, she was the proud holder of the Boston Post Cane as our town's oldest citizen—a cane made of Gabon ebony which was distributed to seven hundred New England villages as part of a newspaper promotion in 1909, passed on upon the oldest's death to the next one in line, and so on down through the century.

Pearl was the best town clerk we ever had here; during the war, with the men away, she apparently functioned like Lord Poo-Bah in *The Mikado,* all the town officers wrapped up into one efficient and busy personage. Her house was a dignified blue Victorian set on the same terrace as the Academy—a kit house sold by Sears, Roebuck around the time of the First World War, and yet, in grace and style, as far beyond our modern prefab houses as Chartres is from a contemporary bank. She lived alone here well into her nineties, visited by her many friends. When my daughter was little I would take her to the swings behind the Academy and see Pearl with her fine white curls peering out at us from her window, waving, smiling; it was, quite literally, like being smiled upon by an angel. The town genuinely mourned when she died, felt a real tie, a last link to the old days, had with her passing been severed . . . but even here she had one last surprise for us. Living alone, never married, she managed to accumulate a sizable amount of savings, and left the town she loved and served so faithfully a permanent endowment to help needy people in distress.

A life lived in the compass of a few square miles. A life lived in the circumference of the world. If you could have lived both Pearl Dimick's life and George Seldes's life simultaneously, there wouldn't be much left to learn of the vagaries, the blessings, time brings. Even now, at the turn of this new century, there are a considerable number of people who have achieved their own century and then some, many with their wits still about them, ready and eager to see their second old century out, their second new century in, having survived what will likely go down in world history as the hundred years of greatest change. This seems to me, even if they have done nothing else with their lives, a remarkable accomplishment, a physical feat far beyond any athletic record, a moral feat—when you consider the life-sapping despair the century has taught us—worthy of the most extravagant celebration.

For the more passing years I witness myself, nearing half their age, the more continuance seems a virtue in and of itself. We live in a time of severed connections—a world of disloca-tion and rootlessness; a distracted, stuttery world; a world that is coming rapidly unglued; a world in which all the adjectives that apply are those of severance, as if the human synapse that has linked generation to generation, culture to culture, age to age, has finally reached its breaking point and snapped. And while I'm no therapist, not on this scale, it seems obvious that if you're looking to heal this synapse the direction you should look is toward the words that suggest the opposite. Words like *suture* and *thread, linkage* and *connection, continuance* and *con-stancy.* Words that were evidenced in the lives of George Seldes and Pearl Dimick. Words the meaning of which were built by the endurance and faith of thousands of forgotten souls like them, millions of obscure destinies, millions of brave hearts.

Within this book are the things I have come to value in my own life, qualities I hunger for, consolations that make up for so much else. There are more. I take comfort in knowing, for instance, that outside the Flanders town of Ypres the "Last Post" is blown on the trumpet every night at eight o'clock as it has been for over ninety years, in memory of the young men and women who tragically died there in the years 1914–18. That in mountain villages in Italy people worship every week in the same small churches they have worshiped in for over a thousand years. That in our own small New England town Christmas is celebrated as it has been since the days of the French and Indian Wars. That the same characters who made an audience in Shakespeare's London of 1599 laugh out loud or cry can provoke the same reaction from an audience gathered in a small American high school four hundred years later. That there still exist on this planet mountain refuges where no man has ever stepped foot. That the sight of wind blowing across meadow grass, the brightness of moving water, have caused a moment of delight in the beholder's eye throughout the history of our species. That Polaris shines in the north for us as it did for our remotest ancestors. That there are many such threads left to weave us into eternity if only we would grasp them.

This has nothing to do with nostalgia, wishing a return to the old days, pining sadly for the past. Each morning the sun rises above the ridges to our east, filling me with a surge of energy and confidence that makes me eager to get at the coming day—and yet the sun has risen there for every day beyond man's understanding, is the very oldest fact of life on this planet, so the new in us flows quite literally from the old, in this and a thousand other examples.

I feel guilty at times that I'm trying to teach my children to value what I value myself—that in teaching them to love things that might soon disappear I will condemn them to more than their share of sadness, make them somehow unfit for modern life. And yet I will continue trying to teach them. Teach them to know and reverence the land, take delight in the roll of land-scape, find in music, literature, and painting man's closest approximations to nature's beauty. Survival depends on it, as directly as if they were lion cubs being taught to hunt on the African veldt. Not only their survival as beings that hunger for more than the trivial and fleeting, but the survival into the future of those qualities in life worth loving and cherishing, which will soon depend on their own passion and strength, not their parents'.

For we live in one of those eras where we have to learn once again that progress is not a continuum, as much as we long for it, but that civilization proceeds in restless fits and starts, and that our own time is suffering one of the worst and most pro-longed of these fits, distracting us, confusing us, making us yearn for something we hardly have the name for anymore, let alone have the key to finding. We are in a *fin de siècle* state of mind, which is only appropriate with the century's turn, but

we're in a *fin de monde* mood as well, so we never know if what's
in store for us are merely bad times or the worst times ever.
"Every human generation has its own illusions with regard to
civilization," wrote the Bosnian-Serb novelist Ivo Andrić in the
dark midnight of 1945. "Some believe they are taking part in its
upsurge, others that they are witnesses of its extinction. In fact,
it always both flares up and smoulders and is extinguished,
according to the place and the angle of view."

∽

Yes, the angle. Always the angle. It's clear now that what I fell
in love with as a young man was not the old rural way of life,
which disappeared forever from these hills in the 1920s with the
introduction of paved roads and electricity, but the afterglow of
that world, which had clung to life, clings to life still, with surprising tenacity. In the country round about my home can still
be found overgrown meadows where no one sets foot from
decade to decade; houses where strong, stubborn people live
without lights or running water because they've always lived
that way, see no reason to change; hill towns where the newest
house is over a hundred years old; upland farms worked by
descendants of the same families who cleared the fields in 1769;
stone walls constructed 250 years ago that still run like granite
sutures across the earth; softwood forests where owls and
ermine hunt; brooks where wild trout survive in miniature;
mountain notches where, in the course of a winter day, you will
never hear a sound that isn't of the wind.

As a boy I used to read writers who lamented the passing
of this old way of life, the genuine country. Growing to maturity, I came north too late to witness this myself, and yet, again,
I've been surprised by how many postscripts managed to live
on—disconnected, isolated, vulnerable, and yet, when you
encountered them, still partaking of these bittersweet scraps of
eternity. Now even these are fast disappearing. A reason for sadness? Yes, but not quite despair; humans will always find new
sources for beauty, for without it we starve. Almost everyone
admires sunsets, but for every million that do, perhaps a thousand will linger on to watch the afterglow that follows upon

this—and out of those thousand, a dozen will realize there is a further beauty in the western sky, an afterglow to the afterglow, a moment when the horizon, cleared of brightness, cleared even of its smudged yellow and red, will still manage to hold to itself a delicate zone of coral and pearl, which is often the most poignant light of the entire day . . . and that even when this disappears there are beauties yet to come in the blackness of night.

All through this book I've sensed a single quality that underlies the qualities the passing of which I've lamented, one that will endure when many of the things, places, and people I love are gone. I've sensed it, drawn strength from it, celebrated it, and yet I've never been quite able to entirely grasp it, give it a name, other than the complicated one that comes out of the thousands of words, the millions of syllables, I've put down here on these pages, in exactly their same order. I realize I've offered a life that cannot serve as a direct model; in trying to forge my own truce with the times, I've left a difficult trail, without prescriptions or markers anyone else can easily follow, and yet perhaps this is its value, the lesson it contains: that these qualities are still there for the grasping at all. My intention throughout has been to tell the story of a country year from the angle of a man of quiet habits living in an isolated pocket among forgotten and enduring hills, and I claim no other province for it than that. Readers can add in their own celebrations, their private wonderings, their cherished loves. I sense these, sense them strongly. Together, between us, there is very little left to say.

∽

Winter again and snowy drifts ring the house, shining under the sun with a matching brightness that makes it seem as if they are stretching to catch the beams halfway, so there is more motion and vivacity in the scene than the quiet would suggest. Out my study window the landscape falls away like the winter side of my grandfather's miniature village, the one that went under our Christmas tree each year, ringed now with a sheltering circle of hills that enlarges it, brings it to life. In the stillness, the snow lies flat on the branches of the oldest trees, giving the lower part of the horizon a papery, striated texture that is almost of birch; above this the sky is white where the scraps of cloud that came with sunrise have been bunched and herded by the cold into enormous cumulus; amidst them, centered in my window, my seeing, my sense, is October, the mountain that crests the horizon, swells it into the shape I find so reassuring, turning it to the kind of gray-blue color, soft with steel, that seems, on days like this one, the tint eternity would choose to ride on toward the future.

Watching these, listening to the sound of my son and daughter playing below the window in the snowy drifts, I feel I should end with a personal statement of belief—that this book has been an exercise in drawing near to this and perhaps I should be brave enough to make that final declaration. For at my back are the books I love. Below me is my family. Out the window stand these hills. Underneath my hands, this last white page. They're all I want of life now, and yet how fiercely I want them and the strength they bring. I place my faith exactly here. I place my faith on the truth of art, the beauty of the natural world, the consolation of human courage, and while I know it's old-fashioned of me, impossibly out-of-date, this is what I believe in and that's the way I was born.